Gifts OF
MOTHER
EARTH

EARTH ENERGIES, VORTEXES, LINES, AND GRIDS

JAAP VAN ETTEN, PhD

Other books by Jaap Van Etten:

Crystal Skulls:
Interacting with a Phenomenon

Gifts OF MOTHER EARTH

EARTH ENERGIES, VORTEXES, LINES, AND GRIDS

JAAP VAN ETTEN, PhD

3 LIGHT Technology
PUBLISHING

*   *   *

ISBN-13: 978-1891824-86-9

Light Technology Publishing, LLC
Phone: 800-450-0985
Fax: 928-714-1132
PO Box 3540
Flagstaff, AZ 86003
www.lighttechnology.com

This book is dedicated to Mother Earth—who always unconditionally loves and supports all of her children.

ACKNOWLEDGMENTS

THIS BOOK SUMMARIZES THE RESULTS OF ABOUT TWENTY YEARS OF RESEARCH. This research has been carried out in several countries and has involved many people, and their number makes it impossible to mention everyone. Whether or not you are mentioned by name, know that I am very grateful for every contribution you have made, however small it may be. A book like this is actually the result of a collective effort. Thank you all from the depth of my heart.

Of course there are always people who have contributed in a very special way. When I mention names, some may feel left out. If you do not see your name, know that you are included in the first group.

I would like to start with mentioning Bas Meyer. Thank you for making the wonderful dowsing rods that have been my companions during my studies. These rods made it impossible to forget you. Thank you also for being my dowsing companion in the initial phase of my research. At that time, I did not realize how crucial that phase would be.

I like to thank Frank Gieling for sharing with me so many days of research. Thank you for your willingness to drive me tens of thousands of kilometers when we were following lines and grid systems throughout The Netherlands. Thank you also for the many wonderful photos you have taken.

Thank you, Andre de Vos, for being such a great companion during my research in The Netherlands and for your ability to give me confirmation when I needed it. Stephen Gladstein, I would like to thank you not only for being such a wonderful hiking buddy during my research but especially for the many enlightening discussions we had. Ted Mercer, I would like to thank you for being so wonderfully supportive during the long trips while researching grids throughout Arizona. Thank you also for keeping me safe during the research day hikes. And thank you for helping me to formulate the results of this research more clearly as a consequence of your many great questions. Your support in the last phase of the research was very important to me.

Special thanks to you, Kristina Arysta, for your support in so many ways. I enjoyed the dowsing we did together and deeply appreciate your courage to disagree with me so I could learn new things. Our discussions were stimulating and helpful and they continued into the last phase of this book.

Thank you, Evita de Vos, for making several of my primitive sketches into professional illustrations (credited within).

I would also like to thank Michael and Amayra Hamilton. They gave me permission to set up, test, and improve the vortex tours at their Angel Valley Spiritual Retreat Center in Sedona, Arizona. These tours have formed the basis of an important part of this book and gave me the possibility to test ideas with willing participants.

There is always support for transforming a manuscript into a book. In the first place, I would like to thank those who were willing to edit the manuscript before it went to the publisher. Debby Mercer, Kristina Arysta, and Sandi O'Connor I am very grateful for your willingness to be honest and clear in your comments on the manuscript. In your own way, each of you has helped me to see what was needed to bring this book in a form that was clearer and more ready for a larger group of potential readers. Thank you very much.

I would like to thank Melody Swanson and her staff at Light Technology Publishing for transforming the manuscript into a real book. Thank you so much for your trust in me and my product and for a great final book.

Lastly, I would like to thank the most important contributor to this book: my beloved Jeanne Michaels. You have a very special place in my life. From that place, you support me continuously. Without your ability to connect with energies the way you do, I would never have been able to complete my studies to make this book possible. In addition, you have spent countless hours reading through the different phases of the manuscript and have given me very valuable feedback that transformed the manuscript from dull and scientific into something that is more easily digestible. Our interactions gave me the opportunity to grow permanently and that is reflected in this book. Thank you, my love.

CONTENTS

INTRODUCTION

THE PURPOSE OF THIS BOOK IS TO HELP PEOPLE REMEMBER THE GIFTS that Mother Earth offers us. We live on her, work on her, and use her, but we do not really love her, connect with her, or feel gratitude for what she offers us: everything we need on a permanent basis. Many people will agree with the statement: "The Earth provides us with everything we need," as long as we restrict it to physical aspects like food, water, air, and the many resources we feel we need to satisfy our hunger for luxury. However, this statement is even truer for the different energies we need, in particular the "subtle energies." These subtle energies are the main focus of this book with the hope that after reading it, you will be better able to remember these energies and their functions in relationship to us. This will enable you to again use these energies as they are meant to be used.

The term "remember" is used for two reasons. Firstly, our ancestors knew of the existence of subtle energies and used them to support their lives and spiritual development. They were true members of the Earth community. We are still in the process of remembering what was natural for our ancestors. Secondly, we can only connect with the different subtle energies and experience their gifts if we remember that they exist. We live in a freewill reality so we need to make a choice to experience something. If we do not know that something exists, we cannot choose to connect with it and therefore cannot enjoy its gifts.

How to Read This Book

This book focuses on subtle energies, and therefore it is a more metaphysical text than a scientific one, even though I have included science wherever it is appropriate and available. The order of the chapters is carefully chosen. This order reflects a journey of remembering, a journey of expanding awareness—a spiritual journey. This journey begins with bringing our basic systems into balance: the physical body, the meridians, and the chakras. These first steps are described in chapters 3, 4, and 5: the lower and higher subtle energy systems. The effects of these systems help us to prepare for our spiritual journeys.

When we are more balanced, it will be easier to connect with higher aspects of our third-dimensional consciousness (chapter 6) and increasingly with the unity, or Christ, consciousness (chapter 7). When we increase our awarenesses, we will create communication lines with higher frequencies. We also learn through the already existing communication lines about the legacy of our ancestors (chapter 8). We will become increasingly aware that there are other beings with a higher consciousness on Earth who support the expansion of our awarenesses (chapter 9).

When we progress on our journeys, we will increasingly influence and affect the crystalline grids (chapter 10) and the morphogenetic grids (chapter11). This will help humankind and their evolutionary journeys (chapter 13 and 14) and Earth and all the living beings on her. In the process we will be able to connect with other dimensions and realities and the beings connected with them (chapter 12). However, before starting the journey, it is important to understand some principles of energies (chapter 1) and to prepare ourselves (chapter 2).

Because the book has been set up as a spiritual journey, I encourage you to read the whole book, even though some of the chapters or information in them may seem to be less "attractive." Nevertheless, each chapter is also an independent subject that can be read separately. As always, follow your own guidance.

Why I Wrote This Book

I have been asked many times why a biologist with a PhD is interested in a field that in this emerging phase, is not yet supported by science. I could give a short answer and simply say that I have learned to love Earth. I have developed the ability to connect with, sense, and define her subtle energies and to feel grateful that all these energies are permanently available to us. I have experienced the gifts of these energies and what they do for people. This could be a sufficient answer, but in the light of this book, I will give a longer answer—although if you truly want to know why I am interested in Earth energies, I suggest you read the whole book and marvel at how beautiful all the systems interact with each other, in particular our human system and that of Earth.

I was born with an intrinsic love of nature. Living in a Western society, I gave form to this love in a traditional way: through the science of biology. However, I could never find full satisfaction in the scientific field because my love of nature was stronger than my love of biology. In 1989 my wife was diagnosed with cancer. She wanted to understand the background of her disease and together we embarked on a journey that confirmed a feeling I had held for a long time: There is a lot that science does not know and not all scientists are open to explore avenues that are outside, or on the edge, of accepted paradigms. After her death, I began the study of subtle energies and felt a deep longing to integrate science and spirituality. I studied the subtle energies of human beings and of Earth. I became interested in the question of how the energies of Earth support life in general and that of human beings in particular. I came to the conclusion that Earth provides us with everything we need, both from a physical perspective (atoms, molecules, and so on) and from an energetic point of view. This perspective became the guiding principle of my studies. I wanted to see whether I was correct about my conclusion that Earth provides us with all the energies we need to live a healthy, balanced, and (consequently) happy life.

Does this mean that the study of Earth energies and their effects on us will focus only on methods unacceptable to science? Will the gap between science and spirituality be too wide to bridge? I believe that we can answer both questions with a no. There are signs that the gap between science and spirituality is beginning to narrow. Quantum physics definitely supports this process. We need to integrate science and spirituality once more in a way that is aligned with our current knowledge and time frame. Again we begin to realize that everything is energy. Even science agrees that this is true. What we call "solid matter" is energy that vibrates at such a frequency that we can perceive it with our senses. Our brain translates what we perceive into something that we have learned to define as "solid." However, solid matter is more than 99 percent empty space.[1] It is only solid because that is how our brains interpret the information coming from our senses.

Metaphysical Ecology

An important quality of energy is that it resonates with similar energy. In our daily lives, many energetic interactions occur—far more than we generally tend to believe. On an energetic level we interact with people all the time. However, I believe that the most powerful energetic interactions that exist are the ones between us and Earth. I became fascinated with the study of these interactions and even gave it a name: metaphysical ecology. This study refers to ecology (the study of the interaction between an organism and its environment) on the level of subtle energies and "meta" refers to over and above the normal physical reality. Metaphysical ecology in this context refers specifically to the interaction of the subtle energy system of human beings with the subtle energies in their environment, that is, the energies of Earth.

The importance of our environment has been greatly underestimated. In his book *The Biology of Belief*, Bruce Lipton summarizes information that clearly shows that the environment is more important in molding what we look like and how we function than our genetic code (DNA).[2] The environment induces the formation of proteins that in turn determine the way DNA expresses itself. This knowledge changes the concept of how we function in this world.

The results of recent scientific studies are changing our ideas about the world. It becomes clearer that our concept of a species as a totally separate unit may no longer hold. Lipton[3] refers to scientific evidence that shows genes are no longer only passed on to the progeny of an individual organism. Scientists now realize that genes are shared not only among the individual members of a species but also among members of different species. Given this sharing, species can no longer be seen as totally separate entities. As a scientist told *Science* magazine in 2001: "We can no longer comfortably say what is a species anymore."[4]

The fact that the separation between species is not as absolute as we thought seems to indicate that we share our genetic destiny with other species living on Earth. Consequently, the current eradication of many species actually forms a threat to the continuation of human existence. We need to learn to honor, accept, and work together with other species to create the circumstances that will guarantee our survival as a species. It seems that James Lovelock's Gaia hypothesis holds more truth than we were initially willing to believe. The Gaia hypothesis is an ecological hypothesis that proposes living and nonliving parts of Earth form a complex interacting system that can be seen as a single superorganism. It was proposed by James Lovelock in the 1960s and was described in two books.[5]

Initially his hypothesis was almost totally ignored. Currently it is more accepted, even though the name Gaia still tends to be ignored by certain scientists. The term "Earth system science" has been introduced to take away a certain New Age flavor that seems to be attached to the name Gaia. Accepting this hypothesis as truth means that tampering with the balance of that superorganism can threaten its survival and consequently our own. At the moment, it seems that humankind is throwing off the balance of this superorganism increasingly rapidly.

The physical Earth is an important aspect of this superorganism. Even when we choose not to believe in the existence of Gaia as a superorganism, the importance of Earth in our lives and in that of all other species cannot be denied.

All living beings on Earth are intricately connected to Earth. Most people have no difficulty believing that this is true for plants and trees. They can even understand that this may be true for animals. It seems, however, that it is more difficult to accept that this is also true for human beings. As mentioned earlier, every atom in our bodies, either directly or indirectly (via plants and animals), comes from the earth. I hypothesize that in addition, Earth provides us with all the energies we need to function in a healthy and optimal way. This concept, that Earth provides us all the energies we need, is not part of our general belief structure. That is why it is so important to realize again the truth of it.

The Explicate Order and the Implicate Order

As mentioned earlier, almost all the energies described in this book are subtle energies. Although subtle energies are not yet directly measurable, there is increasing evidence for their existence. The famous physicist David Bohm[6] is very clear about this matter. According to Bohm, the problem is that most scientists focus on the study of the explicate order only. The explicate order is the world of form. We can connect with the world of form through our five senses. This is what scientists focus on, as I did until I no longer felt satisfied with that approach. At that time, I did not know that I unconsciously looked for what David Bohm calls the implicate order, the world of subtle nature, subtle matter and subtle energies. I believe that the implicate order needs to be studied with the same diligence as the explicate order to be able to understand the universe. Therein resides many of the answers for which we are searching.

The implicate order helps us to see that everything is interconnected. We are not separate from anything that exists or may come into existence, which implies that we are also connected with Earth. Becoming aware of this connection may help humankind to stop exploiting and polluting Earth, because we will realize that such behaviors have an adverse effect on us, whether we believe in Gaia or not. We know that if we pollute our water, then we will have contaminated water to drink. We know that if we poison the earth, we will have contaminated food to eat. We also know that if we pollute the air, we will have contaminated air to breathe. Many people do not know that if we affect the subtle energies of Earth, we will not have the optimal support available to keep our own energy systems healthy and balanced. Even the way we think influences the energies of the environment in which we live. Our thoughts contribute to the energetic condition of Earth as a whole and even that of the universe. Physical, emotional, and mental pollution affects Earth much more than we realize.

Everything Is Interconnected

Although we will focus mainly on the subtle energies, we have to keep in mind that everything is interconnected. There is no sharp separation between electromagnetic energies and subtle energies, and these two types of energies are affecting each other continuously. There is a continuum in energies that have different frequencies and different functions. While the study of electromagnetic energies is called an objective study based on scientific paradigms, the study of subtle energies is a subjective study. There are no clear rules. An experience is personal, and who is to say what is right and what is wrong? We can use subjective data to create a model that can be tested by others for its validity and through further research by ourselves. This is what is presented in this book. It is a subjective model that has been tested in different ways, and wherever possible, scientific data has been included.

When we talk about objectivity versus subjectivity, we have to take into account that quantum physics tells us that an observer affects what is observed—even *determines* what is observed. It is increasingly believed that consciousness creates our experiences of reality by believing that what we observe is "reality." Consequently, we may conclude that everything is subjective. To understand the reality we live in, we make subjective models—even in science—that may change when more observations are made (a dynamic model). Also, our way of looking at the world changes when there are changes in the collective consciousness. These changes in the collective affect our subjective perceptions and interpretations and, consequently, the model. To make our model more independent of the collective, we need to create it from our hearts. Through our hearts, we can connect with our own unique models that can be independent of the collective because we tap into a higher consciousness. This model may contribute to the understanding of creation and to the evolution of the human species.

The model that is presented in this book has been tested in many ways and by many people. These tests have, I feel, increased the validity of this subjective model. I trust that your inner wisdom will allow you to resonate with that which feels true for you and let go of that which does not. I also trust that the information in this book may contribute to the remembering of who you are and a remembrance of the environment you live in: the Earth, or Gaia.

I have chosen to restrict the technical aspects as much as possible. I only provide data when it is needed for understanding. I also have chosen not to include a chapter on dowsing, even though it is the way most of the data in this book has been collected.

This book is meant for those who are aware that we are connected with the earth but are not yet familiar with the diversity of energies available. It is for those who would like to explore the gifts of Mother Earth without the need to first learn different techniques like dowsing. For those who are interested in more technical data and information on how to study Earth energies, I am writing a book called *The Handbook of Earth Energies*.[7] I also trust that a good dowser can use the information presented to explore the different energies described in this book.

People could easily think that this is a book that helps to heal Earth. I'd like to make a clear statement: Earth does not need healing. She can take care of herself without any problem. It is humans who need healing, and Mother Earth provides all the help we need in order to do so. However, we have created many energetic disturbances, and it is our responsibility to rebalance what we have disturbed. This book provides ways to do so. Let us again take full responsibility for our roles in this world: that of leaders in the shift of awareness, the shift of consciousness, that is taking place on Earth. Enjoy your journey through the energies of the world we live in and experience their powers in helping us to become who we truly are: spiritual beings having an interesting journey. Remember the gifts of Mother Earth and become again a true member of the Earth community.

ENDNOTES

1. Most textbooks on chemistry will mention that an atom has 99.999999999999 percent empty space. See also Thomas Knierim's "Spacetime" (published as a PDF file, accessed 2007, http://www.thebigview.com/spacetime/spacetime.html), 30. 1. For another explanation of this topic, see Jefferson Lab engineer Brian Kross's response to the question about empty space on the *Jefferson Lab* website, accessed January 31, 2011, http://education.jlab.org/qa/atomicstructure_10.html.

2. Bruce Lipton, PhD, *The Biology of Belief: Unleashing the Power of Consciousness, Matter and Miracles* (Fulton, CA: Elite Books, 2005), 41-46.

3. Ibid., 44.

4. Ibid., 45.

5. James Lovelock has written a number of books on the subject of the Gaia hypothesis. I recommend *Gaia: A New Look at Life on Earth* (Oxford: Oxford University Press, 1979) and *The Ages of Gaia: A Biography of Our Living Earth* (New York: W.W. Norton, 1988).

6. David Bohm has written many interesting books on the implicate order. See for example David Bohm's *Wholeness and the Implicate Order* (London: Routledge, 1980) and David Bohm and Basil J. Hiley's *The Undivided Universe* (London: Routledge, 1993).

7. *The Handbook of Earth Energies: Finding and Defining the Different Subtle Earth Energies* is currently in preparation. For the most up-to-date publication announcements, please visit http://www.lemurantis.com/books.html.

AN INTRODUCTION TO
METAPHYSICAL ECOLOGY

BEFORE WE START THIS JOURNEY GUIDED BY THE ENERGIES OF EARTH, IT is important to have some descriptions of energies as a base for understanding the energies described in this book and understanding the systems that support our energy journeys. Therefore we start with this preparatory (and for some, technical) chapter before going on to the description of subtle Earth energies and their effect on us.

The environment is a key factor in the lives of all living beings. There is a whole branch of biology dedicated to the study of the interaction of species with their environment; it's called ecology. The environment needs to provide an individual living being with all its basic needs; otherwise, it cannot survive. When we talk about the environment in ecology, we always refer to the physical environment. For example, human beings need air, water, food, and shelter from weather that is too stressful or dangerous for our bodily systems, like extreme hot or cold weather. While animals adapt, move elsewhere, or die when factors become unfavorable, we have the ability to change our environment to suit our needs. We grow food and defend it from competitors (pesticides), get water from aboveground or underground streams and lakes (aquifers), create transportation to provide us with what we believe we need, and above all we create mini environments like buildings. In these buildings are included technologies that protect us from conditions that otherwise would be uncomfortable or even unbearable. In short we change our environment, adapting it to our needs.

We Are in a Time of Scientific Materialism

Science and technology have brought us great comfort and many wonderful things. However, it has also brought with it many problems as well. Some major problems can be summarized in two words: destruction and pollution. In our attempt to create comfort, we have focused almost exclusively on ourselves. We believe that Earth is here to provide us with what we need, and we take without thinking about the consequences. Whatever is in the way of what we want to have or accomplish, we simply destroy, often creating environments that are unlivable for other living beings.

As a society, we do not really care about the waste products we create. We simply throw away that which we no longer need, not caring about effects on the environment. We pollute our air, water, and land.

The phase of scientific materialism in which we now live is a phase of egoism and extreme arrogance. There are very promising signs of change, although for the most part our society still functions within the paradigm of scientific materialism. We are beginning to realize that we are part of the whole world, of the whole universe, and that separation is an illusion. We are beginning to recognize that when air, water, and soil have been polluted, our health and existence may be threatened. Human beings have a tendency to fear what they do not understand. We no longer understand our environment, and we develop more and more technology to create an environment that is predictable and controllable. Living in such conditions has cut us off from nature even more. The more we are cut off, the more fearful we become about being in our natural world, and therefore we see the environment as a threat, as an enemy. It is those fears that have led to our need to control and destroy.

It is time once again to see Earth, our environment, as our friend. As with human friends, we have to get to know this friend in all her beautiful and challenging aspects. This is only possible when we are willing to start the process of reconnecting. The beauty of nature that most of us still enjoy may help us in this process. We are beginning to see that we live in an environment that contains many different energies. These energies have an impact on us and on all living beings of Earth. These energies affect everything, including our safe mini environments, in ways that we are beginning to rediscover. We, in turn, have an effect on the different energy systems of our Earth environment.

Energies contain information. Therefore the energies of Earth contain an enormous amount of information. This is information about all of life, and about Earth itself. This information is needed to ensure that Earth and all who live on her (forming a kind of superorganism) function well. This creates a stable system that we need for our survival. We have destroyed a lot of this information through the destruction of the many species of plants and animals that formed part of this superorganism. The amount of destruction inflicted on these species is equal to the amount of information (energy) that has diminished in the superorganism that many call Gaia. This diminishing amount of information and energy threatens the survival of other species. This could lead to a system that no longer supports the species that we call *Homo sapiens*, the human species.

We will see that information (energy) is concentrated in fields or in a network or grid of energy lines and vortexes. These grids are spread all over the earth. A change in the grid causes a change in the environment. For this reason it is very important to understand at least the essence of the different grids, thereby enabling us to understand how they affect us and how we affect them.

When I studied the different Earth energy systems, it became clear that these systems support our health and well-being. Although I noted that we disturb these supporting energy systems at an increasing rate, it also became clear that we are able to transform all these disturbances. However, we can only do so when we are aware of the different energy systems and understand their functions. The purpose of this book is to increase awareness and understanding of these energies so that we can better support and enhance the lives of all living beings, including our own lives.

Natural and Artificial Energies

This book does not cover all aspects of our energetic environment. That would take more than one volume, and we are still learning and discovering its many aspects. In general, there are two major types of energies that affect us. There are natural energies, energies that naturally occur on Earth, and there are artificial energies. By artificial energies, I mean those energies that are the result of the use of electromagnetic technologies like radar, radio, television, computers, cell phones, microwaves, WiFi systems, and many others. These artificial energies are not part of this book.

Natural energies are found in two different groups: natural electromagnetic energies and subtle energies. These systems are not really separate. There is a whole continuum of energies that are part of All That Is and all these energies influence and affect each other. From a certain point of view, seeing them as separate may also lead to seeing separation in a more general way, which then prevents us from seeing the whole. However, for the sake of understanding different frequency systems, we need to separate them. This is not a problem as long as we keep in mind that all is connected.

The main focus of this book is to look at the subtle energies of Earth and examine how these energies affect our own subtle energies. This is the study of metaphysical ecology, the study of the interaction of our subtle energies with those of Earth ("metaphysical" here means above or beyond the physical). In this chapter, I will describe some energies that are relevant for understanding our interactions with the subtle energies of Earth. I will also give some definitions of terms used throughout the book.

Electromagnetic Energies

Electromagnetic energies have an effect on the subtle energies of Earth and humans. The term "electromagnetic" refers to energies that always combine an electric current and a magnetic field. Magnetic fields are produced by and surround electrical currents. These two phenomena are inseparable. In other words, when there is a magnetic field, there has to be an electric current and vice versa.

Science has named the group of energies with a range of radiation "electromagnetic energies." All radiation is characterized by function and wavelength. Going from radiation with a long wavelength (low frequency and low energy) to a short wavelength (high frequency and high energy), we find radio waves, microwaves, infrared light, visible light, ultraviolet light, x-rays, and gamma rays. These energies are naturally occurring radiation in the universe. Thanks to Earth's atmosphere, the electromagnetic energies that are harmful to us do not reach us. Only visible light and radio frequencies reach the Earth's surface.

Electromagnetic energies have a certain wavelength, which means that the energy moves in a waveform that makes it possible to predict where and when a wave will be. In other words, electromagnetic energies are bound by time and space.

Electromagnetic energies form only a small part of all the matter/energy of the universe. In his book *Infinite Love Is the Only Truth: Everything Else Is Illusion*, David Icke mentions that the electromagnetic energies form only 0.005 percent of the matter/energy estimated to exist in the universe.[1] The electromagnetic energies that form the visible spectrum (light)—the energies that humans see—are again only a small part of this electromagnetic spectrum. Hence we have an extremely reduced vision of reality.

The fact that electromagnetic energies form such a small part of the matter/energy complex of the universe does not change their importance. They seem to be the most important energies in our daily lives. For example, our abilities to see and hear depend completely on electromagnetic energies. All physical activities generate electromagnetic energies, whether they occur in living organisms or in and around Earth. All activities in human beings are also electromagnetic in nature, and consequently many people believe that we are electromagnetic beings. As we will see, this is a limiting idea, but it is a fact that electromagnetic energies are an important aspect of our physical lives. One of the most familiar ways in which humans work with electromagnetic energies is in the field of medicine. Doctors examine the condition of our health by looking at electromagnetic vibrations, such as our hearts with an electrocardiogram (ECG), our brains with an electroencephalogram (EEG), or our muscles with an electromyogram (EMG). Earth has her own electromagnetic fields and energies and they affect every living being on Earth.

Electromagnetic energies are the easiest energies to study, at least from a scientific point of view. We already have instruments to do so, and it is possible to design new instruments to conduct any kind of measurement or research you may desire. These studies may be challenging, but they are possible within the currently defined scientific paradigms and technological possibilities. One pioneer in the study of nature wrote a book that I highly recommend as an excellent source of relevant information about electromagnetic energies in nature: *Exploring the Spectrum: Wavelengths of Agriculture and Life*, by Philip Callahan. [2]

Earth also creates electromagnetic energies as a consequence of activities inside her body. Examples of this include volcanic activities like lava flows, especially those within Earth; geological fault lines, especially those that are active; and underground water streams (flows). All of these examples refer to energies that are localized. Earth as a whole also has a magnetic field, and consequently there have to be electrical currents. The cause of these electrical currents is not clear, although several ideas exist. For more information, I refer you to "Magnetic Field of the Earth" by C.R. Nave. [3]

Whatever the causes of the electrical currents in Earth, we know there is a measurable magnetic field. The magnetic field strength of Earth fluctuates continuously, not only because of the factors mentioned, but also because the North Pole is continuously moving. It wanders as much as 10 miles (15 km) every year[4] and this has lately increased to 20 miles (40 km) per year.[5]

The Role of the Brain

Let us go back to the electromagnetic energies of human beings. There are some electromagnetic energies that are very important in relation to experiencing the subtle energies of Earth. These are the electromagnetic frequencies of the brain.

The fact that electromagnetic frequencies created by the activities of our brains play such an important role in the understanding of our interactions with Earth makes it important to look at these frequencies in more detail. Brain wave patterns can be measured and are reflections of our states of consciousness in the sense of awareness. For example, our mental and emotional state has a strong influence on brain waves. The frequency of brain waves can be expressed in cycles per second, or hertz (Hz). Understanding our brain waves is important because it tells us how our brains function. It also helps us to understand certain challenges people may have. For example, our brains use 13 Hz for active intelligence. Often we find individuals who exhibit learning disabilities and attention problems having a deficiency of 13 Hz activity in certain brain regions. This affects a person's ability to easily perform sequencing tasks and math calculations.[6]

The brain is an organ that makes us aware of what is happening inside and outside of ourselves. Therefore it plays an important role in becoming aware of what happens when we connect with the subtle Earth energies. Without being aware, it seems that nothing is happening and it will not stimulate the longing to continue with this connection. Awareness of subtle energies requires a shift in the activity of our brains. When we are thinking too much, there is no space for awareness of more subtle signals. Therefore our brain activity determines whether or not we are aware of subtle experiences.

Brain Waves and Brain States

Brain activity is described by the frequencies of different brain states. When the brain is active, it creates certain electromagnetic frequencies that we can measure with different instruments. Five main frequency ranges are recognized, each describing the different states of brain activity. I will describe these different states because they are important in the process of connecting with subtle Earth energies. The five brain states are called beta, alpha, theta, delta, and gamma. Most people are familiar with the first four states. Gamma has been studied more recently with the development of more sensitive equipment. The brain wave states and their characteristics can be summarized as follows:

- **Beta state.** In this state, the brain shows frequencies in the range of 12 to 36 Hz. This is the most active state. The patterns are generally very irregular. These are the brain waves of alertness, concentration, and cognition. This heightened alertness is associated with focused attention, peak concentration, clear thinking, processing visual information, hand-eye coordination, and also with anxiety, worry, and fight-or-flight activity. For most people this is the dominant state of the brain during the day—when the eyes are open and we are listening and thinking—when we are analytically problem solving, passing judgments, decision making, and information processing about the world around us.

- **Alpha state.** The brain waves in this state have a frequency range from 8 to 12 Hz with a peak in activity around 10 Hz. The patterns are more regular than with beta waves. The key words are relaxation, visualization, and creativity. Its attributes are deep relaxation, detached awareness, a nondrowsy alertness, a reflective and contemplative energy, an open mental focus, and introspection. The alpha state is the link between the conscious beta (focused attention), subconscious theta, and higher conscious delta (deeper awareness) states. The frequencies of brain activity most likely move into the alpha state when you quietly watch a sunset or contemplate water flowing in a creek.

- **Theta state.** In this state, the brain waves range from 4 to 8 Hz. Key words are meditation, intuition, and memory. This is also called the dream state. Some call this the subconscious mind functioning. Theta brain waves are found during meditative states, in prayer and spiritual awareness, when dowsing, when we drift off to sleep, when we dream, and after we come out of the delta state. This is the subconscious connection to the higher consciousness and the akashic records. It is the state that leads to self-healing. Theta has been identified as the gateway to learning and memory. You need this state to connect on a deeper level with Earth energies. This state is a natural state in children until they are thirteen years old. It is also a state that gives the feeling of oneness and knowing.

- **Delta state.** This is the lowest frequency, ranging from 0.1 to 4 Hz. This state is defined as the higher conscious mind. It acts as a radar or unconscious scanning device for intuition (hunches, your sixth sense), instinctive action, inner knowing, and deep psychic awareness. Some people call it the gateway to the soul. Normally this state is only found in deep dreamless sleep, but it is also found in trance. This state can also be induced during very deep meditation and even during dowsing. Neurons, which are not involved in the processing of information, all fire at the same time. Certain frequencies in the delta range also trigger the release of human growth hormone, which is beneficial for healing and regeneration. It is the dominant rhythm in infants up to one year of age.

- **Gamma state.** The gamma state has the highest frequencies, which means above 36 Hz. Recent research has shown that these frequencies can go up quite high, to about 200 Hz. Initially gamma was defined as the frequency range of 36 to 44 Hz. Most people stick to this definition. Higher frequency ranges are called hypergamma (up to 100 Hz) and lambda (for frequencies from 100 to 200 Hz). Others define the gamma range as being from 36 to 70 Hz. Basically the gamma frequencies are the ones that represent the simultaneous processing of information from different areas. The gamma state could be called high-level information processing. Precognition is also connected with the gamma state. Research shows that long-term meditation develops a high level of gamma brain waves and shows high levels of brain synchrony and coordination.[7]

In summary, we can say that the delta state is the state of deep dreamless sleep while beta is the state of normal daily activities. It has been shown that transcendental meditation brings you into both alpha and theta states—so does Zen meditation, although with Zen there is more beta activity. When falling asleep, you are in alpha, then in theta (dreaming sleep), and finally you move into delta (dreamless sleep). While dowsing, a dowser (a person using a dowsing rod to find Earth energies) is able to have all four states active at the same time. This is true both for dowsing with tools and for virtual dowsing.[8] Each day we need time for our minds to be in each of the brain states to be healthy functioning people.

Most of us are in the beta state during all our waking hours. It is a very important state that helps us to function in this world. However, we need the wisdom to access the other states whenever it is appropriate or important. When we are only in the beta state, we do not have access to other states of awareness. This is the case for most people, many of whom have forgotten how to relax. For many people, relaxing is watching TV. This is not true relaxation. They are still in a beta state, unless they fall asleep in front of the television.

Becoming a conscious healthy being requires the ability to choose which state of brain activity we want to be in. From looking at the given definitions, it may become clear that some brain states help us to connect with information that cannot be perceived with our five senses. Both the theta and the delta states help us to do this. In order to get there, we need to learn to relax in the alpha state. Once we master the different states, we are able to access information other than through the active logical mind—the beta state, which is connected with our five senses. We do this through intuition, accessing our akashic records, and other nonphysical sources of information. These ways of accessing information are often referred to as being psychic. However, they are normal activities of our brains, available to everyone. This does not mean that there are no individual differences. We all can learn to paint, but only a few are truly masters. When we meditate enough and are able to use the gamma frequencies, we will truly be able to coordinate the information we receive.

Increasingly, we begin to understand that the brain is a transmission and processing system. It receives signals and translates them into a new signal. This signal can be an action or an emotion. The human brain can be seen as a bridge between the subtle energy world and the physical world. Therefore the ability to use the potential of our brains is paramount for working with subtle energies.

The Schumann Resonance Frequencies

The functioning of the brain is supported by certain frequencies that Earth creates. These frequencies are called the Schumann resonance frequencies. These frequencies belong to the group of natural electromagnetic Earth energies. They are very important for us because they induce brain states that help us relax, heal, and perceive and experience Earth energies. The system works in the same way as a tuning fork works with sound. Like a tuning fork that has to be struck in order to express its inherent natural frequencies, the same is true for the natural electromagnetic frequencies of Earth. Technically, the striking force is lightning in the resonating cavity that is formed between the terrestrial surface and the lower edge of the ionosphere. Lightning forms broadband electromagnetic impulses that fill this cavity and induces the seven Schumann resonance frequencies, which are between 7 to 50 Hz. These frequencies are named after Winfried Otto Schumann, a German scientist who first predicted them in 1952[9] and later discovered them with a colleague, Herbert König, in 1954. Although Schumann's name is connected to these frequencies, Nikola Tesla worked with these energies much earlier, in 1905.[10]

The strongest and also the most important Schumann frequency is the frequency of 7.83 Hz. This frequency of 7.83 Hz falls in the range that corresponds to the low alpha and high theta frequencies of our brains. Authors such as Benjamin Lonetree[11] and Tony Smith[12] and mention that our brain waves are influenced by and resonate with this particular Schumann resonance frequency. What does this mean? It seems that the frequency of 7.83 Hz is a frequency that helps us to bring our brains into states of deep relaxation equal to that of meditation. The Earth's Schumann resonance frequency and the brain waves that are at the edge of the alpha and theta states seem to be in tune. Is this speculation or is proof available that this is true? As James Oschman, PhD, says: "There is no need for us to hypothesize that geomagnetic fields, modified by terrestrial and extraterrestrial events, entrain brain waves. Scientists from around the world have already done so and continue to build solid supporting evidence."[13]

In summary, we can say that the Schumann resonance frequencies, in particular the 7.83 frequency, are key in helping us experience Earth energies and their effects on us. In addition, these frequencies help us to balance and heal. We do not need special training to connect with these frequencies. Sitting quietly in nature just staring at something is enough to allow our brains to become entrained by the Schumann resonance frequency. It brings us to a relaxed and meditative state, ready to perceive the effects that Earth energies and other subtle energies have on us that would otherwise have remained imperceptible.

The Role of the Heart

In the process of working and interacting with Earth energies, one other organ is very important: the heart. In his book *The Heart's Code*, Paul Pearsall states that the heart is more than a pump. It is actually the most important part of our bodies. It thinks, remembers, communicates with other hearts, and contains stored information that continually pulses through the body. It conducts the cellular symphony that is the very essence of our beings.[14] In other words, all signals that come from the heart have importance. These signals are received throughout the body. Emotions are the key to how the heart functions.

Our emotions are imprinted on electromagnetic waves; electromagnetic waves are the carriers of information, and our emotions determine the quality of this information. The information on the carrier waves in turn affects the quality of the heart's rhythm. Positive feelings like joy, happiness, and gratitude induce a coherent heart rhythm. This coherent hearth rhythm synchronizes everything. If, however, emotions are negative—like anger, frustration, worry, or anxiety—the heart rhythm becomes incoherent and will cause incoherence in other systems of the body. This could lead to dis-ease. The quality of heart rhythm also affects the functioning of the brain. It becomes obvious that coherence is the optimal state for our whole physiology and thus our health and well-being.

In the documentary *The Living Matrix*, Rolin McGraty, PhD, Director of the Heart Math Institute, shares that the heart has its own nervous system independent of the brain.[15] Not only is the heart independent but it actually responds faster to information than the brain does. Studies at the Heart Math Institute showed that the heart responded to signals even before the actual signals (which were randomly presented as positive or negative images) were given. The heart sends the message to the brain and the brain sends it to the body. The response of the body makes the person aware of the quality of the information by what it does to them. These researchers concluded that the heart connects to a field of information independent of time and space. It connects to information that is complementary to that of the brain. It is the master organ that imprints information into the body. The control source for the exchange of information turns out to be the heart. The research of the Heart Math Institute helps us to understand better the flow of information within our systems.

Comparing the Heart and the Brain

When we compare the heart and the brain, the heart is the primary receiver of information. It is very sensitive to our emotional states and reacts by bringing either coherent or incoherent rhythms into the body. The brain receives information from the heart and processes it. The way it processes the information depends on the frequency state in which the brain is functioning. In addition, the brain receives information from the different senses, bodily organs, and tissues directly. The quality of the signals the brain sends to the different parts of the body depends again on the quality of the heart rhythm.

This information indicates that there are different information flows. These flows are all-important when we connect with Earth energies. The heart receives information from subtle energy systems, from the brain, and from other sources. The heart is not bound by time and space, as demonstrated by the research of the Heart Math Institute. Therefore the heart is most suited to receive information from the subtle energy systems, which also are not bound by space and time. Unfortunately, the fact that the heart receives information does not mean that we are aware of that information.

Most people need the brain to become aware of something. When the heart receives information, it passes it on to the brain. The brain passes it on to the body. The body reacts to the information and the brain translates this reaction into awareness (see fig. 1.1). This means that we are not so much aware of the energies themselves but more of how we experience these energies. The way we experience them is to a large degree determined by our beliefs. The body has its own memory. All

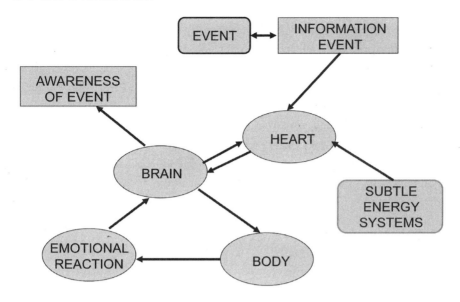

Fig. 1.1: Role of the brain and the heart relative to information flows within humans.

the memories of all the experiences we have ever had create an entity that we call mind, which reflects personality, or ego. The mind functions as a reference system that determines how we define an experience. In this way, we can get caught by the mind, which holds belief structures that are based on past experiences. This may not give us the space we need to be open to new experiences.

There is a way to bypass the system I just described. The mind works mainly through the beta frequencies of the brain. When we connect with the theta and delta frequencies, we tap into a different system of awareness. In that way, we can connect with information from other sources. This is how psychics and people who channel do their work.

When we want to tap into any source other than the mind, we need to be connected with the heart and with the lower frequencies of our brains. When we want to connect with the subtle energies of Earth, we need to be in a similar state of being to become aware of the information each system holds and to become aware of the effects these energies have on us. Working with these energies not only give us the benefits of the energies but also stimulates us to develop these functions of our brains and to open our hearts.

Subtle Energies

The term "subtle energies" does not have a clear definition yet. In his written works, David Bohm postulates that all energies that belong to the implicate order, the world of the invisible subtle energies and forms, and also the world of the unmanifested, can be called subtle energies.[16] I prefer the definition: "Subtle energies are all energies that are not electromagnetic in nature." Stanford University Professor William Tiller, PhD, defines subtle energies as all those energies beyond those presently acknowledged in physics.[17] Subtle energies are different from electromagnetic energies and cannot be studied in the same way. This means that the majority of existing energies are subtle energies because, as we have seen earlier in the chapter, electromagnetic energies comprise only 0.005 percent of the total matter/energy of the universe. Subtle energies are not part of the electromagnetic spectrum and therefore are not bound by the laws of physics, which opens up unique possibilities such as distance healing and receiving information from the future via premonition.

Life force energies—also called chi, ki, prana, mana, orgone, ka, and so on—are an important aspect of subtle energies. Life force is of prime importance for us because we need it to live. We can go weeks without food, days without water, minutes without air, but only seconds without life force. Our health can be defined by the flow of life force through our different body systems. Dis-ease occurs when life force is insufficiently available to promote optimal functioning. Life force is not only found in human beings but also in animals, plants, and in Earth herself. As we will see, the life force energies of Earth support all life on her, including human beings.

It is clear that life force is not a homogenous energy but has many different frequencies and qualities. Because energies are carriers of information, there is by definition a lot of information flowing through our bodies. Energy pathways are also information pathways. This is true for the human energy system and also for the energy system of Earth. All the different Earth energy systems we will talk about are actually information systems. The human subtle energy system consists of three major systems. These three systems are the meridian system, used in acupuncture; the chakra system, used in most energy healing modalities; and the subtle energy bodies. Most people who are active as healing practitioners choose either the meridian system or the chakra system as an entrance for their healing. All three systems are important within the context of this book; each has a direct relationship with certain Earth energies.

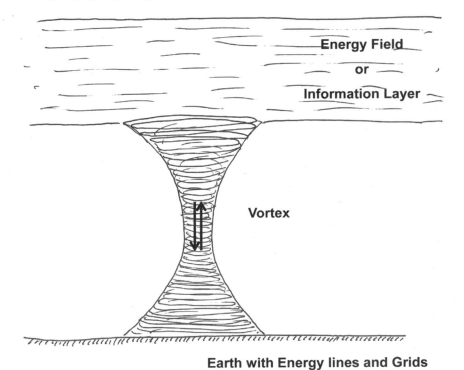

Earth with Energy lines and Grids

Fig. 1.2: A vortex is a connection and a place of energy exchange between an energy field and lines and grids on Earth.

The Three Components of All Subtle Energy Systems

There are many subtle energy systems connected with Earth. All these systems consist of these components: a field, grids, and the connecting vortexes.

- The fields are information systems that are located in layers around Earth. These energy, or information, layers vary in width and hold different frequencies. Each layer holds the optimal information of the system to which it belongs.

- The second part is formed by grids. Grids are networks of lines that we find on the surface of Earth. The lines, with very few exceptions, are partly under and partly above the surface of Earth. These grids hold the information of that part of the field that is used by those for whom the information in the field is meant. For example, all potential of the human consciousness in the third-dimensional reality is found in a field, a layer around Earth. The part of the field that we collectively use is found in grids on Earth.

- The third part is formed by vortexes. Vortexes are the connections between fields and grids (see fig. 1.2). The word vortex comes from the Latin *vertere*, which means "to spiral." This means that vortexes are spiraling connections between two systems, allowing the exchange of energy and thus information between these two systems. Vortexes cover a certain area. The diameter of this area can be small (tens of feet) or very large (from many miles to even hundreds of miles). In general, the area a vortex covers and the distance between vortexes of the same grid are such that the whole Earth surface is covered by the energy. This is a very important point, because it means that you can connect with subtle Earth energies basically everywhere.

When I take people out to experience different Earth energies, they believe that it will be difficult to connect with them when they are back home. They believe that they need knowledge and skills before they can even think about connecting with these energies, but nothing is further from the truth. You can connect anywhere with almost any type of energy, as I describe in this book. You do not have to be able to find the center of a vortex to connect with in order to experience the different Earth energy systems. You do not need to learn how to dowse in order to find the different energies. We can connect with all the different energies simply through intent. However, you may need to know what energies you want to connect to.

An Overview of What's to Come

This book will explain the different energies and what these energies can do for you. The only thing you need to do is prepare yourself and set a proper intent. How to do that will be described in chapter 2. There are many subtle energy systems connected with Earth. Some of them belong to Earth in the same way as our meridians and chakras belong to us. Other systems are anchored on Earth and have a connection with life that exists on Earth. The following list summarizes the different subtle energy systems. For completeness, the overview also includes the electromagnetic energies.

- Portals
- Morphogenetic grids/fields
- Crystalline grids
- Christ consciousness grids
- Other consciousness grids and lines

- Human consciousness grids and lines
- Higher subtle energies, Earth meridian and chakra lines
- Lower subtle energies, like Hartmann grids
- Electromagnetic energies

Earth energies called subtle energies are energies that are similar to the energies of our subtle energy systems. I have separated them into lower and higher subtle energy systems. They are very important for our well-being, and we will look at them in chapters 3, 4, and 5. As mentioned in the Introduction, they form the basis for our personal journeys and development on Earth. The energies of these systems induce healing and transformation to help us connect with the largest group: that of the consciousness systems. We will look at our current third-dimensional consciousness (chapter 6), the Christ, or unity, consciousness (chapter 7), communication lines we create through our conscious or subconscious intents (chapter 8), and consciousness of other species that we have a special relationship with (chapter 9). These grid systems are very important because they hold information that helps us to express who we are, expand our awarenesses, and evolve spiritually.

The expansion of awareness through connection with the consciousness grids will enable us to connect and work with other grid systems. Of these, the crystalline grids (chapter 10) are an interesting subject because these grids are still in development, and we play an important role in their development. The morphogenetic grids (chapter 11) are important because they are the matrices for the existence of all species on Earth, including the human species and beings that many people doubt exist: beings like elementals, devas and Mother Nature. The morphogenetic grids hold the key to the evolution of humankind and that of Earth as whole.

Portals (chapter 13) are doorways into other realities, other dimensions, or even other star systems. They are included because they are integrated parts of the Earth energy systems and support personal growth and development by allowing us to connect with other information systems. Before we embark on this journey, let us look first how we can prepare ourselves for an optimal experience.

ENDNOTES

1. David Icke, *Infinite Love Is the Only Truth: Everything Else Is Illusion* (Ryde, Isle of Wight, UK: David Icke Books, 2005), 24-25.

2. Philip S. Callahan, *Exploring the Spectrum: Wavelengths of Agriculture and Life* (Kansas City, MO: Acres U.S.A., 1994).

3. C.R. Nave, "Magnetic Field of the Earth," from the HyperPhysics website hosted by Georgia State University, accessed January 31, 2001, http://hyperphysics.phy-astr.gsu.edu/Hbase/magnetic/MagEarth.html.

4. "Earth's Magnetic Field," *Wikipedia*, last modified January 31, 2011, http://en.wikipedia.org/wiki/Earth%27s_magnetic_field.

5. Dr. Tony Phillips, "Earth's Inconstant Magnetic Field," *NASA Science*, http://science.nasa.gov/headlines/y2003/29dec_magneticfield.htm.

6. Neurohealth Associates, "The Science of Brainwaves: The language of the brain," accessed February 8, 2001 http://www.nhahealth.com/science.htm.

7. Antoine Lutz, Lawrence L. Greischar, Nancy B. Rawlings, Matthieu Ricard, and Richard J. Davidson, "Long-Term Meditators Self-Induce High-Amplitude Gamma Synchrony during Mental Practice," *PNAS* 101, no. 46 (November 16, 2004): 16369-16373. The article is also available online at http://www.pnas.org/content/101/46/16369.full, and a summary of it was published in *The Washington Post* by Marc Kaufman on January 2, 2005, under the title "Meditation Gives Brain a Charge, Study Finds" (*The Washington Post*, January 3, 2005: A05, http://www.washingtonpost.com/ac2/wp-dyn/A43006-2005Jan2).

8. Ed Stillman, "Dowser's Brain-Wave Study: Your Key to Dowsing Independence and toward a Unified Theory for Dowsing Success," *Sedona Journal of Emergence* 10, no. 10 (October 2000): 71-78.

9. W. O. Schumann, "Über die strahlungslosen Eigenschwingungen einer leiteden Kugel, die von einer Luftschicht und einer Ionensph%orenh₁lle umgeben ist. *Zeitschrift f₁r Naturforschung* 7a (1952): 149-154. For those interested, on online search for "Schumann resonance" can reveal many additional references to the Schumann resonance and Schumann's work in online articles.

10. See for example "Schumann Resonances," *Wikipedia*, last modified January 14, 2011, http://en.wikipedia.org/wiki/Schumann_resonance.

11. Benjamin Lonetree, *Seven Subtle Variations: A Scientific Study of Schumann Resonance, Geomagnetics and Vortex Energy in Sedona* (2002), 1-23, also published online at *Sedonamolies*, http://sedonanomalies.com/E-Book%20Web/seven_subtle_vibrations.htm. An excerpt of the booklet can also be read at the *ArizonaEnergy.org* website: http://www.arizonaenergy.org/AirEnergy/SchumannAZ.htm.

12. Tony Smith, "Schumann Resonances, Geomagnetic Reversals and Human Brain States," *Lowndes County Historical Society and Museum*, accessed December 2008, http://www.valdostamuseum.org/hamsmith/Schumann.html.

13. James Oschman, PhD, "What is 'Healing Energy'? Part 3: Silent Pulses," *Journal of Bodywork and Movement Therapies* 1, no. 3 (1997): 179-194.

14. Paul Pearsall, PhD, *The Heart's Code: Tapping the Wisdom and Power of Our Heart Energy* (New York: Broadway Books, 1998), Back Cover.

15. Greg Becker and Harrey Massey, *The Living Matrix: The Science of Healing*, directed by Greg Becker (Hillsboro, OR: Beyond Words Publishing, 2009), DVD.

16. David Bohm has written many interesting books on the implicate order. See for example *The Undivided Universe* and *Wholeness and the Implicate Order*.

17. William A. Tiller, "Subtle Energies," *Science and Medicine* 6, no. 3 (May/June 1999), accessed November 2008, http://www.tillerfoundation.com/subtle-energies.html.

HOW TO CONNECT WITH
EARTH ENERGIES

I CONSIDER THIS TO BE THE MOST IMPORTANT CHAPTER OF THE BOOK. It indicates how to connect with any of the subtle Earth energies described in this book. The next chapters tell you about the various subtle Earth energies that exist so you can choose the ones you would like to connect with. Connecting with Earth energies is a spiritual journey and, as with every journey, it is important to prepare. This chapter helps with that preparation.

We can connect with subtle Earth energies from almost anywhere. However, it is better to connect with these energies out in nature. As we will see, human activities in cities often reduce the available energies considerably. In addition, a city has many disturbing factors that can easily distract you from connecting deeper with Earth's energies. Conversely, when in nature, the Schumann resonance frequency supports a good and easy connection.

Once you are in nature, let yourself be guided to a place you feel attracted to, a place that feels good. We often do this naturally, without realizing why a certain place is more attractive than others. Places you are attracted to will always offer you experiences that support you. Such places can be attractive because they have a certain combination of energies that are important for you in that moment. It could also be that you've been attracted to the center of a vortex. I have met people who did not know anything about Earth energies; however, when they showed me their favorite places in nature, they had naturally selected centers of vortexes.

Although we do not need to sit at the center of a vortex, these centers do have some advantages. In the center of a vortex, the energy of the grid it is part of is so strong that it overwhelms all other energies present. However, this is only important for those who really want to experience a particular type of energy purely. For most people, this is not important; they simply want to connect with energies to help them heal, balance, and grow, and that can take place anywhere in nature, and in most cases larger city parks will work well. We can find all major types of subtle energy almost everywhere due to the size of vortexes. The energy of each vortex often spreads over large areas, and the vortexes are close enough together to overlap.

Vortexes also are connections between the grids on Earth and the field of potential that is located above us. Most people will connect more easily with the grids than with the field. The grids hold those energies of the field that we work with now or have been working with in the past. This connection makes these energies more familiar, and therefore we will have a stronger tendency to connect with them. However, the field contains the full potential of a system and may be more supportive. We can always connect with the field through intent and explore the energies there. Connecting with the field also is the best way to bring more of the field's potential into the grid, which allows other people to connect with these new energies more easily. When a person connects with the field, they become the bridge between the field and the grid. They bring more of the potential into the grid for available use. This can happen anywhere, although it is easiest and most powerful at the center of a vortex.

Those who do not want to dowse but nevertheless would like to go to the center of a vortex have yet another option. Basically all sacred sites are centers of vortexes. That does not mean that you will know what type of vortex it is, but they are great places to explore. The disadvantage is that many sacred sites attract larger numbers of people, although there are still sites that are quiet.

There are many different grid systems, but most people will connect with only a few. Unless you have a deep interest in studying and experiencing the different types of Earth energies, there is no need to try to connect with all of the different systems. The energies of the grids that have a more direct effect on us are the most important. They help us to become more balanced and healthy and also help us to understand more of who we are. Most important are the energies of the Earth meridian grids, the Earth chakra grids, and the different consciousness grids. For those who like to connect with crystalline energies, there are crystalline grids and vortexes. We will also look at other systems, because they are important for different reasons.

There are other factors that influence our connections with the energies of Earth. We live in a freewill reality, which means that although there is a great amount of energy available to us, we need to make conscious decisions to connect in order to experience the energies more fully. Because we are not aware that we are walking through a sea of energy all of the time, we do not fully experience the wonderful energies that always surround us. There will, however, always be some benefit. Usually people will be affected by the different energies through resonance to a certain degree. Resonance explains why people feel so much better when they are out in nature. Most people who are out in nature have made the decision to relax, to let their minds be at ease. This creates conducive circumstances to be open to receiving the wonderful, healing energies that nature, Mother Earth, offers us.

Preparing to Connect: a Meditation

Whether you are able to sit somewhere in nature, go to a sacred site, or find the center of a vortex, the preparation to connect with the energies of your chosen place is the same. The preparation is the same even when you work with a vortex essence (see next section). Many people have their own ways of making connections that they prefer to what is presented here. Always follow your heart and your own truth, and do what feels right. Your preparation is to become a conduit between heaven and earth. You need this alignment, whether you use the energies for personal growth or choose to contribute to the transformation or activation of Earth energies and the collective human race.

I will give you a meditation that I have used, with different variations, during the many vortex experiences I have guided people into. I am presenting the extended version; you can always adapt it to fit your personal preferences. This meditation is designed to help you connect with all the different energies present in the location where you are sitting. While you are doing this, you will also activate these energy systems, helping them to expand and to bring in more energy from the fields. You also can choose to connect with a specific type of energy, for example, meridian energies or chakra energies, or even a specific meridian or chakra. I have included this as an option in the meditation.

There are four major components in this meditation: connecting with your heart from this place of love, connecting with Earth, connecting with the universe (cosmos), and connecting with those energies of the vortex (or sacred place) where you are sitting for your highest good. This means that you intend to connect only with those energies that support changes and transformations that move you toward experiencing a joyful, happy, spiritual life filled with love and abundance in this physical reality.

The meditation goes as follows: Make yourself as comfortable as possible in the given circumstances (see fig. 2.1 and 2.2). For most people, being comfortable promotes a better flow of energy than the attempt to hold an uncomfortable position because it is supposed to be "better." Take some full breaths to help you relax and arrive as completely as possible in the here and now. During the in-breath, allow your belly to expand, and during the out breath, let the belly completely relax. With every exhalation, relax deeper and as much as possible let go of your thoughts, possible physical tensions in your body, and your emotions. Do not force yourself and do not fight your thoughts, as this will make your beta waves become even stronger. Simply allow your thoughts to be background noise, something that exists but that you choose not to pay attention to.

Once you feel relaxed, become aware that with every inhalation, you bring life force into your system. You can direct the life force in any direction, but for now direct it to the heart center. The heart center is a combination of the heart chakra, the physical heart, the thymus gland and a plexus, or network, of nerves that belongs to this center. By directing life force to this center, you activate it, allowing you to experience love in all its qualities and aspects. Allow the love to expand through your whole system, moving it into every corner of your body, charging, healing, and balancing every cell to the degree that is possible in this now moment.

Allow the energy of love to expand beyond your physical body and permeate all your subtle energy bodies, filling your whole aura with the energy of love. From this place of love make a connection with Mother Earth in your own way. You can imagine this connection: you can touch the earth, the rocks or the grass; you can connect with the center of Earth; whatever works for you. While in this connection, send love and gratitude to our Mother Earth who provides us with all we need in this physical reality. Be open to her response; she will always send love back to you. From this place of love, also connect with the universe, the cosmos. We receive all the spiritual energies we need from the universe. Again, make the connection in your own way. Once you feel connected, send love and gratitude out to the universe. Again, be open for the response; you will receive love back.

Now your system is aligned with Earth and the universe; you are a connection between heaven and Earth. Acknowledge that you are a living antenna that receives energy from Earth and sends it out into the universe while receiving energies from the universe to send back into Earth. Now invite into your system those energies of the location/sacred place/vortex you are sitting on that are for your highest good. Allow some time for the energies to enter and permeate your sys-

Fig. 2.1 and 2.2: Meditate on an Earth energy location in your favorite position.

tem. A couple of minutes for most people is enough, but you can take as long as feels right for you. Realize that this intake of energies lasts only a couple of minutes; the process that is set into motion may take days or even longer. When you feel complete, take a deep breath, and when you feel ready, open your eyes. If you are with other people, share your experiences. Sharing with others will deepen the experience and bring it more into your awareness. However, this may not be true for everyone, so again, feel and do what is right for you in every moment.

When you visit a number of places, you can do this meditation at every place you select, but you do not really need to. It is helpful, however, to do a short version of this meditation at every place you choose to connect with Earth energies. It helps to refocus your system again to make your interactions with the selected energies most optimal. A very short version can be said as an affirmation: "I open myself for the Earth energies. I open myself for the universal energies. I allow via my heart those energies of this location/sacred site/vortex that are for my highest good to enter into my system."

Each meditation will open you to a deeper experience and connection with the energies of Earth and into a deeper understanding of yourself and your own energy system. Do these meditations without expectations. Your experience may be totally different from what you think might happen. For example, if you sit on a fourth chakra (heart) vortex, you may expect to feel your heart area. This is not necessarily true. It may be that you experience all kinds of other reactions. These reactions may reveal what prevents you from truly opening your heart. See every experience as a valuable contribution to a deeper understanding of yourself, of Earth, and of the energies that are connected with her. Experience how she is truly our mother, the nurturer, the provider.

Vortex Vibrational Essences

Not everyone is able to go out into nature regularly to connect with subtle Earth energies. In addition there are people who would like to connect with a particular type of vortex but do not know how to find such a vortex. For these people, there is yet another possibility, which is to work with vibrational vortex essences. Vibrational essences carry the qualities and vibrational frequencies of the object, place, event, or even the being that they have been asked to hold. They are called essences because they actually hold and can therefore transmit the essence of whatever they have been made from. These vibrational essences serve as portals, or doorways, to help you to directly connect with a particular being, object, or place. So not only do these essences transmit these qualities but you can also use them with the intent to connect directly with the Source. This means that vortex essences connect you with the vortexes they are made from. The vortex harmony essences[1] I am aware of carry the frequencies of different Earth meridian and Earth chakra vortexes. Because their energies resonate directly with our meridians and chakras (as we will see in chapters 4 and 5), the essences are wonderful tools for healing and balancing our meridian and chakra systems.

Some people may find it difficult to believe that the essence of a vortex can be caught by water. We begin to understand that water is actually a liquid crystal that, like the crystals we know, is able to store information. The work of Masaru Emoto demonstrated how sensitive water is to energies.[2] We also know the power of water as an information storage device through homeopathy. Many people have begun to discover the power of water and its ability to store information. We see an increasing number of vibrational essences appearing. People make essences of almost anything, and that includes angels, sacred sites, crop circles, and other energies that are connected with Earth.

The vibrational essences are often made by simply placing a bottle of water at a particular place or next to a chosen object of power. There is no doubt that the water will take on information of the place or the object. However, in most cases it brings only a part of the potential energies into the water. To increase the amount of energies that are taken in by the water, some people use rituals and invite their guides to assist. The quality of the water plays an important role in the quality of an essence. The nature of the quality that determines optimal information storage is a subject in itself, one that sparks many different opinions; such a discussion goes beyond the subject of this book.

Another factor that plays a role is conscious intent. Through conscious intent it is possible to create an optimal condition for information storage within the water and to activate the vortex in such a way that the essence of the vortex is available to be transferred into the water. This is an art that takes training and time to master. Finally, to make the strongest, fullest vibrational essences of vortexes, you need to be able to find the center of the vortex. At the center of a vortex, the purest essence of that vortex can be downloaded. When you move away from the center, the energies of other vortexes begin to have an influence as well, and the vortex essence becomes a vortex blend. Although this is not a problem in itself, it may make the experience of those who work with the essence rather confusing. Once all the conditions are met, it is possible to create a vortex essence that gives a similar energetic effect as the actual vortex. For those interested, such vortex essences are available.[3]

Protecting Your Energies during Meditation

Many of the actions of human beings have been wonderful, but sometimes their actions have been negative. Such events have happened all over the world. Negative actions have been perpetrated by individuals or groups but also on a larger scale, like wars and genocide. All these events have left their energetic imprint on the land. Even sacred places may have been used in negative ways in the past, leaving negative energetic imprints. Examples include human sacrifice and ritual killings, black magic, and the destruction of spiritual places.

It is important to acknowledge the possibility that each place we select may hold both positive and negative energies. Because there is the possibility that such negative energies exist, some people believe they need to protect themselves before they can open themselves up to the energies of a place, particularly with some of the sacred sites. David Furlong, who has a deep connection with Earth energies, believes that protection is essential, and he gives two exercises for protection in his book.[4] He denies that the need to protect has anything to do with fear and compares energetic protection with the protection that clothes give against unfavorable temperatures.

The subject of protecting against negative energies has kept me busy for many years. Over time I have used many different systems of protection. I finally found a solution that works for me all the time. It started with the realization that we are only affected by an energy, be it positive or negative, when there is something in us that resonates with that energy. This means that whenever we are affected by energies, they tell us something about ourselves and the condition we are in. As we are all in a process of healing, there is only one way we will not be affected: when we are in a state of unconditional love. Love is the best protection, and therefore it is the first thing we do in meditation: We begin by bringing ourselves into a state of love. The more powerfully you are in a state of love, the stronger the protection. When you are in a powerful state of love, other systems begin to resonate with this vibration, because weaker systems will always resonate with stronger, more powerful systems. Using this kind of protection is therefore a wonderful way to help you to increase love vibrations in yourself while helping everything around you at the same time.

Some people have wondered how they can stay in a state of love when they are exploring Earth energies and sacred sites. The answer is the same as the one for the question of how to stay in a protective energy: We need to train ourselves to be able to do so. This is true for any new system we choose to use. Before we can embrace that system fully, we must train. I prefer to train myself to be in a state of love because love not only protects me but it creates a state of being that gives me joy, happiness, and abundance all of the time. In the meditation, another protection has been built in: the intent to connect only with those energies that are for our highest good. Such protection means that I will not experience something unpleasant unless it is for my highest good, in which case the experience will benefit me on my spiritual journey.

However, love as protection only works when love for self is strong enough. Many people are in the process of building up that love for self. Therefore many people would prefer to have additional protection available. Let me share a protection that has proven to work for me and many others. I call it the Archangel Michael protection. Traditionally Archangel Michael is seen as the protector. To create this protection, ask Archangel Michael to help you to place two protective layers around yourself and around your energy field. The first one is blue in color and the second one, which will become the outer one, is purple. In my experience, this protection is very powerful and will protect you when you work with energies in general and with Earth energies in particular. However, please do not give up your training in creating love as the ultimate protection.

ENDNOTES

1. For more information on vortex essences, see the discussion "Vibrational Essences" on my website *Lemurantis*, http://www.lemurantis.com/vibrational_essences.html.

2. Dr. Masaru Emoto has written several books demonstrating the power we have to change the quality of water. See, for example, Masaru Emoto's *The Hidden Messages in Water* (Hillsboro, OR: Beyond Words Publishing, 2004). See also Masuru Emoto's official website in English at http://www.masaru-emoto.net/english/e_ome_home.html and the official English website of *The Hidden Messages in Water* at http://www.hado.net.

3. See "Vibrational Essences" at *Lemurantis*, http://www.lemurantis.com/vibrational_essences.html.

4. David Furlong, *Working with Earth Energies: How to Tap into the Healing Powers of the Natural World* (London: Piatkus, 2003), 34-40.

LOWER-FREQUENCY SUBTLE
ENERGY SYSTEMS OF EARTH

ON THE JOURNEY OF EXPLORING EARTH ENERGIES FOR HEALING, transformation, and expanding awareness, we start with the lowest vibrations of subtle energies. These vibrations are held in grids that are small in size because the lines are small and close together. These are not the type of grids that you would consider connecting with for an Earth energy experience. However, these grids are very important because they have a direct effect on our health and well-being, and whether we know it or not we are experiencing their energies to various degrees all the time. As a consequence, people in many areas of the world are experiencing slight to serious health problems that seem to be caused by these grids. Knowing and understanding these grids will help to create circumstances that may improve the health and well-being of many people. These grids, when in balance, can help us to create a solid foundation for our spiritual journeys.

Of all the grids that will be described in this book, the grids in this chapter have been studied the most, especially the Hartmann grid. These grids have received a lot of attention in Europe and also increasingly in other parts of the world. The reason for this focus is that these grids supposedly have a negative effect on our health; therefore, they are mentioned in most books and articles of Earth energies. It is said that the energies of these grids cause geopathic stress,[1] which means stress caused by Earth radiation—by Earth energies. I define four different grids that belong to this group. Of these, three are well known and are described as the Hartmann, Curry, and Benker grids. The fourth grid has not been described before. I will describe these grids in more detail because they have such a deep impact on our health and because not all definitions of these grids—both definitions of the grids themselves, and predictions of their effect on our health—have always been clear.

The Hartmann Grid

The Hartmann grid is probably the most frequently mentioned grid system. There are many articles that offer the same basic information about them. In some, the discovery of the grid is mentioned, the grid is described to a certain degree, and then it is shared that the nodes (the intersections of the lines) of this grid are harmful. It is because of these negative effects on humans that this grid has been given so much attention.

The grid system was discovered by Dr. Ernst Hartmann, a respected German medical doctor, who described the grid shortly after World War II. He discovered it while doing experiments with people who had two electrodes on their skin. He was measuring the galvanic skin response (a way of measuring the electrical resistance of the skin) during different activities. When his test subject walked through a room, he saw a change in the response and this change happened at regular intervals. At certain points, the response was more intense, and when these points were connected, they formed a grid. This is how the Hartmann grid was discovered.[2]

In general the Hartmann grid is described as a subtle energy grid, sometimes an electromagnetic energy grid, that has lines that alternate as positively (yang) or negatively (yin) charged (see fig. 3.1). A yin line has its energies mainly below the surface of the earth, whereas a yang line is mainly above the surface. The energy of these lines penetrates everywhere, whether over open ground or through buildings.

This grid is viewed as being so important that it is covered in almost all books on Earth energies, dowsing, and geopathic stress. Some people go as far as to call it the global grid or even the universal grid.[3] It is true that it is indeed a global grid, but as we will see, there are many global grids. Michael Smith is a person who calls the combination of the Hartmann grid and the Curry grid (we will look at this grid in the next section) the "global grid." He even compares the nodes of this system with acupuncture points on the body.[4] Michael Smith also noted in his research that the lines are not all equidistant but rather vary from region to region and tend to parallel the contours and topography of the landscape as they go around the planet and converge at the poles.[5]

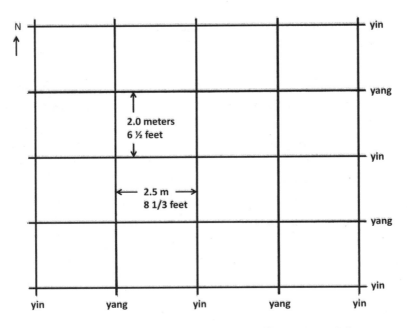

Fig. 3.1: Hartmann grid with alternating yin and yang lines. The north–south lines are spaced at a distance of 8.3 feet (2.5 m) and the east–west lines at 6.5 feet (2.0 m).

Measurements

The lines of the Hartmann grid are about 8 inches (20 cm) wide. The north–south lines are spaced at a distance of about 6.5 feet (2 meters) while the east–west lines are 8.33 feet (2.5 m) apart (see fig. 3.1). In between the lines is a neutral zone. However, these measurements are not constant across different publications. These differences in measurement have been explained by the results of the research of Dr. Zaboj Harvalik. In his book *The Divining Hand*, Christopher Bird describes the research that Harvalik has done on this grid.[6] He compared the size of this grid as measured at different localities. He found that the universal grid, as he called it, was oriented to magnetic north. Based on measurements of places from Iceland to Switzerland, he was able to prove that as the lines proceed northward, the north–south dimension remained constant at two meters while the east–west dimensions necessarily shortened.

The findings of Harvalik are very interesting and seem to explain the variations between different researchers. However, the results found in the Sedona, Arizona, area do not match. Using twelve measurements I found that the north–south distance was only 4.3 feet (1.3 m) and the east–west distance 6.08 feet (1.8 m). I also noticed that the variation in the distances was large. It seems that there were local variations in addition to the variations Harvalik mentioned, which is in alignment with Michael Smith's findings.[7]

Besides measurements of the distances between lines, there are also references to the measurements of the size of the lines, but most of this data is incomplete. In the Sedona area, I found that the width of the line was on average 2.125 feet (65 cm) with a total height of 6.17 feet (1.88 m). The total height is independent of the line being yin or yang. The width I measured is quite different from the width of 8" (20 cm) that is generally mentioned. However, Juan Bueno mentions that there are many factors that affect the width—and I assume the total height as well—such as earthquakes and solar eclipses.[8] Bueno states that Hartmann energy can be detected at a height of 6,670 feet (2,033 m).[9] I believe that he is referring to the vortexes that are located at the nodes. Therefore the negative effect from such nodes can be experienced even on the higher floors of multistory buildings.

The Curry Grid

The Curry grid was first discovered by Siegfried Wittman and the physician Manfred Curry. Curry was a researcher with the Medical and Bio-Climatic Institute in Germany at the time when he worked on the Curry grid. These lines have a harmful influence on human physiological processes, such as brain, nerve, organ, and the immune system function.[10] Curry's ideas were initially met with skepticism, but his reputation grew when he accurately diagnosed people's problems based on the location of their sleeping areas at the cross points of the Curry grid.

Curry lines have alternate yin and yang lines just like the Hartmann grid. However, instead of being oriented north–south and east–west, the lines are oriented northeast–southwest and northwest–southeast (see fig. 3.2). It is generally believed that when nodes of the Curry and Hartmann grids coincide, the detrimental effects are even stronger.

Measurements

Besides the general statement that the distance between Curry lines in both directions is about 13.33 feet (4 m), there is not much other information available on the distance between these lines. Eva St. Claire and Peter Carlton mention the distance as being 11.5 feet (3.5 m).[11] In Sedona I also found the grid to be square, but the length of the sides was on average (for 24 measurements) only 8 feet (2.4 m). It seems that this grid, like the Hartmann grid, has quite a bit of local variation.

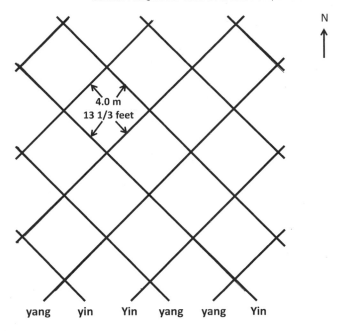

N

4.0 m
13 1/3 feet

yang yin Yin yang yang Yin

Fig. 3.2: Curry grid with alternating yin and yang lines. Both north–east and south–west lines are spaced at a distance of 13.33 feet (4 m).

There is not much information on the size of the lines, either. In Sedona I found that the northeast–southwest lines and the northwest–southeast lines do not differ much in size. They are 2.92 feet (0.88 m) wide and have a total height of 9 feet (2.7 m).

The Benker Grid

The Benker grid, or Benker cubical system, is named after the Austrian researcher Anton Benker. The grid is formed by energy lines that, according to Western European information, are spaced about 33 feet (10 m) apart (see fig. 3.3). The grid is called a cubical system because people imagine the grid as square blocks on top of one another. The lines are aligned magnetically north–south and east–west. The lines are like the walls of the blocks and are about 3.25 feet (1 m) wide. Similar to the previous two grids, each line alternates yin and yang.

It is believed that the nodes of these lines are strong geopathic zones. These nodes create areas that are especially harmful and damaging to the immune system if a person is exposed to them over extended periods of time—for example, at your sleeping place, your workplace, or your favorite place to relax while watching TV or reading a book. From this perspective the system is similar to the Hartmann and Curry grids.

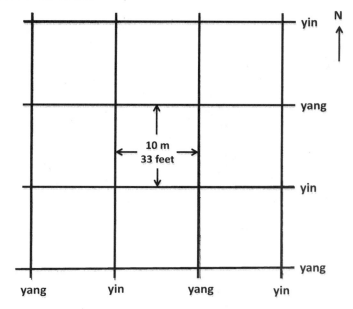

Fig. 3.3: Benker grid with alternating yin and yang lines that are in both directions spaced at a distance of 33 feet (10 m).

Measurements

Similar to the previous two grids I found different sizes in the Sedona area, suggesting that the Benker grid may have local variation. The distance between the north–south lines and between the east–west lines is the same: 25.67 feet (7.8 m). The north-south lines and the east-west lines do not differ in size. They are 7.83 feet (2.35 m) wide and have a total height of 25 feet (7.6 m).

How Harmful Are Hartmann, Curry, and Benker Grids?

Many authors agree that these three grid systems can be harmful to human health. However, from the start of my studies, I found it difficult to believe that Earth would have systems that are harmful to one of the species that lives on its surface to the degree that this species would get sick and even die. Because the lines of these three grids are so close together, it is not easy to find a place where there is no intersection of at least one of these grids. Additionally these three grid systems seem to reinforce each other's negative effects. During my research in Europe, I came to admit that these grid systems are indeed very challenging if not harmful to our health and well-being.

While living in the Sedona area, I decided to gather more details about these grids outside of the town. I was surprised to notice that these grids felt quite different. Actually, these grids and their nodes did not feel negative at all. What was going on? Was I measuring the same lines? There was no doubt about it; these were the three "bad" grids, and they were not bad at all! The question arose: What causes these differences between the situation in Europe and Sedona?

I made many observations of these three grids at a place just outside of Sedona, taking many measurements over time. Initially I did not find any negative energies or negative effects at all. However, once in a while, there were complaints that the energy in certain buildings and rooms on the property was disturbing—employees became tense and tired. When I checked the energies I found that the disturbance was caused by nodes where at least two of the three mentioned grids (Hartmann, Curry, and Benker) coincided. In all cases, there was a correlation between the nodes and the stress and emotional tension of the employees. Additionally, these rooms had electro-stress; for example, one of the rooms had four computers and a server. The affected area expanded slowly, covering an increasing area. However, when I sent energies of love into the grids, the disturbances disappeared. Combining the observations in this location with observations at other locations, a clear picture formed. The three grids are extremely sensitive to electro-stress and human emotional tension, easily going out of balance especially in densely populated areas, like cities. In Europe, these disturbances are widespread across many countries.

Once the grids are off balance, they stress the human system, which in turn stresses the grids. When people stay in these disturbed energies over extended periods—for example, sleeping there—the effects of these disturbed grids could lead to dis-ease. After all, dis-ease is the result of a system that is off balance to such a degree that it expresses itself in the form of discomfort, pain, and dis-ease. These observations taught me that it is not Earth that creates dis-ease; we do it ourselves. In ecology, we say that we tend to pollute our own nests. It turns out we do the same with our subtle energy environment: We pollute it and have to live with the consequences.

I like Michael Smith's description: "What continues to impress me about these energy meridians (Hartmann and Curry grids) is how alive they are, how they interact with and absorb their immediate surroundings on multiple levels—elementally, chemically, mentally, emotionally, electromagnetically, and traumatically. They convey and radiate the energies they absorb much like a river transports leaves and debris that drop or blow into it as it flows across the land."[12]

I agree with him fully, and I was happy to find a person who also understands that we are responsible for most, if not all, the disturbances we find in these grids.

Much has been said and written about how to deal with the effects of these disturbed grids. In my experience, the best way to rebalance them is through intent and love. Rebalancing is easy in a small area where there are no surrounding areas that invade your balanced living space, which is not a common situation for most people. Nevertheless, realizing that we can undo the effects of disturbances in these grids is an empowering idea. Although we as a species cause the disruption of these grids, we also have the ability and the power to rebalance them. As much as our negative emotions affect the grids and disturb their energies, it is equally true that love, gratitude, and positive thoughts can affect the grids in a positive way and rebalance them. We can, in our daily meditation, rebalance the three grids in our own homes. Even if we need to continue to rebalance, we are creating a positive environment for ourselves, and we may stimulate others to do the same. Regular meditation, especially in a group, can rebalance the grids over a large area. What a gift this is for us and others!

Early in my studies I noticed that the power lines of our electricity network have a very disruptive effect on these grids. Because the three grids are already disturbed in many areas, those living near power lines may not easily notice the additional effects. This is one of the reasons why it is not easy to determine the effect these power lines have on us. We can only measure the direct effect of power lines on the grids in areas where there are no other disturbances. Unfortunately, there are few remaining undisturbed areas left to set up such a study. It will take a long time before we as a society are willing to admit that the alternating current electrical system was not such a good invention from the perspective of human health and the health of other life forms. Will we ever be willing to admit that and change it? At the moment, we seem to only be creating additional disturbing fields in the form of cell phone towers and WiFi systems.

In summary, when we experience the negative energies of the disturbed three grids, we have a few choices. We can behave as victims and consequently we will only increase the negative effects. We can believe that there are people and gadgets out there that can help us—there are indeed companies and individuals who claim they can. They use all kinds of gadgets and in many cases charge quite a fee. Often this approach does not lead to the desired results. We still feel like victims and give our power away to others. The third approach is that of empowerment. We know that we have the power to change the situation by sending love and positive energies out into the environment so that the grids will rebalance themselves. In case there are other powerful disturbing factors like high voltage electrical lines, cell phone towers, and so on, we may make the wise choice to move. Why welcome more stress than is necessary? I hope you would make a choice that supports you, turning a challenging situation into something positive.

How to Transform Disturbed Energies

When I mention that we can transform the disturbed energies of the Hartmann, Curry, and Benker grids through love, many people ask how. The simplest way to transform the energy of these grids is through meditation with intention. You may use the first part of the meditation in chapter 2, which includes relaxation, connection with love, and alignment between Earth and cosmos. Then instead of inviting the energies of the place you sit on, you set the intent to send love into the Hartmann, Curry, and Benker grids. Make sure that you clearly state the names of the three grids. To the best of your ability stay in this state of love and send love into these three grids for about ten minutes. Initially this duration may seem long and even challenging but after a while it will become easier. You can extend the duration of the meditation as desired. Doing this regularly will keep the energy of these grids in your home in balance. When you meditate frequently over longer periods of time, you will expand the size of the area in which the grids become balanced. This process will be even more powerful when you meditate with other people, expanding the area over which the grids are balanced.

Basic Yin and Yang Grids

There is another grid system that I have placed in the group of lower subtle Earth energies. This system shares some similarities with the three previously mentioned grids, but there are also differences. I have called this system the basic yin and yang grids. This system has five vibrational levels. The lines of each level have sublines like wires in a cable (see fig. 3.4). The number of sublines varies from three to seven; therefore, I've named the sublines three through seven. I have never found lines with only one or two sublines.

It seems rather strange to use the name "basic yin and yang grids," because I already stated that all three previously mentioned grids have lines that are yin and yang. I named these grids before I knew there were more systems with alternating yin and yang lines. I decided to keep the name because the effects that are expressed through the energies of these lines are basic yin and yang. The yang

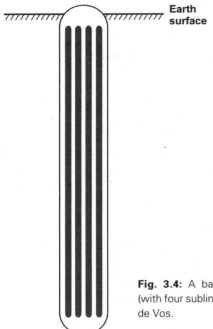

**Earth
surface**

Fig. 3.4: A basic yin line level 4
(with four sublines). Created by Evita
de Vos.

lines of this system powerfully display the masculine principles of activation and
stimulation. The yin lines powerfully display the feminine principles of being,
receiving, and nurturing.

In general, the lines of the basic yin and yang grids are not recommended
places to live on, especially not on the nodes. Only when you are completely
healthy and balanced would it be acceptable for you to be on these nodes.
Unfortunately, few people are so healthy and balanced. The yang lines seem to
have the most direct effect on our health. The higher the level of these lines (the
more sublines there are) the more intense their effect on our systems. People
sleeping on a node or on a line of a higher level are prone to problems, which
may manifest as illness. Because these lines and nodes activate everything,
they can turn small problems into serious problems. I believe that the lines in
Western Europe that acquired the nickname "cancer lines" are basic yang lines.
Some people believe that the name "cancer line" applies to the lines of one of
the three previously mentioned grid systems. I believe that to be true as well,
but the effects of the basic yang lines are much stronger, especially those of the
higher levels.

There are known cases where every house on one side of a street had at least one
case of cancer or serious illness. I found that the line that causes such an effect was

Fig. 3.5: A Beech tree with cancer on a cross point of level 4 and level 5 basic yang lines.

typically a basic yang line with five or more sublines. Because there are no official references or descriptions of these lines, there are no formal confirmations of this. There are, however, reports of a relationship between Curry lines and cancer.[13] In this situation, the Curry grids and also the Hartmann and Benker grids are related to individuals and not to a situation where all of the houses in a row had a similar problem.

People may get cancer if they live on a basic yang line with a higher number of sublines. Trees on such lines are also prone to developing cancer and dying (see fig. 3.5). This is not true for all species of trees. It will require more study to understand more fully which trees are affected and why. One factor that definitely contributes to the sensitivity of trees to these lines is stress. In the Sedona area, I noted that during droughts, the trees on such lines were dying instead of developing cancer. The yang lines stimulate growth, and when there is insufficient water to support the speeding up of growth, the tree will die.

The basic yin lines help us to create a state of deep relaxation and being, making them wonderful places to connect and meditate. However, too much energy from the basic yin lines may lead to apathy in human beings. They can also lead to illness, but I have insufficient information to know the specific correlation between these lines and certain health problems. Because these lines have not yet been clearly defined, there is no information available from other sources.

Ants and bees seem to be attracted to these lines. Ants build their hills on basic yin lines, and you can follow these lines by walking from anthill to anthill. Although I have not done extensive research on this topic, I know a species of ant in Arizona, the red harvester ant (*Pogomyrmex barbitus*), and a species in Europe, the red wood ant (*Formica rufa*), who build their nests on these lines. Many websites mention that ants, bees, and wasps do like lines of geopathic stress.[14] Bees are said to produce more honey when you place their beehives on these lines. Before World War II, the Germans did a lot of research on what they called Earth radiation, both positive and negative. I was impressed by a book written by Hanns Fischer and published in 1933 that talks about Earth radiation. Based on his research, he concluded that bees and ants have no problem with negative energy lines (geopathic stress). The formic acid found both in bees and ants works as a protector against cancer and rheumatic problems. He also mentioned that mistletoe protects trees on geopathic stress zones against cancer. In those days and in earlier times, mistletoe was used for the treatment of cancer.[15]

I prefer to see the energies of this system as positive instead of negative. I agree that they are not suitable to sleep on or to stay on for a prolonged period of time, especially not when your system is off balance. Short exposure, however, can be very beneficial. The energies of the basic yang lines may even help to heal a person, because they stimulate the whole human system into greater activity. However, you have to dowse or to sense the amount of energy that is optimal for your system at that particular moment in time. If you are not able to do this, it would be better to stay away from these lines. Short exposure may also help us to become aware of those aspects of our systems that are not in balance because we may feel them more clearly. This will allow us to take care of problems in the most optimal way. If we approach these lines with awareness and positive intent, these lines are supportive. However, when in a state of unawareness and negative and fear-based emotion, these lines can be quite damaging to our health.

The basic yin and yang lines are similar to the Hartmann, Curry, and Benker grids in that they all have alternate yin and yang lines (see fig. 3.6). All four of these grids have a challenging effect on our health. They differ from one another in that the basic yin and yang lines have sublines whereas the other three grids do not. The basic yin and yang lines also have five different levels due to the fact that the sublines vary from three to seven, thus differing from the other three grids, which have only one level.

The lines of all five levels are oriented north–south and east–west. These five levels differ in the number of sublines they contain and also in the distances

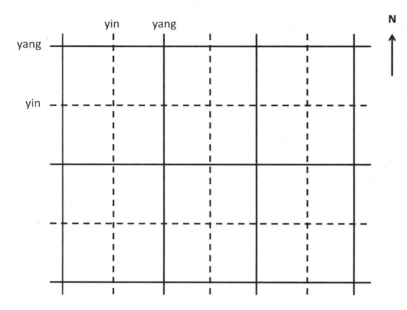

Fig. 3.6: A basic yin and yang grid with alternating yin and yang lines.

between the lines of each grid. This is fortunate because the effect of the lines on humans and other beings increases as the number of sublines increases. I have not studied the grids of all five levels in detail. I know that the distance between the lines of level three (grids with three sublines) in the Sedona area is close to 13 feet (4 m), for those of level four it is around 60 feet (18.3 m), and for those with five sublines it is 570 feet (174 m). The distance between the lines of a grid with six sublines is about 11 miles (17.2 km) and that of the highest level is about 60 miles (96.5 km). With those harmful lines so far apart, it should be easy to avoid them. However, when they run through cities, people build on top of them and are not aware of the deleterious consequences, even when people become ill.

Use Thought to Change the Energy of the Grid System

The grids of the lower subtle energies of the earth seem to create challenges. The energies of three of the four types of grids that belong to this group of Earth energies are rather easily thrown off balance. If that happens, then they become a threat to our health and well-being. Understanding that *we* are directly or indirectly the cause of these disruptions gives us the opportunity to look at the way we live mentally, emotionally, and technologically. These grids help us to become aware of whether or not we live in harmony with the energies around us, forming a beautiful warning system. However, looking at these grids in this way is uncommon. People try to find all kinds of solutions, like placing copper pipes or spirals to prevent the lines from flowing through their houses. The attempted solutions rarely help, because the diverted energies often cause problems for someone somewhere else. Instead, a better method might be exploring how people can change their ways of living.

The most empowering discovery is that we are able to change the disturbed energies ourselves without any gadgets. We have the possibility to rebalance the energies and transform their disturbing effects by sending love. For some people this may sound unbelievable. However, we are beginning to discover that the power of intent only has limitations if we choose to believe that such limitations exist. The work of Dr. Masaru Emoto shows us that we can change the quality of water through our thoughts—through prayer and especially through love and gratitude.[16] If we can do this with water, we can do this with the energies in the three grid systems discussed in this chapter.

The fourth system, the basic yin and yang lines, is a natural warning system. It helps us to see whether we are in balance or not. The energies of this grid system can help us to feel, sense, and discover those aspects of our systems that are inharmonious. This awareness gives us the opportunity to take actions and make changes where needed.

This is a warning system, and should be used as such, and it is not a system that we should expose ourselves to over long periods of time. Most people have challenges that stem from emotional and physical imbalance. The energies of the basic yin and yang grids can increase these challenges and make visible those issues that have not yet manifested. Prolonged exposure could lead to serious illness and even death. Therefore it is important that we learn once more to become aware of the energies around us and understand the proper condition to connect or not. Although the systems described in this chapter may pose challenges, at the same time they are powerful teachers that can help us to understand more deeply ourselves and the environment in which we live, thus preparing us for a journey of further exploration of the subtle energies of Earth.

ENDNOTES

1. Mariano Bueno, *Stoorvelden in onze woning* [Disturbing fields in our house], (Deventer, NL: Ankh-Hermes, 1990), 53-57. This book is translated from Spanish original, *Vivir en Casa sana* (Barcelona: Ediciones Martinez Roca, 1988). [See note at bibliography.]
2. Ibid, 53-57.
3. Christopher Bird, *The Divining Hand: The 500-Year-Old Mystery of Dowsing* (Atglen, PA: Whitford Press, 1993), 347.
4. Michael Smith, *A Year in the Field: Apprenticeship in the Energy Arts* (Gilroy, CA: Bookstand Publishing, 2009), 27.
5. Ibid., 28.
6. Bird, *The Divining Hand*, 347.
7. Smith, *A Year in the Field*, 27.
8. Bueno, *Stoorvelden in onze woning*, 56.
9. Ibid., 55.
10. Eva St. Claire and Peter Carlton, *Geopathic Stress: Unlock the Key to your Health* (Toronto: Savoy House, 2001), 27-28.
11. St. Claire and Carlton, *Geopathic Stress*, 26-30.
12. Smith, *A Year in the Field*, 29.
13. There are many articles online that mention a relationship between geopathic stress and ants, wasps, and bees. Two examples are Lauren D'Silva's 2008 article "Geopathic Stress" in *BellaOnline* (http://www.bellaonline.com/articles/art39881.asp) and Avril Webb's 2007 "Geopathic Stress in Our Homes" (accessed January 31, 2011; original publication website no longer online, reprinted as PDF at http://www.sheerprevention.co.uk/cdata/23461/docs/1453477_1.pdf).
14. St. Claire and Carlton, *Geopathic Stress*, 26-30.
15. Hanns Fischer, *Aardstralen en de Wichelroede* [Earth radiation and the dowsing rod] (Den Haag, NL: De Mystieke Wereld, 1938), 82-85. Translated from the German original, *Die W,nschelrute: Traktat ,ber das magische Reis* (Diessen vor M,nchen: Verlag Jos. C. Huber, 1933).
16. Dr. Masaru Emoto has written several books demonstrating the power we have to change the quality of water. See, for example, Masaru Emoto's *The Hidden Messages in Water* (Hillsboro, OR: Beyond Words, 2004).

HIGHER SUBTLE EARTH ENERGIES 1:
EARTH MERIDIAN LINES
AND VORTEXES

THE SECOND STEP ON THE JOURNEY OF OUR INTERACTION WITH SUBTLE
Earth energies is the connection with energies that have been named "Earth energy
meridian lines and vortexes." This grid system holds energies that have direct
effects on our meridians. Our meridian system fulfills a very important function:
It distributes life force through our physical systems, which is essential for maintaining good health and the proper functioning of our organs.

The Earth meridian grid system is complex and unique. It can be found everywhere on Earth and is so pervasive that it is surprising this system has not been
described before. At the same time, I have to admit that it took me many years
before I found it and even longer before I began to get an idea how this system is
constructed. A key element in defining a grid system is understanding the characteristics of the lines in the system—namely the presence of sublines or the way in
which a line flows through the landscape. To fully understand the Earth meridian
grid system and its functions, we have to consider the human meridian system.

The Human Meridian System

The simplest way to describe the human meridians is as a system of channels
through which life force flows. This system coordinates the internal organs and
connects them with the more superficial organs and tissues, integrating the whole
physical body. The meridians form one of the most basic subtle energy systems
that we have. It is the subtle energy system closest to the physical body; therefore,

problems in the flow of energies in this system often have direct physical effects. These meridians form the basis of Traditional Chinese Medicine (TCM), which has been used for thousands of years in China. Acupuncture forms an important part of TCM and is a way to work with the flow of energy in the meridians.

The origin of the meridian system is shrouded in the clouds of time. Some people believe that the meridian system is a more workable version of the far more complex system of nadis used by the Hindus. Knowledge of nadis seems to have existed for over 5,000 years, while knowledge of the meridians is estimated to be around 2,000 years old. It is believed that nadis and meridians actually represent the same system,[1] with the meridian system being part of the nadi system. The Hindu nadi system consists of as many as 72,000 to 350,000 different pathways, depending on which text you read. Not all of these pathways are important. As Swami Muktananda states: "Of the 72,000 nadis, 100 are important; of these 100, 10 are more important; of these 10, 3 are most important; of these 3, the central channel, the sushumna, is supreme."[2]

Nadis and meridians are channels through which life force flows. Hiroshi Motoyama talks about chakras and nadis to describe the subtle energy system of human beings. He also sees the flows of the nadis as corresponding more closely to the meridians than, for example, to the flow of the nervous system.[3] This idea confirms that nadis are a subtle energy system and not a physical electromagnetic manifestation. The same is true for the meridians.

In general, people in the West are more familiar with the Chinese meridian system than with the nadis. Also, as we will see, the meridian system corresponds with an energy system that we find on planet Earth while there seems to be no correspondence with the larger system of the nadis. For this reason, I will focus mainly on the meridian system.

It is important to understand how meridians work, as they provide a general system outlining the workings of human subtle energies. Different modalities have been developed to work with the energy flow in the meridians. Of these, acupuncture, shiatsu (acupressure), and Jin Shin Jyutsu are the best known. What I present in this chapter is a personal summary based on basic principles of the TCM. Books that formed the basis of the knowledge I share here include: *Chinese Medicine: The Web That Has No Weaver* by Ted Kaptchuk[4] and *The Touch of Healing* by Alice Burmeister and Tom Mente.[5] However, many other sources and personal experiences have contributed to my views on this subject.

According to the Chinese, the meridians are pathways or channels that do more than just carry chi through the body. They comprise an invisible network that links together all the fundamental substances and organs. These channels are unseen but work with physical reality. Because the meridians unify all parts of the body, they are essential for the maintenance and harmonious balance of the whole being. Meridians connect the exterior with the interior, which is the basis of acupuncture theory. Through points on the surface of the body (exterior), you will affect what goes on inside the body (interior).[6] These points on the surface are called acupuncture, or acupressure, points.

Traditional Chinese medicine states that there are twelve meridians of major importance. These are the regular meridians that correspond to the five yin organs and the six yang organs. Officially speaking, the twelfth, the pericardium, is an independent organ,[7] but in general it is described as the sixth yin organ. There are also eight extra meridians of which only two, the governing vessel and the conception vessel, are considered major meridians. That is because they have independent acupuncture points while the other six share acupuncture points with the other major meridians. When an acupuncturist is working with a client, he basically uses the acupuncture points on these fourteen meridians. Traditionally, the number of acupuncture points on these fourteen meridians is 361. However, other schools describe different numbers of acupuncture points.[8] There are more meridians than these fourteen but they are not used in acupuncture. There are internal meridians, extraordinary meridians, connecting meridians, and divergent meridians in the body. Generally there are seventy-one meridians described, but again this number varies across different traditions.

The Twelve Major Meridians

Only twelve meridians seem to be important for our understanding of the interactions of our energy systems with the energies of Earth. As we will see later in this chapter, the energies of Earth only directly support the twelve organ meridians. There are twelve Earth meridian lines that resonate with our twelve organ meridians. I have not been able to find any sign of lines or vortexes that resonate with the governing vessel or the conception vessel.

A way to understand the meridians is to group them together based on certain characteristics. The first step is to divide them into two major groups: the yin meridians and the yang meridians. In the yin meridians, the energy flows upward, yin being feminine and receptive. In the yang meridians, the energy flows downward, yang being masculine and active. Each of the two groups can be divided into three meridians of the hand and three meridians of the foot, thus forming four groups of three.

One group of meridians is called the three yin meridians of the hand. The energy of all three meridians flows to the hand from the chest. The chest meridians are the lung meridian (LU), the pericardium meridian (PC), and the heart meridian (HT).

Another group is called the three yang meridians of the hand. The energy of these three meridians flows away from the hand and goes to the head. These meridians are the large intestine meridian (LI), the triple warmer meridian (TW)—also called the triple heater or triple energizer meridian—and the small intestine meridian (SI).

Next there is the group formed by the three yin meridians of the foot. The energy in these meridians flows from the foot to the abdomen and the chest. These meridians are the spleen meridian (SP), the liver meridian (LR), and the kidney meridian (KI). Finally there is the group of the three yang meridians of the foot. The energy in these meridians flows from the head to the feet. These meridians are the stomach meridian (ST), the gallbladder meridian (GB), and the bladder meridian (BL). The meridians work in pairs, so there is a yin and a yang aspect to each particular type of energy (see table 1).

The yin-yang pairs have a strong relationship. Pathways corresponding to the yang organ are often used to treat disorders of its related yin organ. The meridians work as a team and rely on each other to contribute to the whole. Besides regulating the function of organs, meridians are seen as energy flows that govern a part of our personalities and the way we function in the world. This is reflected in the different emotional states that affect the functioning of the meridians. It also affects the quality of the information that flows through the meridians. The energies of the emotional state affect the quality of life force and the information it carries, information that is spread through the meridians to other parts of the body. Once systems like meridians and organs are off balance, they in turn affect the emotional state.

Yin – Yang	Hand/Foot	Connected emotions
Heart – Small Intestine	Hand	Pretense or trying too hard
Kidney – Bladder	Foot	Fear
Pericardium – Triple Warmer	Hand	Despondency/ despair
Liver – Gallbladder	Foot	Anger/frustration
Lungs – Large Intestine	Hand	Sadness or grief
Spleen – Stomach	Foot	Worry

Table 1: The six yin-yang meridian pairs, their connections to the hand or foot, and the emotions connected to each pair.

A Description of the Functions of the Twelve Meridians

Let us define the functions of the twelve meridians, realizing that different schools and traditions may have different visions. This summary compiles different systems and modalities into one. As the meridians work in pairs, the balanced and unbalanced emotional states or attitudes are the same for both meridians of the pair.

- **Heart–Small Intestine Meridian:**

  The heart meridian is called the ruler of the meridian system. It creates the circumstances to allow the other meridians to do their jobs. When this meridian does not function well, the whole system has problems functioning properly. It gives us the feeling that nothing is really safe or secure. Given what has been said about it in the first chapter of this book, that the heart is defined as the master organ, it is not surprising that the heart meridian is the ruler of the meridian system.

  The small intestine meridian helps us to sort out what we need. This is true for food but also for information and emotions. Working with the small intestine meridian can help us if we are in a muddle. It passes on to the large intestine that which is impure and unneeded.

  When the heart and small intestine meridians are in balance, we live with our hearts open and receptive, without judging ourselves or others, without the need to compare or compete. We allow ourselves and others to be who we and they are. If there is an imbalance in these meridians, we may find ourselves having an attitude of pretense, trying too hard, or being judgmental.

- **Bladder–Kidney Meridian:**

  The bladder meridian helps us eliminate our tears and fears. A strong bladder meridian gives strength to the whole body by distributing the energy stored in the kidney meridian. It also deals with the distribution of water; it is part of our cleansing system. If the energy in this meridian is not moving properly, we may feel tired.

  The kidney meridian stores life force energy for the whole body. If not functioning properly, we do not have the energy to do anything.

  If the kidney and bladder meridians are flowing fully and harmoniously, a person will be in the flow of life. If there is disharmony in these two meridians there will be fear (False Evidence Appearing Real). This is often the basis for all disharmonies in the body.

- **Pericardium–Triple Warmer Meridian:**

The pericardium meridian (also called the heart protector meridian) protects us from shock and hurt. When this meridian is not functioning properly, one can easily get hurt or feel hurt. When we feel anxious, this often comes from the improper functioning of this meridian.

The triple warmer meridian (also called the triple heater or triple energizer meridian) maintains and regulates the temperature of the body's main sections and a person's emotional state. It is like a guardian of all the organs.

This pair of meridians brings harmony to the whole being in terms of our relationship with the universe. If these meridians are challenged, they can bring feelings of despair and despondency.

- **Gallbladder–Liver Meridian:**

The gallbladder is the meridian of judgment and vision. It controls personal decisions and mental reactions. It helps us to see the future with flexibility and hope. If we have trouble seeing things or if we are rigid in our attitudes to situations, this may come from a gallbladder meridian that is not functioning well. Without a vision, there is no hope.

The liver meridian is the meridian of planning and action. It takes the information of the gallbladder and plans what needs to be done, moves forward, and does it. If we have difficulty in getting things done or procrastinate decision making this may come from the liver meridian.

When these meridians are in harmony, there is good production and delivery of blood to and around the body. Blood carries nutrients to all of the body, bringing balance and harmony. When these meridians are disturbed there, is anger and frustration.

- **Lungs–Large Intestine Meridian:**

The lung meridian is the receiver of the chi. It is our connection to all that is pure, to the heavens, to all that is spiritual. This meridian helps us to see and appreciate quality in ourselves, others, and the outside world. The record of every thought, word, and deed passes from the lungs and into the blood to be carried around, affecting other parts of the body.

The large intestine meridian is the waste disposal system for the body, mind, and emotional self. When the small intestine has sorted the pure from the impure, the large intestine makes sure we have space for the new by removing the old. This meridian affects the ability to let go of what is no longer needed.

This pair of meridians helps us to let go. By letting go, we become open to receive the energies of life. When we disrupt the natural rhythm of that process, we experience sadness or grief.

- **Stomach–Spleen Meridian:**
  The stomach meridian is our source of absorption. This may be the pure chi of food, the ability to absorb information, or the ability to take things in emotionally. It affects the ability to nurture ourselves and others and also the ability to feel full and satisfied. Its function also represents reason and intelligence— think of instinct or gut feeling.
  The spleen meridian is the center of transportation and distribution. The spleen transforms food and drink by extracting food, chi, and food essences, which are then distributed to lungs, heart, and liver. This process is central to the production of both chi and blood, and therefore the spleen meridian is the source of the body's energy. It also works with our nervous system. It houses our thoughts, the ones that influence our capacity for thinking, studying, concentrating, focusing, and memorizing.
  When this pair of meridians is working harmoniously, we feel nurtured and at ease. When there is disharmony, we experience worry.

The Meridian Flow

In the descriptions given so far, it seems as if each meridian is separate from the others. This is not true. In reality, there is one flow of life force, chi, that continuously moves through the twelve meridians. It takes twenty-four hours for this flow to complete its cycle. All of the meridians are active all of the time. However, in a twenty-four-hour period each meridian will take the lead for a two-hour time period. If a particular meridian is in a weakened condition, during the two hours when it is in the lead, the body will feel more challenged.

The time of the optimal activity in each meridian has been given in table 2. The times given are commonly used; for an example see Kaare Bursell's website.[9] Not everyone will agree with the timetable as it is presented here. Some people state that the time frame is one hour earlier than the times as given here; for an example, see Tuberose.com.[10] We are dealing with biological systems, and this means that there is substantial variation between individuals. The given time is an average. Most individuals will approach the given times, but not everyone will. The time given is local time. When you move to another time zone, your system will not be in harmony with the time cycle of that place.

Time of day	Yang Meridian	Yin Meridian	Negative Emotion
12PM - 2PM		Heart	Pretense
2PM – 4PM	Small Intestine		Pretense
4PM – 6PM	Bladder		Fear
6PM – 8PM		Kidneys	Fear
8PM – 10PM		Pericardium	Despair
10PM – 12PM	Triple Warmer		Despair
12AM – 2AM	Gallbladder		Anger
2AM – 4AM		Liver	Anger
4AM – 6AM		Lungs	Sadness
6AM – 8AM	Large Intestine		Sadness
8AM – 10AM	Stomach		Worry
10AM – 12PM		Spleen	Worry

Table 2: The time of optimal activity of each of the twelve organ meridians. It is indicated whether the meridian is yin or yang and the associated emotion when that meridian is challenged.

This is why you experience jet lag. It takes awhile for your system to adjust to the new time cycle.

This table is useful in several ways. When we observe discomfort at certain times of the day or night, we most likely have challenges with the meridian that is the lead at that period. This can help us to understand our condition, which helps us to find solutions.

People who wake up around 4 AM may have a sadness that asks for attention. In the same way, people who wake up around 2 or 3 AM may be angry or frustrated about something. When we sleep, we are in contact with the subconsciousness, and this may bring up issues that trigger these meridians. When we repeatedly wake up at the same time, we may have a weakened meridian. That means we have been given an invitation to resolve an underlying issue.

Acupuncture/Acupressure Points

Acupuncture points, or receptors, form an important part of the meridian system. Acupuncture points are the actual points with which acupuncturists work. The number of these points used varies across the different traditions. Traditional acupuncture works with 361 acupuncture points[11] (I also have seen reports of 365) on the fourteen meridians they work with: the twelve organ meridians plus the conception vessel and the governing vessel. Some people believe that there are far more acupuncture points and mention numbers up to 2,000, or even tens of thousands.

Mikio Sankey believes that the acupuncture points are developing into spin points.[12] In my opinion, they are already spin points, because the acupuncture points spin like vortexes. They are places where energy and information travels in and out of the system, exchanging energy with other systems. This is the principle used when acupuncture points are needled during acupuncture. The more spin points spin in an undisturbed way, the easier the energy goes in and out via these spin points. An optimal functioning of these points is an important basis for expanding consciousness. I do agree with Sankey that the frequency of spinning will increase during spiritual development.

The Earth Meridian System

Without question, the human meridian system is important to human health. Different healing modalities like acupuncture, acupressure (Shiatsu), and Jin Shin Jyutsu support the human meridian system. There is also a natural system that supports the balance and healing of the human meridians: the Earth meridian system.

I can still remember standing on the little knoll north of Airport Mesa in Sedona. I was told that this was one of the famous vortexes. I felt that this was true but I had no clue how to define the energy of this vortex. It was 1998 and the only vortexes I knew at that time were those connected with triad lines (see chapter 6). There was a line going through the vortex and I knew it was not like any of the lines I had studied up to that point. I checked for sublines but I could not find any. I also found the vortex to be much larger than the largest vortex I had encountered so far. The one I found on this knoll at Airport Mesa had a radius of almost 7 miles (11.2 km).

It was impressive to stand there and feel the powerful and special energy. It felt like a confirmation that Sedona was a special place. I still think Sedona is special, even though the type of vortex I connected with is more common than I'd thought. Later I learned that the vortex at Airport Mesa is a combination of many different vortexes and that the one I was standing on belonged to a system of lines and vortexes that resonate with our organ meridians. For that reason, I have named this type of vortex with connecting lines "Earth meridian lines and vortexes." These lines and vortexes exist all over the world.

The term meridian is used by other people but it is mainly used to compare, in a general way, the principle of energy lines and systems on Earth with our human meridian system. I use the term "meridian lines and vortexes" because these Earth meridians resonate specifically with our organ meridians, and this is not how it has usually been defined in the literature. There are several references to meridians on the Internet and in books. An example from Judy Jacka's *The Vivaxis Connection*[13]: her book:

> In ancient times, it is possible that people understood how to work with Earth energies by holding rituals at sacred places situated on ley lines. We can think of these sites as acupuncture points on the surface of the Earth meridians; perhaps, through ceremonies and beacon fires, the energy was distributed from one meridian to another. The standing stones are like acupuncture needles placed in special points on ley lines to transmit energy.

This is even more clearly described by Philip Gardner and Gary Osborn in "The Grid Lines of Force: Their Ancient Discovery and Primitive Use"[14]:

> Now let us go back to early man's use of these power points in the grid. After a while, stones were placed at these points on the instruction of the shaman, and this was another instinctive leap forward. These standing stones, or "menhirs" as they are called, acted very much like the acupuncture needles that are used in the same meridian channels of energy that connect together all the organs in the human body. Like the acupuncture needles, they found that these stones could stimulate the flow of energy at the location of these crossing points.

There are many more examples of similar phrases. However, none of these statements define meridian lines as a type of line. Instead they use the word "meridian" as a generic term to indicate energy lines in general and their function. I did not find a specific relationship to menhirs and the lines I call Earth meridian lines. These menhirs are found on all types of energy lines, depending on what the ancient people located there wanted to achieve. What they wanted to achieve can only be guessed at based on what we perceive at this moment in time with the knowledge we have gathered so far.

Once I'd started this more detailed study of the Earth meridian lines, it became clear that the system of meridian lines and vortexes was more complex than I'd initially thought. First I looked mainly at the vortexes themselves. I found two distinct types of vortex. These two types differ in size and in their connection with

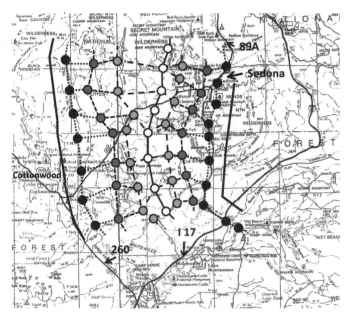

Fig. 4.1: The seven lines with vortexes of an Earth meridian (gallbladder meridian) in the area between Sedona, and Cottonwood, Arizona.

other vortexes of the same type. The difference in size was slightly over a factor of two. The vortex I found on the small knoll north of Airport Mesa belonged to the larger type. The average size of the radius of twenty-six of these larger vortexes is 6.7 miles (10.8 km). These vortexes are found on a line, and there are no other lines connected with these vortexes. This means they are located on a line, but not on a node. [**Author's note:** Remember that a node is a place where lines come together or a place where similar lines intersect.] The smaller vortexes have an average radius of 2.93 miles (4.72 km) based on the measurements of twenty-eight vortexes. These vortexes are found on nodes. At these nodes, I have found up to three lines going through the vortex, but mostly there are only one or two.

At this point in my research, I found the situation confusing and decided to follow the different lines to determine if these lines and vortexes created a pattern. This was the time-consuming part of the research, but the results were rewarding. I found a complex pattern of lines and vortexes. As I previously stated, the vortexes were found at the nodes of the lines. Initially it seemed that each of the twelve meridians formed a grid similar to the Hartmann and other grids like the ones we looked at in the previous chapter. However, this was not the case. I found seven lines that were connected to each other (see fig. 4.1). They formed a system

**Earth
Surface**

Fig. 4.2: A transverse cut through an earth meridian (cable with seven wires); the dotted lines indicate the connecting flows between the lines. Created by Evita de Vos.

that seemed to be the meridian that flows through the landscape. The seven lines within this meridian are more or less parallel to each other. However, there are many irregularities, most likely induced by other energies in the landscape. On each of the seven lines, the vortexes are located at nodes at a fairly regular distance from each other. At the vortexes are connecting lines bridging with neighboring lines. The large vortexes I mentioned earlier are vortexes where the connections are missing. During my research I noted that when the vortexes and lines are more activated, the number of connections also increases. Consequently, there are fewer large vortexes, and in Sedona, where I conducted the majority of my studies, they seem to have disappeared. In Sedona, the many ceremonies, meditations, and other spiritual activities have increased the energies to such a degree that all vortexes are interconnected and, consequently, there are only small vortexes.

Around the seven lines is an energy field. This energy field, together with its seven lines and the connecting lines, form a system that compares to a cable with seven wires (see fig. 4.1). Although normally wires are not connected with each other, in this system they are (see the broken lines in fig. 4.2). These cables vary in width from 13 to 15 miles (21 to 24 km) and have a height that varies between 1.1 and 1.2 miles (1.8 to 1.9 km). This means that the cable is more like an undulating ribbon flowing through the landscape. It moves deep under the surface of the earth and can also be completely above the surface of the earth. This undulation can be in the length or the width of this ribbon (see figs. 4.2 and 4.3).

**Earth
surface**

Fig. 4.3: The flow of a yin earth meridian line (cable) in relation to the earth surface. Created by Evita de Vos.

All vortexes are located within the cable on the wires, and within a cable, all vortexes spin predominantly in the same direction. Based on the dominant spinning direction of the vortexes, we can find two types of cables: yang (masculine) and yin (feminine). The yin cable can be completely under the ground or above the ground, but overall, it is usually more below the surface than above. The vortexes on these lines spin predominantly clockwise. This means that both spinning directions exist, but that the clockwise one is stronger than the counterclockwise one and determines the overall quality. The yang cables can also be completely above or below the surface of the earth, but overall, they are more above the surface of the earth than below. These vortexes predominantly spin counterclockwise. The distance between the vortexes is such that the energy field of each vortex overlaps with neighboring vortexes of the same type to at least some degree. In this way, they create an energy field that goes beyond the cables. This is true for all twelve different types of cables (meridians). Of course the energy is most intense at the center of each vortex.

The twelve Earth meridians are related to our twelve organ meridians. For that reason, I have given the twelve Earth meridians the same names as our organ meridians. For example, the Earth's lung meridian got its name because it resonates with our lung meridian. Earth meridians are, however, a bit less exclusive than our organ meridians. Sometimes two or even three of our meridians resonate with a particular Earth meridian vortex. Nevertheless, there is always one of the organ meridians that resonates most strongly with a particular Earth meridian. Therefore each Earth meridian has been given the name of the human meridian that it resonates most strongly with.

Personal Experiences with Meridians

During my work as a facilitator for vortex experiences (I gave vortex tours), I noticed that the meridian vortexes were extremely important. Each meridian vortex, independent of the type of vortex, activates the whole meridian system. I am always amazed at the powerful effect this activation has on people. They feel more relaxed, more present, and lighter—often at the same time—stating that their bodies feel heavier but in a pleasant way. Because the flow in the meridians is stimulated, the whole physical system is stimulated. Depending on people's issues, I sometimes include an extra meridian vortex, and people usually have an experience of feeling better. This is often induced by the release of stuck negative emotions, which the meridian vortexes undoubtedly facilitate.

It is often difficult for people to discern the more specific effects of the particular type of meridian they are sitting on. It took me many years to understand how people's experiences relate to a specific type of meridian. Often there is seemingly no relationship between people's experiences and the particular type of meridian. I believe that this is due to the stimulation of the whole meridian system giving us so many changes that the relationship to a particular meridian gets obscured.

After many observations I have come to the conclusion that it does not really matter what type of meridian you select. Sitting on a meridian vortex or inviting meridian energies when you sit somewhere in nature always gives a general stimulation of the whole system and improves your well-being. It helps people to become more aware of their physical bodies, which is very important. The body gives us signals telling us how well we are doing. However, we need to listen to the signals. A tense body gives less clear signals than a relaxed body. There is no doubt that the Earth meridian energies help us to relax and improve bodily awareness. I highly recommend connecting with these energies on a regular basis.

The Twelve Earth Meridians Promote Physical Well-Being

The meridians are a very important part of our subtle energy system. They form a bridge between the physical body and the higher subtle energies. The meridians transport life force to organs and other parts of the physical body to ensure their optimal functioning. The meridians are connected to our emotions, especially those we call negative, like fear, worry, and anger. These emotions jeopardize the flow of energies through the meridians and consequently have an adverse effect on the function of organs and tissues.

There are many meridians. Of these, twelve are called the organ meridians. These twelve organ meridians actually form one flow supported by the earth through twelve energy flows that I have called Earth meridians. These Earth meridians have a direct effect on our twelve organ meridians through the principle of resonance. Thus Earth provides us with the possibility of creating a healthy meridian system if we choose to open ourselves to these energies. This healthy meridian system creates a healthy physical system that is grounded by connection to the earth, forming a perfect foundation from which to continue with the exploration of different Earth energies.

ENDNOTES

1. Mikio Sankey, *Esoteric Acupuncture, Volume I: Gateway to Expanded Healing* (Kapolei, HI: Mountain Castle Publishing, 1999), 33-40.
2. Ibid., 34.
3. Hiroshi Motoyama, *Theories of the Chakras: Bridge to Higher Consciousness* (Wheaton, IL: The Theosophical Publishing House, 1981), 281.
4. Ted J. Kaptchuk, *Chinese Medicine: The Web that Has No Weaver* (London: Rider and Company, 1983).
5. Alice Burmeister with Tom Mente, *The Touch of Healing: Energizing Body, Mind, and Spirit with the Art of Jin Shin Jyutsu* (New York: Bantam Books, 1997).
6. Kaptchuk, *Chinese Medicine*, 77.
7. Ibid., 78.
8. Ibid., 110.
9. Kaare Bursell, "Healing with the Day," *The Alchemycal Pages*, accessed January 31, 2011, http://www.alchemycalpages.com/heal10.html.
10. Tuberose Natural Healing Store, "Meridians," Tubersose.com, accessed February 10, 2001, http://www.tuberose.com/meridians.html.
11. Kaptchuk, *Chinese Medicine*, 110.
12. Sankey, *Esoteric Acupuncture*, 25.
13. Judy Jacka, N.D., *The Vivaxis Connection: Healing through Earth Energies* (Charlottesville, VA: Hampton Roads Publishing Company, 2000), 183.
14. Philip Gardner and Gary Osborn, "The Grid Lines of Force: Their Ancient Discovery and Primitive Use," *World-Mysteries.com* (2008), accessed January 31, 2011, http://www.world-mysteries.com/sci_gridlines.htm.

5

HIGHER SUBTLE EARTH ENERGIES 2:
EARTH CHAKRA LINES
AND VORTEXES

IN TERMS OF RESEARCH INTO EARTH ENERGIES, ONE OF THE MOST REMARKABLE discoveries for me was learning about the direct interaction between the higher subtle energies of Earth and the human subtle energy system. In the previous chapter we discussed the complex Earth meridian lines and vortexes that interact directly with our twelve organ meridians. In this chapter, we will look at another subtle energy system that receives support from the earth: our chakra systems. This Earth energy system is therefore called "Earth chakra lines and vortexes," or the "Earth chakra system." The Earth chakra system is another important support on our journey toward increased health, balance, and expanded awareness.

Chakras are very important energy centers in our human systems. They give us information about the quality of the energy flowing through our systems. The chakra system works on a higher vibrational level than that of the meridians. As we will see, it works on four different levels. In order to understand this Earth chakra system and how it interacts with our chakra systems, it is helpful to begin by looking at the human chakra system.

In general, the human chakra system is seen as consisting of seven chakras, although some research mentions more chakras. These additional chakras are often secondary chakras, of which there seem to be many. Barbara Ann Brennan defines twenty-one of them.[1] I will describe only the primary chakras of the twelve chakra system. This is in alignment with what we find with the Earth chakra system. I believe that the Earth energy system determines the energy systems of all beings living upon her. Human beings reflect her energy system most optimally, and therefore humans have twelve chakras that reflect the Earth chakra system. The five chakras, in addition to the seven chakras normally described, are connected with the five subtle energy bodies. In this chapter, we will look both at the seven body chakras and the chakras of the five subtle energy bodies before looking at the Earth chakra energy system.

The human chakra system is of key importance in terms of our functioning in this world, and therefore we will pay significant attention to it. Information on the human chakra system helps us to understand our daily life experiences. Without understanding the human chakra system, it is difficult to evaluate the importance of the Earth chakra system. Knowledge of the chakra system can also help us to understand the way the consciousness works and especially how it is organized, as we will read in chapter 6.

The Seven Human Body Chakras

Much has been written and said about chakras. Almost every alternative healing modality works with chakras. They have become an increasingly important aspect in discussions about health and healing. Many psychics claim they can see chakras. While working with people, both in healing sessions and in working with Earth energies, I have received insights that have helped me to understand chakras, their functions, and their energy flows. These insights in combination with information from other sources have led me to describe chakras in ways that differ from descriptions you may find in other articles and books. Therefore I have not included many references, unless I refer to a specific author's ideas.

The word "chakra" comes from ancient Hindu texts, the same texts that use the term "nadis" for channels of energy. It is a Sanskrit word that means wheel or disc. I find it fascinating that most books on chakras do not talk about meridians and most books on meridians do not talk about chakras. Even though their origin in antiquity may have been the same, their individual developments have separated them over time. It is valuable to align these two systems and compare direct and indirect relationships. After all, a human being is a functional unit with different aspects and qualities that work together as a harmonious whole. If the aspects do not work harmoniously, imbalances will be created. When we experience imbalance, we are invited to look at which aspect is no longer in balance and what causes this imbalance. Chakras are one of the easiest ways to understand the cause of imbalances and are therefore very important. Usually there are emotional issues that cause imbalances, and this in turn may cause diseases. Because chakras are the easiest system to understand and to sense, most healers work with the chakra system.

The seven body chakras are actually part of a center. This center is formed by three things: a chakra; an endocrine (hormonal) gland or glands; and ganglia (also called a plexus), a node of nerve ganglia branching forth from the spinal column. Actually only the lower five chakras are connected to the plexus; the two higher chakras are connected to the brain and the hormonal glands located in the brain. A chakra, together with its hormonal gland and the nervous system, all interact with one another. The way this happens is determined by the condition of the chakra and the energy/information coming through. Of course the condition of the chakra will also determine what energy/information is able to come through.

If a chakra does not function properly, it will have a negative effect on the functioning of the hormonal gland. If such a condition is severe or chronic, it may lead to a dysfunction of the hormonal gland. The hormones produced by the gland are regulators of specific body processes. If there is a disturbance in the regulation, it may lead to a disturbance of the organs related to these processes. Dysfunction of a chakra will set a chain of events into motion in the physical body, the meridian system, and other chakras because everything is interconnected and related to everything else.

A Chakra Is a Vortex

A chakra is a vortex (see fig. 5.1), meaning that it is a place of information exchange between systems. For us, this refers to the exchange between our physical bodies, the subtle energy bodies, and the outside world. Each chakra acts as an antenna for certain frequencies. This means that the type of chakra and its condition determines the kind of energy coming in, as well as the kind of energy sent out. That in itself makes it important to ensure that our chakras work in balance and in a healthy way for optimal quality energies.

Chakras also receive energy/information from our own subtle bodies. We will describe these subtle bodies later in this chapter. Each subtle body has its own frequency range and the different chakras are able to tap into the energies of these subtle bodies. It becomes clear that each chakra is able to operate on several levels at the same time. I see a chakra not as one single vortex but consisting of four vortexes, each operating at different vibrational levels. These four vortexes are so close together that it appears as if there is only one. The lowest vibrational level, or vortex, interacts mainly with the physical system, which also includes

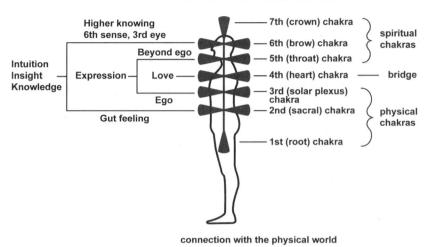

Fig. 5.1: The seven chakras, their relationships, and their functions. Created by Evita de Vos.

the etheric and astral bodies. The other three levels (vortexes) work with the emotional, mental, and spiritual bodies respectively. The vortexes of this chakra complex spin in both directions, clockwise and counterclockwise, in the same way as most Earth energy vortexes do. When they interact with the outside world, they interact with different aspects of the human collective consciousness and other energy fields. We can even interact with the energies of stones, crystals, plants, trees, and animals.

The Chakra Pairs

The chakras can be grouped in different ways. The second to the sixth chakra have an opening both at the front and at the back side of the body. The first and seventh chakras can be seen as the lower and higher aspects of our connection with the world around us; the lower (first) chakra represents our connection with the physical world and the upper (seventh) represents our connection with the spiritual world, the world of All That Is.

Some of the chakras work in pairs. Together the third and fifth chakras work with different aspects of expression. The third chakra expresses from the perspective of the physical world (ego) and the fifth chakra from that of the spiritual world beyond ego, the expression of who we truly are. However, the condition of the third chakra strongly affects the way the fifth chakra functions. The second and the sixth chakras form a pair that works with intuition, insight, and knowledge. The second chakra intuits in the physical reality (gut feeling) and the sixth chakra is for intuiting in the spiritual world (the sixth sense, the third eye, higher knowing, intuition). Also here we see that the way the second chakra functions affects the functioning of the sixth chakra. The fourth chakra, the heat chakra, forms the bridge between the physically oriented chakras and the spiritually oriented chakras. To bridge the physical and the spiritual worlds/aspects of reality, all we need is love! We see again that the heart creates balance and coherence. When we are in fear—which means when we are not in a state of love—we disrupt the balance and create incoherence.

The seven chakras also help us to orient ourselves in reality. The paired chakras can be shown as three axes (see fig. 5.2). Each axis determines the place of any point or object in space. Indigenous people define them as the four directions, the above, and the below. They use these directions in their ceremonies. The two ends of each axis always represent two opposites. In the case of chakras, these two opposites are the physical aspect versus the spiritual aspect. The three axes of the chakras consist of the unity axis (formed by the first and the seventh chakra), the information/knowledge axis (formed by the second and the sixth chakra), and the expression axis (formed by the third and fifth chakras). The first chakra is the below and the seventh chakra is the above. The four directions are formed

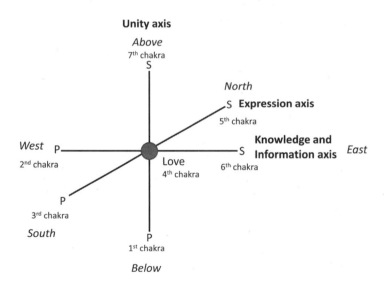

Fig. 5.2: The three axes (six directions) that show how the seven chakras help us to orient ourselves in this world (P = physical; S = Spiritual).

by the second and sixth chakras, which represent the east–west axis/directions, and the third and fifth chakras, which represent the north–south axis/directions. The six directions are balanced through love, which is represented by the intersection of the three axes. Love also brings balance between the physical and spiritual chakras.

The fact that chakras are directly connected with the hormonal glands and the nervous system adds to their importance. Because hormones are the regulators of many physiological systems, the condition of the chakra system is to a large degree responsible for the functioning of our complete physiology and biochemistry. In addition, they have a strong effect via the nervous system on large parts of our bodies. These centers are so important that their proper functioning should have the highest priority in all healing processes.

Chakras and Our Personal Development

There are several approaches that may help us to understand the function of the chakras. One of these approaches conceptualizes chakras as representing stages of development throughout our lives. This way of looking at chakras makes it easier to understand them and also to understand the relationship between the chakras and issues that occur in our lives. Therefore I would like to describe the chakras primarily from this perspective.

When a child is born, the chakras are in place but they are not yet fully developed and functioning. They are in a neutral state; they have not yet been colored by experiences. Most people, when they are born, lose the awareness that they are spiritual beings having a human experience. By losing this awareness, they also lose the awareness of their connection with Source. Nowadays many of the new children—children who have been given names like Indigo, Crystal, or psychic children—maintain an awareness of their spiritual connections to various degrees. As this connection facilitates the possibility of experiencing enlightenment, it seems that these children could have an advantage as they embark on their spiritual journeys. However, these children also go through the same stages of development as everyone else. As we go through these stages of development, most of us are unable to develop our chakras in a way that allows the experience of enlightenment, oneness, and connection to Source.

According to esoteric tradition, it takes seven periods of seven years to complete a full cycle of chakra development. Most, if not all, humans have life experiences that keep the chakras from fully developing. Whatever happens at the end of seven periods of seven years, comprehending the seven phases or periods of development helps us to understand our human journeys and the role the chakras play in it.

The first period, which lasts from birth until a child's seventh birthday, focuses on the first chakra. While the focus is on the first chakra, within each year, the development of this first chakra is in connection with one of the other seven chakras, moving through all seven chakras in the seven years of this first period. This means that during the first year of our lives we develop the first chakra from a first chakra perspective. In the second year, we develop the first chakra from a second chakra perspective, in the third year from a third chakra perspective, and so on, until the period of seven years is completed and the first chakra has been activated almost completely. Maybe it is better to use the word "programmed" instead of "activated." What actually happens is that our experiences program the way the chakras function. This program is connected with the belief structures associated with experiences during development. The same pattern exists for all chakras.

The next period of seven years, from the seventh until the fourteenth birthday, focuses on the second chakra while also going through the seven steps of the seven chakras. The period from the fourteenth year to the day of the twenty-first birthday focuses on the third chakra, again with seven steps. This goes on until the cycle of seven periods of seven years is completed. In theory, we are at that moment fully functioning, fully realized people. We all know that this rarely happens. When we start a new cycle, there is often a strong longing for change. This is the famous period around the age of fifty, give or take a few years, when people go through what is called a midlife crisis and/or menopause. Let us look now at the essence of what happens during each of the seven periods. The process is more complex than what is described here, but this chapter will give you a general idea, which is enough to understand the basic functioning of the chakras and the relationship between our chakras and those of Earth.

Developing the First Chakra (1 to 7)

The first period of seven years, the period of development of the first chakra, revolves around feelings of safety and acceptance. The first chakra is a unity chakra: We are one with our physical world, with Earth, and with all that exists on it—plants, animals, stones, mountains, rivers, and people. We also are one with planets and stars. In this first phase, we learn what it means to be part of the world around us and how to connect with it. When we do not feel accepted by our families or environment, we feel separated and develop feelings of lack—lack of safety and lack of acceptance.

In this first period, everything is focused on wanting to feel accepted and safe in this world. For a child, the world used to be the community and the environment he or she was born into. In our modern society, this community has mostly been reduced to the family and sometimes even to a single parent. As a consequence, parents now carry a responsibility that used to be taken on by a whole community: to help a child feel safe and accepted in this world and to feel one with it. Needless to say, even the best parents have their shortcomings, especially in relation to this sense of feeling one with the world. Few parents feel one with the world around them, so how can they teach that feeling to their children?

When I talk with people about their upbringing, especially about those first seven years, many will tell me that they had good childhoods. Therefore they do not understand why when I see that their first chakra is out of balance, I then relate that to the early years of their lives. However, children experience the world in different ways than adults. Very young children do not have an adult's developed mind, the development that helps people to understand and process experience. Children experience situations directly, without analyzing them.

Children also perceive things literally. When parents say to their children that they are bad boys or bad girls, children literally believe themselves to be bad. Children translate this as "my parents do not love me" or "my parents do not accept me." When this happens, often the first chakra will be out of balance. Unfortunately, few people have a fully developed and balanced first chakra. This means that we have not yet dealt fully with all of the issues from our childhoods. As the health of each higher chakra is determined by the previous ones, the first chakra has now induced imbalance in other chakras, imbalance that we need to deal with in order to align our systems. When children feel they are not loved or accepted, they will experience the world as being unsafe. They will feel separated from the world instead of developing the feeling that they belong to this world. Because this chakra gives a feeling of belonging, it is also called the group chakra or the "we" chakra.

Developing Personal Relationships (8 to 14)

The second period focuses on the development of our personal relationships with other people and with our environment, work, and money. This is the relationship period. In this period, we also develop our sexuality. We shift from "we" (the community, the world) to "I and other." This period determines how we will relate to our partner(s), friends, nature, home, food, money—anything that is outside of us. If feelings of separation, lack of safety, or lack of acceptance have developed during the first period, they will have a profound effect on the way we experience relationships. If we do not know how to relate to situations and at the same time want to fulfill a need we have, we often give ourselves away in order to get what we want.

As children, we feel unaccepted and unloved for being ourselves and feel we have to act in certain ways in order to receive the love we need. Girls, as they grow up into women, experience this even more strongly. This is very disempowering and weakens the second chakra even more. Women are nurturers and therefore feel a strong urge to take care of others. Often they forget themselves in their attempts to support others. However, they still have needs, and the fact that they insufficiently fulfill those needs because they give others priority eventually weakens their second chakras. This may create feelings of disempowerment, unhappiness, and even resentment.

Developing Self-Worth (15 to 21)

The third period of seven years focuses on the third chakra. This is the period in which we develop our self-esteem, self-worth, and belief about what we deserve. We grow toward independence and individuality. We search for our personal truth and values, which form the basis of how we see ourselves. This is the period of the "I," the ego. In current spiritual literature, many see the ego as something bad, something to get rid of. But the problem is not ego as such—it is the unhealthy distortions of ego that need to be transformed. We need the ego to be able to deal with the physical world. So we need a strong healthy ego in service to higher self rather than a dominating ego that is in charge.

In our society, many parents do not allow their children to develop strong, healthy egos. Children need to fit into society, especially the community they've grown up in, and this may be based on social, religious, or educational rules. Again, children are not allowed to be who they are but must be who they are told to be. This produces inner tension, and children come to believe that something is wrong with them. This may lead to low self-esteem and, consequently, to deformed egos. Healthy egos can easily surrender to Spirit in later periods when we have a deeper connection to our spiritual paths. Development during this period will depend to a large degree on development that has occurred in the previous two periods. In other words, the condition of the first and the second chakras will have a major influence on the condition of the third chakra.

The first three periods are mainly focused on those things that we need in order to function properly in the physical world. We are supposed to have mastered how to deal with these needs by the time we are twenty-one years old, which is the age of adulthood. This challenge, however, is that our experiences have programmed what we need. That means that needs are what we believe we need and not necessarily what we truly need in order to be a functional human being. When we have feelings of "I need," our true basic needs have not been met. The fact that so many of us feel needy has led to our current consumption culture. When we are needy, we are never satisfied, even when we have more than we need.

Changing Conditional Love into Unconditional Love (22 to 28)

The first three periods are primarily oriented physically. We develop the persona or the ego and learn to interact with the world around us. An aspect of these three periods is that love is mainly conditional: "I love you when you give me what I need. If you do not give me what I need, I do not love you anymore." Most of us have experienced this with our children or have observed children saying these words. However, many adults are still stuck in this phase of conditional love and experience this in their relationships.

The possibility of changing conditional love into unconditional love presents itself during the fourth period, during the development of the fourth chakra. The degree to which we are able to develop the ability to feel unconditional love depends to a large degree on the condition of our lower three chakras. If we are still very needy due to disturbances in the development of the three lower chakras, it will be more difficult to develop feelings of unconditional love.

We can also characterize the fourth period as the beginning of a shift from a more physical and ego-oriented way of living to a more spiritual and loving way of living. We grow increasingly toward unconditional love for self, everyone, and everything. The fifth to the seventh period will connect us increasingly with the spiritual aspects of ourselves, expanding the ability to love unconditionally.

Expressing Who We Are (29 to 35)

The fifth period is about expressing who we are. In the fifth period we are able to go beyond expression from the point of view of the ego. Having opened our hearts to the best of our abilities, we learn to express ourselves more clearly, with more love and compassion and with an increasing spiritual connection. This phase is when we learn to express our true selves instead of the people others have taught us to be.

This period is also about learning to express our emotions while staying in connection with our hearts. Many believe that the fifth chakra is about speaking our truths. If our chakras have not been able to develop properly, then our truths are still expressing our egos. The real opportunity this period offers us is to express our abilities and our qualities more fully. Speaking our truths is part of that. We will continuously develop the fifth chakra during the remaining part of our lives, and that is also true for the next two chakras. We keep exploring the abilities connected with these three chakras for our whole lives.

Developing Intuition (36 to 42)

The sixth period is the period of understanding, wisdom, and insight. We become more intuitive and begin to tap into sources of information beyond those we access with our normal five senses. For that reason, the quality of the sixth chakra is also called the sixth sense or the third eye. We begin to reap the fruits of our experiences in life and are able to see the patterns we have created. This is often also a period of deep spiritual longing.

Connecting with Our Souls (43 to 49)

This spiritual longing becomes even stronger in the last of the seven periods. This is a period of looking for and fully connecting with our spiritual beings, or souls. It is the period in which all our experiences lead to a sudden deeper understanding of life. We begin to realize more fully that we are spiritual beings who cannot die; we only transform.

In this period, we may also realize that the only way to fully express our spiritual beings through these physical bodies is by letting go of the ego's control. This can bring up deep fear. If we still have many fears and unresolved issues from earlier periods of our lives, we may not be able to let go of our controlling egos. Looking around us, we notice that hardly anyone who has completed the seven cycles seems to be able to let go of this controlling ego. So we enter a new cycle of seven periods, starting again with the first chakra. We have the opportunity to deal with those issues we were not able to deal with in the first cycle. In some cases, this leads to big changes in people's lives. It is a period of menopause and of midlife crisis. While many see these experiences as negative, they are actually gifts. They offer us openings, ways to get unstuck, and a higher view of our patterns, offering us opportunities to let go of ego and open more fully to our spiritual beings. This can, however, also lead to a strengthening of existing patterns, making people even more rigid. It is all a matter of choice; the opportunity for change is there.

The Seven Body Chakras

Caroline Myss[2] connects the seven steps of development with the seven Christian sacraments and the seven steps of the tree of life as described by the Kabbalah. This comparison is similar to what has been described above. We go through a natural flow that guides us through different stages of our personal and spiritual developments. This process has been recognized by different traditions and has been expressed in their teachings and rituals.

It is not easy to find any two books or any two articles that describe the seven chakras in exactly the same way. You will find differences in the way chakras function, the way they are characterized, and the way in which a given chakra is connected to other systems. Fortunately, most authors do agree on the general principles. Many differences can be attributed to a longing to make everything simple. However, in nature, there are many variations, and everything is related to everything else. Let me give an example: Every chakra is related to a hormonal gland. The adrenals are one type of hormonal gland. The adrenals produce adrenaline, the hormone of fight or flight. We are all familiar with the expression: "That gave me a real adrenaline rush." There is no agreement on which chakra this hormonal gland is connected to. You can find texts that connect the adrenals to the first chakra, second chakra, and third chakra. The question is, who is right? Actually, they are all right. Any stress in the three lower chakras may affect the adrenals. However, if we ask which energy center the adrenals belong to, the answer becomes clearer. The adrenals, the third chakra, and the solar plexus all work together. Other differences are based on the writer's personal vision, the model he or she likes to work with.

Table 3 gives an overview of the seven body chakras, their Sanskrit names, their locations in the body, the hormonal glands connected to each, and their associated colors. The colors given are generally accepted with the exception of the color associated with the seventh chakra. Although many people mention purple, I have also seen the color white mentioned on the Internet. This brings up an interesting aspect of the body chakras.

	Chakra	Sanskrit name	Location	Glands	Color	Element
1	Base or Root chakra	Maludhara	Base of spine	Gonads	Red	Earth
2	Sacral or Naval chakra	Svadistana	Below the naval	Certain cells in gonads	Orange	Water
3	Solar Plexus	Manipura	Just below the breastbone	Adrenal Pancreas	Yellow	Fire
4	Heart chakra	Anahata	Center of the breastbone	Thymus	Green	Air
5	Throat chakra	Vishuddha	At the throat	Thyroid	Blue	Ether
6	Third eye or Brow chakra	Ajna	Slightly below mid-forehead	Pituitary	Indigo	
7	Crown chakra	Sahasrara	Just before the top of the head	Pineal	Violet and/or white	

Table 3: Overview of the seven chakras, their Sanskrit names, their locations in the body, hormonal glands they are connected with, and their associated colors and elements.

When we look at the colors of the seven chakras, we see that they are the colors of the rainbow. As you may remember from science lessons, we get the colors of the rainbow when white light is diffracted. We can demonstrate this with a prism or we can observe this in nature when sunlight shines through water droplets, creating a rainbow. The colors are different aspects of oneness. They have been separated but when combined, they create white light. However, when the vibration of the colors changes and they are no longer a pure color, it is not possible to create the white light, the oneness. The colors of our chakras change when our systems are no longer functioning as one. This happens when we begin to believe in separation and see each chakra as an independently functioning unit. The chakras become separated and disturbed when we let ourselves be guided by fear. When we transform fear into love, the chakras attain their full vibration and color and we experience once again the white light of enlightenment, of oneness.

The Spiritual Triangle of the Subtle Energy Bodies

Different people have different ideas about the number of our subtle energy bodies and their functions. Most authors agree with four subtle energy bodies: the etheric, emotional, mental, and spiritual. Some authors reference up to twenty-one different bodies with variations of every number in between.

I will discuss five subtle bodies as they relate to characteristics of the Earth energy system described later in this chapter. The five subtle energy bodies are the etheric, astral, emotional, mental, and spiritual bodies. Different terminologies are evident; however, for me these names resonate. I am aware of only one other author, Judy Jacka, who uses five subtle bodies, but her terms and descriptions are different,[3] so I am not sure whether we share the same ideas.

Although I risk confusing readers, I will mention another approach to describing the human system. This system is commonly used and is described very well by Herbert Puryear and Mark Thurston in their book *Meditation and the Mind of Man* based on the readings of Edgar Cayce.[4] In this system, there are only three aspects: the physical body, the mental body (mind), and the spiritual body (spirit). Connected with these three aspects are three levels of consciousness: conscious (physical), un- or subconscious (mind), and super-conscious (spirit). Comparing this to the five-body system I mentioned, the physical body is a combination of the physical, etheric, and astral bodies. The mind is similar to the emotional and mental bodies, and spirit is the spiritual body.

As valid as the system of body, mind, and spirit may be, from an energetic perspective, especially in the light of the connected Earth energy system described later, I find it more appropriate to use the system of five subtle energy bodies, with each connected to the physical body. This means that there are in total six bodies. One way to describe the relationship between these six bodies is through the six-pointed star, the Star of David (see fig. 5.2). The Star of David consists of two triangles. The triangle that points upward is considered to be the masculine triangle and represents connection with the cosmos, the invisible spiritual realm. The triangle that points downward is considered to be the feminine triangle and represents connection with the earth, the visible physical realm. The physical body and the five subtle energy bodies can be related to the six points of the Star of David. The three energy bodies that make up the physical system are the physical body, the etheric body, and the astral body.

The three subtle energy bodies that make up our spiritual system are the emotional body, the mental body, and the spiritual body. This trio is what people call the soul. They are an expression of a larger aspect called the oversoul. Each over-

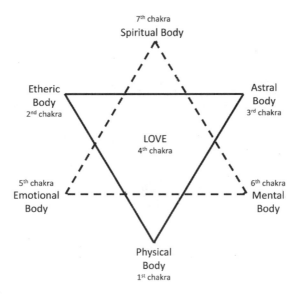

Fig. 5.3: Star of David showing the relationship between the physical bodies (solid-line triangle pointing downward), the spiritual bodies (broken-line triangle pointing upward), and the chakras.

soul is an expression of a higher dimensional unit, one that has been given many different names. Ultimately everything is an expression of All That Is (see fig. 5.3). The number of levels of expression is beyond my understanding. Although interwoven, the two triangles also have their own unique characteristics and maintain a certain degree of independence. We can see them as two units that work together. We all know that this working together can create interesting challenges and that we need love to make it all work.

The three physical bodies are a creation of Earth. They represent what we might call our animal aspects—survival, or how to live in physical reality. Earth by her very being is capable of creating and maintaining life. Science talks about the oceans as being the cradles of all life on Earth. Although science may not understand all aspects of creation, it does agree that Earth is at least equally responsible for the creation of life. This means that all life on Earth is actually an aspect of her and is intricately connected to her.

Besides our connection and communication with Earth, the physical triangle also represents development. All physical forms and physical expressions go through stages of development. These stages are represented in cycles. We see these cycles in light and dark during the twenty-four-hour cycle; in the seasons (the year cycle); and in the cycle of birth, growth, old age, and death. All cycles

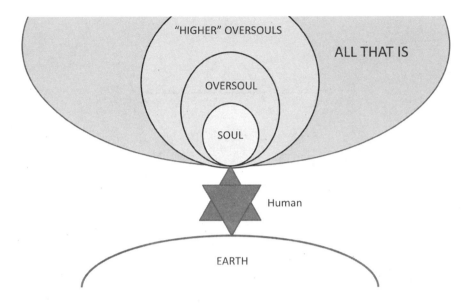

Fig. 5.3: The human being represented by the six-pointed star and its connections with the physical (earth) and spiritual (oversoul, higher oversouls, and All That Is).

lead to experience and adaptation, which result in the larger cycle we call evolution. This evolution takes place at a species level and also on the much larger levels of Earth itself, the solar system, and even the universe.

The spiritual triangle represents a completely different aspect. It represents a nonphysical entity that is called a soul. Some traditions believe that the soul is similar to those we call angels. We can look at souls as angels who have chosen to connect with a physical being—the human, as represented by the physical triangle—in order to experience the three-dimensional physical reality aspects of creation. Angels (and thus the original souls) had a direct connection with the Creator, with All That Is, with Source. It seems that these souls were supposed to stay connected to Source in the same way as the physical body is supposed to stay connected with the earth. We are very aware that in both cases most of us have lost these connections. Fortunately, we now live in a time of remembering and reconnecting.

These two systems, the human body and the soul, need to have a connector. This connector is love, the force that underlies all of creation, all connections, and everything that exists. Through love, we can reconnect with the earth and reconnect with Source. We then become wonderful new beings, those who can cocreate with All That Is in physical reality.

The six points/bodies and the center of the Star of David are also related to the seven chakras as seen in figure 5.2. The physical body is related to the first chakra, the spiritual body to the seventh chakra, and the center to the fourth chakra. The etheric body is related to the second chakra, the astral body to the third, the emotional body to the fifth, and the mental body to the sixth chakra.

The Five Subtle Energy Bodies as Related to the Twelve Chakras

The five subtle energy bodies appear like layers around the physical body, although in reality they permeate each other (see fig. 5.4). The smallest is the etheric body, or etheric double, which extends about half an inch (1 to 1.5 cm) outward from the physical body. This is the body that holds the meridians. This body is as temporary as the physical body. When we die, this body stops functioning and dissolves. We connect with this body mainly through the meridians. In addition, the etheric body connects with the astral body through the eighth chakra.

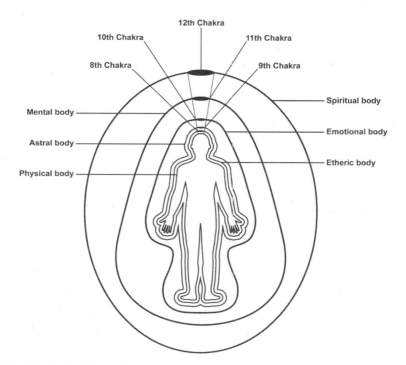

Fig 5.4: The physical body with the five subtle energy bodies and the chakras 8 through 12. Created by Evita de Vos.

The astral body is much better known than the etheric body. Many books have been written about the subject of astral travel and out-of-body experiences (OBE).[5] Some people call the astral body the double, so we actually have two doubles. We can connect our awarenesses to this astral body and will it out of our physical systems in order to let it have its own unique experiences—this is called astral traveling. I would recommend doing this only with proper training and guidance. However, people do have spontaneous OBEs during sleep or under specific, often stressful circumstances. The astral body also belongs to the physical, which means that it is temporary. After death, it dissolves. The etheric body dissolves within hours after death, whereas it takes around three days before the astral body disappears. This is one of the reasons why people of many traditions will wait at least three days before they bury or cremate their deceased.

This body is a bridge between the physical and the spiritual. People who suddenly die or those who hold tightly on to life sometimes do not detach themselves from the astral body and in their perceptions are still alive. The astral body and the soul become one entity that roams around, often disturbing the living. Normally the astral body is invisible, but sometimes the frequencies are lowered to such a degree that a phantom, or ghost, becomes visible. Hollywood has used this theme of dead people staying connected to their astral bodies in different movies like *Ghost*[6] and *Passengers.*[7] The astral contains emotions that are connected with the meridians. These emotions are the physical realities that we work with daily. These emotions, along with counterparts, are:

- pretense/honesty, straightforwardness
- fear/courage
- despair/faith, hope
- anger/forgiveness
- sadness or grief/acceptance
- worry/trust

The astral body stretches 1 to 1.5 inches (2.5 to 4 cm) outside of the physical body. Like the etheric body, it has a direct effect on the physical body via the meridians. The astral body is connected to the etheric body through the eighth chakra and with the emotional body through the ninth chakra as seen in figure 5.4. The ninth chakra is located about two inches above the top of the head.

The emotional and the astral bodies are often perceived as one body because they both deal with emotions. I believe that the astral body deals with emotions connected with the physical world/reality and the emotional body deals with emotions of the spiritual world. The emotional body plays a role in the creation of a loving state of being and the emotions stemming from such a state, emotions such as joy, happiness, gratitude, and the feeling of abundance. This differentiation may be the reason people usually discuss this concept in terms of a lower and a higher emotional body. From my perspective, the lower emotional body is the astral body and the higher emotional body is the emotional body. These two bodies are interdependent, because the emotions of the astral body impact the condition of the emotional body to such a degree that the spiritual and mental aspects of the soul do not reach the physical system. All emotions that we do not allow to flow and do not fully experience are stored in the emotional body, affecting its size, its color, its ability to radiate joy and happiness, and its function as a bridge between the spiritual and physical aspects of our beings.

The size of this body fluctuates strongly depending on our emotional states, health, and where we are on our paths of evolution. It can expand up to 3 feet (0.9 m). This body is connected with the physical body through the chakras. It is connected with the astral body through the ninth chakra and with the mental body through the tenth chakra (see fig. 5.4). This tenth chakra is located about 4 to 8 inches (10 to 20 cm) above the top of the head. The mental body stretches beyond the colorful emotional body. It is believed to hold all mental aspects and is often associated with the mind. Like the emotional body, the mental body is often separated into lower and higher. I do not believe that this is true. The lower mental body relates to mental processes that are connected to the emotions of the astral body. I believe that the lower mental body is also part of the astral body and consequently belongs to the physical and not to the spiritual system.

The higher mental body is what I refer to as simply the mental body. The spiritual processes connected with knowledge, understanding, and intuition belong to the mental body. The fact that this body is connected to the sixth chakra makes it easier to understand. When we talk about beliefs, we are referring to the lower mental body, the astral body, and thus to the physical system. The higher mental body is not connected to belief structures. It can be described as a system in which each moment flows dynamically, guided by a deep connection and understanding of universal energies and creative powers. It is this flowing with understanding in each moment that allows us to use the creative energies of the emotional body to create a reality of happiness, joy, gratitude, and abundance.

This body is connected with the emotional body through the tenth chakra and with the spiritual body through the eleventh chakra (see fig. 5.4). The location of this chakra in terms of distance above the top of the head varies, and its size depends on the overall spiritual state of the person.

The size of the spiritual body fluctuates more than that of any other subtle energy body. This body basically holds the person's full potential, both of "who we are" and of "who we have chosen to be" in this lifetime. In this third-dimensional reality a fully developed and active spiritual body can only be achieved when the soul and physical body function as one. This is called enlightenment. At that moment, the body radiates a powerful light and shines in its fullness. When this happens, everyone around you feels it, as much as everyone can unconsciously feel your presence and react to it. You will only be able to achieve this by being in unconditional love. This state of enlightenment is also the state in which you experience complete oneness.

The spiritual body communicates with the physical body through the chakras. However, in many people, the chakras are not developed enough to connect so directly. This means that the connection has to go through the higher chakras, the eighth to eleventh chakras. This in turn is only possible when those chakras are open. Meditating and transforming emotions and old belief structures enable us to open these gateways, helping us to reconnect to our spiritual essences.

The spiritual body is connected to the mental body by the eleventh chakra. The spiritual body opens to our oversoul through the twelfth chakra. The location of this chakra is too variable to give a proper indication.

The Twelve Chakra System

It has become commonplace to mention the existence of twelve chakras. People do mention many minor chakras, like the higher heart chakra, the hand chakras, and the feet chakras, but they are not considered to be major chakras. However, there are several websites promoting the idea that we have chakras that exist between the seven chakras normally mentioned, adding up to a total of twelve. For an example of this, see Duane Groce's article: "The Twelve Chakras."[8]

Another way to describe the twelve chakras is to add to the seven chakras an additional five chakras that access higher aspects of ourselves, such as the over-soul, the monad, and other higher-dimensional aspects (see the Internet article "The Spiritual Chakra 8 to 12" by Tom Deliso[9]). He describes the eighth chakra as being the energy center of divine love, the ninth chakra as being the soul blueprint, the tenth chakra as being divine creativity and synchronicity of life, the eleventh chakra as being the pathway to the soul, and the twelfth chakra as being the connection to the monadic level of divinity.

From these descriptions, it may become clear that what I have described is some-where between these two views. In my view, the eighth to the twelfth chakras are no longer directly connected to the physical system but are part of the connection between the physical body, aspects of the soul, and ultimately the connection to the oversoul/twelfth chakra. I have found only one other description similar to mine, that being a book excerpt written by Patrisha Richardson: "Subtle Bodies and Chakras."[10]

Beyond the physical body, there are additional etheric chakras in the aura. As mentioned earlier, most sources disagree as to the number and location of these. They appear to me only in the aura of clients who are advanced on their spiritual path. When they do appear, I see five additional chakras—the eighth, ninth, tenth, eleventh, and twelfth—located above the head. To me those upper chakras appear as "plates," or flat discs, of light.

I agree with her and perceive these chakras in a similar way (see fig. 5.4). I believe that when we have brought these twelve chakras into harmony, we are complete in this physical reality and can ascend to higher dimensions. The Earth and the grid systems on Earth give us many clues about our energy systems. All descriptions I have given are in alignment with the energy systems found on Earth. So let us now look at these systems.

The Earth Chakra System

Initially the Earth chakra system seemed to be a simple system. It took many years before I realized that in addition to the Earth chakra vortexes and lines I'd found, other systems existed. It was only a couple of years before writing this book that it became clear that the Earth chakra system is more extensive and more important than I'd initially thought. The first type of vortexes I found that resonated with our chakras I called chakra lines and vortexes. Each line of this system is a single line; they do not form cables like the Earth meridians do. Compared to the Earth meridian lines and vortexes, the chakra lines and vortexes are simpler.

Although the energies are rather easy to recognize, there was initially some confusion. In the human energy system, the chakras are comparatively large and powerful centers. The Earth chakras I found are comparatively small and all are on lines. There are many of these chakra vortexes. Later I found that Earth has larger chakras that do not have surface lines. These larger chakras seem to be more similar to our chakras. Both the smaller chakra vortexes and the larger chakra vortexes resonate with our chakras. This means there are different Earth vortex systems that resonate with our chakras.

Another confusing aspect involved my expectations. I had expected to find seven different systems related to our seven chakras. However, I found twelve different systems. It took a lot of discussion with others, meditations, and psychic readings to realize that there were actually twelve chakras. The Earth chakra system guided me into understanding that we have twelve chakras: the seven chakras connected to our physical bodies and the five chakras that connect the different energy bodies with each other. This Earth chakra system also guided me into a deeper understanding of our subtle bodies.

Earth Chakras on Surface Lines

Initially it seemed that there was no clear pattern in the Earth chakra lines and vortex systems. I studied this system mainly in the Sedona area, and at the time, I did not know that the situation in that area was rather exceptional. Sedona seems to have a special attraction for these lines. Following the lines over longer distances, I noticed that these chakra lines were never straight. However, in the Sedona area, the lines are even more twisted than anywhere else. Later studies showed that the lines have a general direction: They flow more or less north–south or east–west. But in the Sedona area, this general direction is lost. North–south lines can go east–west and in reverse, and lines zigzag through the area. Vortexes on the chakra lines are found on nodes, as we have seen with other systems.

After this initial confusion, I realized that the chakra lines form a kind of grid with lines going roughly north–south and east–west. The distance between the lines is about 10 miles (16 km) in both directions. This distance varies considerably because the lines are not straight and flow irregularly through the landscape. It seems that other energies in the landscape have an influence on the way lines flow, but at this moment, I do not understand all the factors involved.

This grid system also has yin and yang lines. The grids seem to have alternate yin and yang lines similar to those we have seen in the lower subtle energy grids, but here there are more irregularities. Sometimes there are two yang lines or two yin lines next to each other, however, not all the vortexes on a line have the same spinning direction. Nevertheless, we still see that the vortexes on a yin line spin predominantly clockwise and those on the yang lines counterclockwise.

The size of the chakra vortexes fluctuates considerably, especially when we compare the vortexes in cities with those in nature or compare vortexes found in different countries. We will look at the factors that determine these variations in chapter 13. I discovered that there is an optimal size for these chakra vortexes. The size is similar for all twelve chakra grids and is slightly over 12.5 miles (20 km). Based on the size of the vortexes and the distance between the vortexes, it is estimated that when the size of the chakra vortex is about 50 percent of its optimum, the area is completely covered with that chakra energy. When all twelve chakras have vortexes that are more than 50 percent of their optimum, all chakra energies will be available everywhere, even though intensity may vary. If the size of a chakra vortex is less than 50 percent of its optimum, there will be gaps in the energy fields, which mean that in these gaps, the energy of that chakra system is no longer available. As we will see, there are several countries where this is the case.

We have seen that the energy lines of the lower subtle energy grids are straight, having a more or less constant height above and below the Earth surface, whereas those of the meridians can flow completely above or below the surface of the earth. Chakra lines are in between. They do not flow as deeply underneath or as high above the surface of the earth as the meridian lines, but they are far from straight. The difference between the yin and yang lines of this chakra system is similar to the other grids. A yin line runs more below the surface of the earth and the yang line runs more above the surface.

Chakra lines exhibit yet another interesting phenomenon. Different chakra lines can share the same vortex. I have found several examples of this over time in different parts of the world. These combinations do not seem to have a pattern. I have found a tenth chakra with a twelfth chakra, a fifth chakra with a twelfth chakra, a first chakra with an eleventh chakra, a seventh chakra with an eighth chakra and a seventh chakra with a ninth chakra. It seems fair to assume that any combination is possible. However, these doubles seem to occur less than 5 percent of the time. It is still a rare phenomenon, although I am aware that I may have missed some of these double vortexes, especially when the energy of one of the two chakras dominates strongly.

This sharing of vortexes does not seem to be logical. If lines are all roughly 10 miles apart and the lines are all more or less north–south and east–west, they are not supposed to share vortexes, or they should share all of them. The reason they can share vortexes is because the lines are not straight. The distance of 10 miles (16 km) is an average and can vary from about 8 to 12 miles (12.9 to 19.3 km). There are sufficient possibilities for lines to touch or cross and share the location of a vortex.

Earth Chakra Vortexes versus Human Chakras

During my chakra studies I came across vortexes that had chakra energy but were much larger than what I'd usually found. I also could not detect any surface lines. I found three different types of chakra vortexes without surface lines and the largest of these three types spread over an area with a diameter of 500 miles (804 km) or more. These larger chakra vortexes have, like the smaller ones, a spinning direction that is dominant in one of the two directions: clockwise or counterclockwise.

Having studied these four types of vortexes for a while, I believe that they are all part of one chakra system through which Earth supports us on our earthly journeys through our own twelve chakras. The chakra vortex with the surface lines is the one that I call the lowest level (level four). This level seems to work mainly on the relationship between our physical system and the physical world around us.

The level three chakra vortexes have lines just under the surface of the earth. The radius of the area these vortexes cover is between 25 and 40 miles (40 and 64 km). These vortexes also have energies that resonate with our chakras but seem to support specifically the relationship between our emotional bodies and the world around us. The lines of the level two vortexes are deeper below the surface of the earth than those of level three. The radius of the area these vortexes cover is between 55 and 90 miles (89 and 145 km). While they also resonate with our chakras, they seem to mainly support the relationship between our mental bodies and the world around us. Finally, the level one chakra vortexes, as I mentioned, have a radius of more than 250 miles (402 km) and cover large areas. These are the chakras that stimulate spirituality in the most optimal way.

When I described our chakra system, I mentioned that a chakra is actually a complex set of vortexes connecting the physical body with the different subtle energy bodies. We see this system reflected in the four levels of Earth chakras. It seems that our energy systems truly reflect that of the earth's. In this phase of the research, it seems that the energy of each of the chakras of levels two to four covers the whole world. The amount of data that has led to this conclusion is rather limited, however, and more data is needed. Nonetheless the initial research makes it very likely that this is the case. It is possible that there are gaps in certain areas. As we will see, human activities have an effect on the size of the vortexes, especially level 4 vortexes, and this may cause a discontinuity in the fields at this level in certain areas, especially in densely populated areas. The effect we have on the other levels seems to be more limited or even nonexistent.

Based on my initial data, it seemed that the level one chakra vortexes were very rare and unique. I only found a few of these vortexes. One of these was a chakra twelve vortex that was located on Bell Rock, one of the four famous vortexes of Sedona, Arizona. When I brought spiritually oriented people to this vortex, they all really liked it and had wonderful experiences. So I was pleased and surprised to find more vortexes of this type and level. One was found in Amsterdam, the Netherlands, right in the center of the red light district in de Oude Kerk (the old church). I found another one of the same type in the cathedral on Zocalo city square in Mexico City.

Even though I found more vortexes of level one of the same type, I was still not sure whether the energy of level one vortexes would cover the whole Earth. A discovery in Arizona makes it more likely that this may be the case. I found a seventh chakra level one vortex with a spinning direction that was predominantly counterclockwise at one of the sacred sites of the Hopi Nation: Prophecy Rock. I found a similar vortex just south of the Havasupai Reservation. The distance between these two vortexes is almost 150 miles (241 km). The radius of each of these vortexes is more than 250 miles (402 km), so their energies overlap strongly. This finding, which is the only one so far, suggests the possibility that the energy of the chakra vortexes of level one covers the globe.

When I discovered the level one chakra vortexes I believed that they were the main vortexes of Earth and were comparable to our twelve main chakras. The fact that I found more than one vortex of a certain type seems to indicate that the situation on Earth is different from that of our physical bodies. There seem to be no main vortexes. There are four different levels of Earth chakra energies that are created by many vortexes.

Several people have mentioned that they believe Earth has chakras in the same way the human body does. Some people mention seven or twelve chakras, although most mention only seven. Author Amorah Quan Yin, is one of the few people who mentions twelve Earth chakras.[11] I have compared the information given by four people[12] who discuss the first seven Earth chakras. Interestingly these four authors do not agree on any of the chakra locations. Only Uluru in Australia was twice mentioned as the location of the third chakra. Of the four authors, one mentioned Haleakala as the place of the fourth chakra while Amora Quan Yin mentioned a different location in Hawaii. Certain places are mentioned frequently, although for different chakras. Giza is mentioned by all four authors, but in all cases, for different chakras. Mount Shasta, Mount Fuji, and the Himalayas were mentioned three times, but again always for different chakras.

David Furlong has an interesting understanding of Earth chakras.[13] He believes that many places have what he calls a chakra association. Almost any place has an energy that can be associated with one of the chakras. This can be done on a small scale but also on a large scale. For example, he shows a chakra line in

Ireland where all eight chakras appear on a straight line. The line goes from the southwestern to the northeastern part of the island of Ireland.[14] He is one of the few people who believes that there are eight chakras. He bases his belief on the fact that many traditions work with the number eight, like feng shui and the I Ching.

Besides placing chakras within countries or landscapes, he also sees chakra associations in continents and countries as a whole. For example, he associates Europe with the sixth chakra and North America with the fifth, the throat chakra.[15]

Another author who has written a great deal about Earth chakras is Robert Coon, who lists thirteen chakras.[16] The thirteenth chakra synthesizes the other twelve. Of these twelve planetary chakras, eight are placed on two energy flows that he calls the two great serpents: the rainbow serpent and the plumed serpent. These two serpents create an infinity symbol. He calls the four additional chakras elemental spinner wheels, and they are named after the four elements of fire, water, air, and earth. Interestingly, the places he mentions for the twelve chakras are to a large degree the same locations mentioned by the previously cited authors. It seems that people see certain power spots as possible chakras without agreeing which chakras these are.

Obviously people tend to look at the Earth energy system as being similar to that of human beings. This perspective is not true for the chakra system. Although Earth has energy systems that support our chakra systems, in all its aspects, the systems are not the same. We have to look at Earth as unique and approach the study of her energies with open minds, without preconceived ideas. In general, we can say that there are similar energy systems in Earth and in us, but they are expressed differently.

Personal Experiences

Most people I take out on vortex experiences have some knowledge of chakras. This does not mean that they are able to feel the type of chakra vortex they are sitting on, which is no surprise. Like the meridian systems, the chakra system is interrelated. For example, when you sit on a third-chakra vortex or attune to third-chakra Earth energy, you may experience reactions in several other chakras, or even have feelings that are seemingly unrelated to the chakras. I have therefore learned to let people know that it is preferable to hold no expectations and instead to simply be open to whatever happens. I share this up front in order to prevent people from expecting to feel a particular chakra, because the opposite may happen.

As mentioned earlier, visiting a meridian vortex before visiting a chakra vortex will enhance the chakra experience. This is important when you visit a level four chakra vortex, but it is especially recommended before you visit a level three chakra vortex and even more so for levels two and one chakra vortexes.

Even when I do not share with people the type of chakra vortex we are to visit, the fact that they know that it is a chakra vortex creates an expectation. The expectation is that chakra vortexes will have stronger effects than other types of vortexes. My experience is that this is not necessarily true. If and how much people experience certain energies, depends on many factors. Good preparation is important in order to get maximum benefit and optimal awareness from a visit. Nonetheless, most people will only feel the effects in general terms, like feeling more relaxed, more grounded, or seeing and hearing more clearly. Those who have greater body and energy sensitivity may feel specific energies in specific places. However, these experiences may be unrelated to the type of vortex visited. Whatever other people's experiences are, you will always have your own unique experience. Remember to always be open and grateful for the gifts you receive.

The Earth Chakra System Provides Balance

The chakra system is one of the most important subtle energy systems in the human body. In our society, this system is easily thrown out of balance. We can rebalance this system through different healing modalities. However, the most powerful support can be found in the system we call the Earth chakra system. It provides support to help us keep the chakra system in balance or to rebalance it when it is off. It also helps us to deal with issues related to our chakras. Of course we have to be willing to open ourselves to these energies for full support.

The chakra system consists of twelve different chakras, both in humans and on Earth. Although I believe that Earth is a conscious being, I do not believe that her energy systems are identical to ours, even though she supports us energetically in every way we need. I do not support the idea that Earth has twelve single chakras as we do. Based on my research, I believe that there are four Earth chakra systems that hold different chakra qualities and energies. These four systems support our chakra system in every way we need on our journeys to become fully realized spiritual beings in physical bodies.

ENDNOTES

1. Barbara Ann Brennan, *Hands of Light: A Guide to Healing Through the Human Energy Field* (New York: Bantam Books, 1988), 44.

2. Caroline Myss, *Anatomy of the Spirit: The Seven Stages of Power and Healing* (New York: Three Rivers Press, 1996).

3. Judy Jacka, N.D., *The Vivaxis Connection: Healing through Earth Energies* (Charlottesville, VA: Hampton Roads Publishing Company, 2000), 76.

4. Herbert B. Puryear and Mark A. Thurston, *Meditation and the Mind of Man*, rev. ed. (Virginia Beach: A.R.E. Press, 1978).

5. The books of Robert A. Monroe, such as *Journeys Out of the Body* (1971/1977), *Far Journeys* (1985), and *Ultimate Journey* (1994) are well known, for example. Other interesting books on this subject include *Projection of the Astral Body* (1969) by Sylvan Muldoon and Hereward Carrington, Joe H. Slate's *Astral Projection and Psychic Empowerment* (1998), D.J. Conway's *Astral Love* (1996), and many others.

6. Bruce Joel Rubin, *Ghost*, starring Patrick Swayze, Demi Moore, and Whoopi Goldberg and directed by Jerry Zucker (Hollywood: Paramount Pictures, 1990).

7. Ronnie Christensen, *Passengers*, starring Anne Hathaway and Patrick Wilson and directed by Rodrigo Garcìa (Culver City, CA: TriStar Pictures, 2008).

8. Duane Groce, "The Twelve Chakras," *The Inner Switchboard: A Path to Healing* (2007), accessed February 2, 2011, http://www.innerswitchboard.com/chakras2print.html.

9. Tom DeLiso, "The Spiritual Chakra 8 to 12," *Hermes Trismegistus Wisdom's Door Website Collection Volume 1* (Dunnellon, FL: Hermes Trismegistus / Tom DeLiso, 2008), accessed November 2008, http://www.wisdomsdoor.com/hb/hhb-20.shtml.

10. Patrisha Richardson, "Subtle Bodies and Chakras," *Transforming Darkness into Light : A Guidebook for Spiritual Seekers* (Emeryville, CA: Absolute Truth Publications, 2000), excerpted at *Soul2Soul*, accessed November 2008, http://www.harusami.com/soul2soul/althealing/sub_chak.html.

11. Amorah Quan Yin, "The Crystalline Cities of Light," *Pleiadian Lightwork* (2007), accessed February 2, 2011, http://www.amorahquanyin.com/sites.html. 11.

12. The four works consulted are Amorah Quan Yin's *Pleiadian Lightwork* (see reference 11); Robert Coon's *Earth Chakras: The Definitive Guide* (Warburton, VIC: Robert Coon, 2009), excerpt available at http://worldalchemy.bravehost.com/earth_chakras.html; Sean David Morton's "Chakras of Planet Earth," *Toronto Dowsers* (September 2004), http://www.dowsers.info/toronto/chakras.htm; and StarStuffs' 12. "Earth Chakras," *StarStuffs* (2007), http://www.starstuffs.com/chakras/earthchakras.html.

13. David Furlong, *Working with Earth Energies: How to Tap into the Healing Powers of the Natural World* (London: Piatkus, 2003), 66-74.

14. Ibid., 71.

15. Ibid., 74.

16. Robert Coon, *The Rainbow Serpent and The Holy Grail: Uluru and the Planetary Chakras*, rev. ed. (Warburton, VIC: Robert Coon, 2008).

6

HUMAN THIRD-DIMENSIONAL COLLECTIVE CONSCIOUSNESS GRIDS:
THE TWELVE TRIAD SYSTEM

IN THE FIRST PHASE OF THE JOURNEY OF CONNECTING WITH EARTH ENERGIES, we looked at energies that can be defined as "natural subtle energy systems of Earth." These systems belong to Earth herself and are part of her energetic makeup. These energies also support all who live upon her. They help us to heal and balance our physical bodies and our subtle energies such as meridians, chakras, and subtle energy bodies. These changes prepare us to expand our awareness and connect with grid systems. These grid systems are called consciousness grids. Consciousness grids do not belong to Earth in a direct way but rather support life or aspects of the lives of those who live in or upon her. Of these grid systems, the ones connected to human beings are of prime interest to us. In this chapter, we will look specifically at the grid systems that hold what is called the third-dimensional collective human consciousness.

As with all energy systems, there is a field, a layer of energies, above Earth, and there are grids that hold the active part of that field. The field holds the energy and information of the essence of who we are as physical human beings as well as all our experiences and knowledge in the third-dimensional reality at this moment in time. The active part is that part of the human collective consciousness field that we actively use and that to a large degree determines our overall awareness and beliefs, and consequently the behavior of our species. Due to the dualistic nature of this third-dimensional reality, we can use this active part in a positive or negative way.

We have dynamic interactions with both the field and the grid. The grid reflects where we as a human species are from a physical, behavioral, and awareness point of view. Of course this changes continuously due to human activity. Not all information in the field is also available in the grid. The grid holds only that part of the field of our potential that we are able to work with within this time frame. However, we can access the information in the field either directly or more easily through the vortexes. If we want to master this third-dimensional reality, we need to master the information in the field and bring the grids and the field into harmony as a basis for transcending this dimensional consciousness in order to expand into the fourth and fifth dimensions.

In general, people connect more easily with grids than with fields. A grid holds energies that feel more familiar because they hold the energies with which we regularly work. The aspects of the grids we connect with depend on our emotional states. The grid holds energies that are based on fear as well as love. When we live regularly in a fear-based emotional state, whether consciously or unconsciously, we resonate with the energies from the grid that reinforce living in fear. To break free from these patterns, we need to go into a state of love. When we go into a state of love, we resonate with the love frequencies in the grids, and consequently the grids start supporting this state of love. Love makes it easier to expand beyond information from the grids and to connect with energies that are not yet available in the grid. In doing so, we bring new information into the grids that will then become available to other people, then contributing to the shift in awareness of humankind as a whole. We have used the terms "consciousness" and "awareness," And to understand the information presented in this and other chapters, it is important to define what is meant by these terms in the context of this book.

Consciousness and Awareness

The main factor that determines how we feel physically, emotionally, mentally, and spiritually is consciousness. Many books and articles have been written on the subject of consciousness, but so far a full understanding has eluded scientists. The word "consciousness" is used in different ways, so I would like to start with the definition I have chosen to use. What I present here may not feel right for everyone. Whether you resonate with the definition or not, it is helpful to know how I use the term in order to understand the information given in this book.

I see consciousness as that from which everything comes and that which contains all that can and may ever come into being. It is All That Is and All That Is Not (yet). We can call it the infinite Source, because it has no limitations. When we talk about the Creator or God, we refer to the infinite Source.

We are an expression of consciousness and as such contain consciousness. From the perspective of a holographic universe,[1] we know that every part contains the information of the whole. That means we are consciousness in its infinite form. However, that is not what most of us experience, not even when we believe this statement to be true. In this third-dimensional reality we experience limitation and therefore believe that we are limited.

Let us first look at the term "consciousness" as it is used in a more general way. We say that we are conscious when we are awake and aware. In our daily use of the term, we usually equate consciousness with awareness. We also are aware that there is a subconscious or unconsciousness that we connect to in dreams, in meditation, and with certain techniques like hypnosis or self-hypnosis, or through use of certain drugs (not recommended). In addition, there is something we call higher consciousness that, depending on the person defining it, refers in various degrees to an aspect of what I call consciousness.

The infinite consciousness expresses itself in infinite ways at many different levels. We can call these levels "levels of existence," "dimensional levels," or "consciousness levels." It is generally accepted and believed that we live in the third dimension, which is where we experience duality, as explained by Drunvalo Melchizedek.[2] We are moving into the fourth dimension where we experience oneness while still in physical form, and we are on our way to the fifth dimension where we become etheric beings, no longer in the physical. Although consciousness expresses itself in many ways and at many levels, there is no real division. We make divisions and labels in attempt to describe the whole.

In a sense, we are the infinite exploring different expressions and aspects of itself. We are always part of it and will sooner or later become aware of that. In that way, I do not believe that we expand in consciousness. We actually become more aware of aspects of consciousness as we journey on our paths. I call this path the evolution of awareness. I believe that this is the true evolution: Every created system always evolves back to the Source from which it was created. In this way, it feels accurate to say that we move from the third dimension to the fourth and the fifth and then on to the next levels until we fully reconnect with Source. Humankind lives at the lowest vibration at which we still can be aware of our connections with Source. However, most people have lost this connection. From this bottom of the barrel, we now move to higher levels of vibration/consciousness and ultimately to the highest vibration of consciousness from which everything started: the Source, the Creator, the infinite.

The State of "Isness"

How did creation start? This is a question that both religion and science has tried to answer from the beginning of humankind. There may be no real answer, but some insights may help us to have a certain understanding. I like to describe the process of creation as follows: It started at the moment that infinite consciousness became aware of its existence. We can only talk about consciousness when something or someone is aware of itself. We have no real term for a being that is unaware. Some call the state before awareness the great void, or "isness." Isness, the unaware beingness, is like the fabric of existence itself. We talk about consciousness when the fabric knows that it is the fabric. This immediately creates the idea of reflective self-awareness, which creates differences in the fabric. These differences are like threads. At the same time, based on the principle of the holographic universe,[3] every single thread also contains the whole, the isness.

As soon as isness became aware of itself, it started to explore itself through expressing itself. This process continues because what has been created is in turn also able to create; thus the infinite expresses itself infinitely. One of these expressions is physical reality. The principle of the creation of physical reality is beautifully described by Drunvalo Melchizedek in his *Flower of Life* books.[4]

It seems that we have not always done such a good job of collectively and individually creating. Unconditional love, happiness, joy, and abundance are always at our disposal, but not many people make this their way of living. What prevents us from living a life of love, happiness, joy, and abundance? What are our challenges? It is the fact that we forget to use our free will to live in a state of unconditional love. For many of us, the choices we make often lead to lack, unhappiness, depression, and many other undesirable states due to being locked into habitual patterns of tuning in to the fear aspect of the collective grid.

In its exploration of itself, infinite consciousness has created physical reality. In terms of dimensions, this includes the third and the fourth dimensions. Aspects of infinite consciousness—that is, individual souls—incarnate in human bodies. Those souls, spiritual beings, were supposed to maintain their relationship with Source, with Creator. Unfortunately these souls became entangled with the lower vibrations and lost their connection to Source. The mind, which is a human aspect, got the upper hand, and many have forgotten they are actually spiritual beings. So instead of the human form ascending through its interaction with the soul, the soul descended into the physical reality and became trapped in the physical third-dimensional world.

To escape this trap, we have to become aware of the fact that we are spiritual beings in human bodies—we have to reconnect with Source. Instead of being guided by the mind, we need to be guided by the heart. The heart is the connection with the soul that can guide us to remember who we really are. The mind is supposed to support our journeys in this dimension rather than directing them so that the body and the soul can ascend together to higher vibrations and dimensions. The biggest challenge for the soul to bring the human aspect in alignment with itself is the mind.

Mind and Brain

Like the term "consciousness," the complex aspect of ourselves that we call "mind" also has different definitions. My definition of mind is that it is the sum of all experiences an individual has had in life. Experiences are our interpretations of what is happening in the present. Our experiences do not tell us what is actually happening but rather tell us what we believe is happening. They tend to strengthen beliefs we already have. In the third dimension, our minds work with opposites, with duality, and based on our previous experiences, they will tend to label every experience as good or bad. This intensifies our beliefs and strengthens duality.

Because the mind is that aspect of a human being that registers everything that has happened, it is completely in the past. Therefore it will interpret every experience based on experiences from the past. The mind has the tendency to create belief structures based on these experiences and call them reality. The mind begins to imagine that these belief structures are reality. Therefore the mind makes these beliefs the guiding principles for our daily activities. The function of the mind is to protect us from harm. From the perspective of the mind, belief structures are there to protect us and therefore need to be obeyed. As a consequence, the mind begins to dictate the direction of our lives. It tends to override the more subtle signals from the soul, and we become entrenched in belief structures based on past experiences. Because the mind has experienced something, it thinks it knows how things work and it tells us what to do. However, how can experiences of the past guide us in a new direction? What the mind sees as new is only a reshuffling of certain aspects of the old. To quote Einstein: "We cannot solve problems by using the same kind of thinking we used when we created them."[5]

Much of what we have learned to call truth is not based on personal experience but is instead borrowed from the experiences of others. We are conditioned by belief structures belonging to our parents, teachers, religions, and society. Our challenge is to let go of these conditioned beliefs and to replace them with personal beliefs that support the journey of discovering who we really are. The mind has been recognized as the source of many problems for eons. Looking at aspects of the mind began with the development of Western psychology and the research of people like Sigmund Freud and Carl Gustav Jung. Since then, many methods have been developed to help us deal with the mind. A more modern variant of working with the mind is summarized in Rhonda Byrne's book *The Secret*.[6] This book is based on the law of attraction: What you send out is what you get back. This book invites us to work with positive thoughts and imagination to manifest what we say we want. The shortcoming of this approach is that it uses the mind to defeat the mind, which goes only so far. Hence these systems all have their limitations.

We cannot let go of the mind, but we can give it new instructions; we can reprogram it. The directions for this reprogramming have to come from somewhere other than the mind itself. They have to come from the soul, which speaks through the heart. In other words, it is not about controlling the mind but rather about allowing the mind to surrender and follow the guidance of a higher aspect: the soul or higher self.

The whole complex of the mind, the set of beliefs that determines how we see the world, is like wearing a pair of sunglasses: It colors our perceptions of the world. Even when we know the world does not really look like what we see through the sunglasses, we become accustomed to it and ultimately believe that this is the true world.

The mind has a loud voice and dominates the lives of most people. Consequently they do not hear the much softer, never-dominating voice of the heart, which is the voice of the soul, the spirit, our inner guidance. We can hear the voice of the heart most easily when we are in a meditative state: the brain state of theta or delta. When the mind dominates, we are mainly in the beta state; sometimes we are in alpha. Therefore it is very important to train the brain to go into the state we want it to be in, so we can choose to listen to the heart and use the mind only to give form to the directions of the heart.

You may wonder why the soul does not say to the human mind: "Dude, I am done with you. You go your way and I will go mine." That would be nice, but it obviously doesn't work that way. The soul seems to have a need to experience something in this Earth realm, in this third-dimensional physical realm. This something is to experience an aspect of the infinite through the physical body it has chosen to express itself through. We may call this the soul purpose.

It is not the personality that has lived lifetimes. The soul chooses many experiences in this realm to contribute to its expression and experiencing of an aspect of the infinite. A soul may choose to have these experiences in physical reality until it feels that it is complete, whatever that might mean. Only then is it time to explore other aspects of the infinite expression.

Within this reality we may need belief structures. As long as these belief structures are in alignment with our soul purpose, with who we are, we will experience joy, happiness, love, and abundance. However, when they are not in alignment, we will not experience these positive feelings. These misaligned beliefs create tensions that have an effect on energy systems like meridians and chakras and can lead to physical dis-ease and emotional problems, including depression. For this reason, it is important to replace misaligned beliefs with beliefs that are aligned with who we are. There are a few things we can do to achieve this.

Firstly, we have to be willing to look at ourselves and at the way we think. Our emotional and physical conditions give us signals that invite us to look at ourselves and our belief structures. What we experience is a reflection of what we think and believe, and through observing ourselves, we can begin to understand these beliefs. Once we know these beliefs and understand where they come from, we have gained the possibility of changing them for something that is more aligned with what we choose to create and to be. It is interesting that many people are not willing to look at themselves and their belief structures until they experience something unpleasant, either emotionally, in terms of unhappiness, depression, and anxiety, or physically, in ways like dis-ease and pain. Even then, many people try to eliminate their problems without any willingness to understand that these signals of discomfort are invitations to look at themselves and to make changes based on what they see.

Secondly, it is important to meditate in order to train our brains to actively use theta and delta frequencies to communicate with the soul. Thirdly, there are systems that help us to heal and balance all that has been brought out of balance due to the stress of doing things that are not in alignment with who we are. There are many healing modalities, but as I have already mentioned, I believe that the best healer is Earth. There is no doubt that we are able to remember past events and what we have learned by living them. In general, we believe that it is our minds that tap into these stored memories; they are kept somewhere, somehow, in our brain. However, there is a growing idea that our memories are not actually stored in our brains but are instead kept in the field, as described by Lynn McTaggert in her book *The Field: The Quest for the Secret Force of the Universe*.[7] Memory (information) is simply a coherent emission of signals from the zero-point field (also called the field). We developed this coherence ourselves.[8] Our brains seem to have a specific connection with coherent memories of ourselves, more so than with the memory fields of others. I believe that the field is an aspect of consciousness and memory is a personalized aspect of it. The sum of all memories forms what I prefer to call collective human consciousness. It is one of the fields that exist as a layer around Earth. The active part of this field, the one that we work with in our daily lives, is held in the human collective consciousness grid system. I call this system the triad system.

The Triad System

I first became acquainted with this term "triad" through Havelock Fidler's research in his book *Earth Energies: A Dowser's Investigation of ley lines.*[9] The term was used for the first time by Guy Underwood, who described in his book *The Pattern of the Past* different lines that all had triplets of what he called hairlines within the lines.[10] Because the hairlines always occurred in a fixed number of three, he called each group a triad. He gave no explanation as to why there were always three hairlines together. Interestingly, all the lines that both he and Havelock Fidler found had three sets of these triads.

Reading this research started me on the process of defining lines based on the presence or absence of sublines, of which these triads are examples. Discovering lines with triads opened a whole new aspect of my research. I found lines with a number of triads varying from one to thirteen. Like other lines we have seen, they are either mainly above or mainly below the surface of the earth. Some lines are neutral and are above and below the surface in equal amounts. However, there are also lines with triads that float above the earth, which I call communication lines (see fig. 6.1). Another way of describing a triad line is through the analogy of a cable. The triad line is like a cable with one to thirteen wires. Each of the wires always contains three copper threads that we call a triad. See figure 6.2 for an example of a line with three of these triads.

There are three types of grid systems that have triads. All three systems have connections with our consciousnesses. The grid system I call the human collective consciousnesses, or twelve triad system, holds the third-dimensional consciousness of the human species and is the subject of this chapter. The second triad grid system has lines with thirteen triads and is called the unity or Christ consciousness grid. It holds the fourth dimensional human consciousness. We will look at this grid in chapter 7. The third grid system is called communication lines, which are the floating triad lines that we will look at in chapter 8 (see fig. 6.2).

The number of triads in a line can easily be recognized. Every dowser with some experience can count the number of triads. The number of triads that can

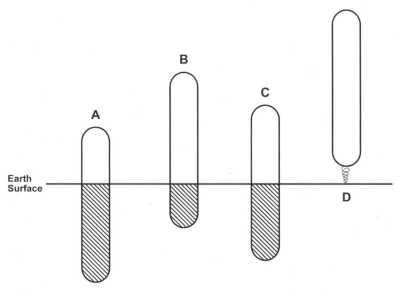

Fig. 6.1: Triad lines that are mainly below the surface of the earth (A) (yin), mainly above (B) (yang), about equal (C) (neutral), and floating above the surface (D) (communication lines). Created by Evita de Vos.

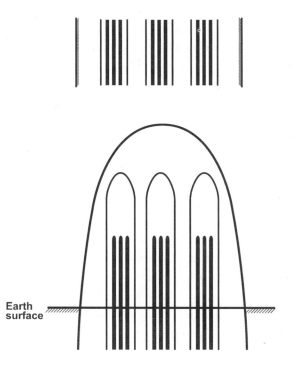

Fig. 6.2: A transverse section of the part of a yin three triad line that is above the surface of the earth (below) and a longitudinal section of this line as you will experience/dowse it when you walk perpendicular through the line (above). Created by Evita de Vos.

be found in the lines of this grid system varies from one to twelve, hence the term twelve triad grid system. When we integrate the twelve levels of this consciousness, we ascend our awareness to the thirteenth level, which is the fourth dimension, the unity or Christ consciousness.

The triad system is very important. It is our direct access to the collective human consciousness and is a powerful and expansive source of information. All human third-dimensional potential and everything that has ever passed through human awareness while living in this dimension is stored in a field and is accessible through the vortexes of grids on Earth. We can use the collective consciousness like the Internet to gather information that can enable us to express who we are and realize who we are not.

This grid system is very important for each individual human being and for humankind as a whole. It is directly related to our spiritual evolution. Although the study of this grid is not complete, the principles of the grid system are, at the moment, quite well understood, and they are presented here.

The Twelve Triad System

The third-dimensional human consciousness grid consists of twelve levels. The characteristics of each of these twelve levels can help us to understand how we interact with reality. Because the chakras have a similar function, the twelve triad grid reflects aspects of the chakra system as well. Consciousness in third-dimensional reality seems to be closely related to the energies experienced through the chakras.

The triad system is the most complex system of lines and vortexes that I have come across. It is also very important, because it helps us to understand the link between consciousness and our energy systems.

The different numbers of triads represent different levels of our collective consciousness. Each level functions as a doorway into the third-dimensional consciousness grids and field. This parallels the chakra system. Each chakra, due to its unique frequency range, allows you to experience the world in a way that is in alignment and resonates with that particular frequency range. It means you look at the whole of an experience but through that particular chakra, or gateway, you see only that which can be seen from the perspective of that particular perception system or chakra. Of the twelve chakras, the twelfth chakra will give most access to the world, because it is the most inclusive.

We see a similar situation with the twelve triad grids of consciousness. Each triad level gives access to certain aspects and qualities of the collective third-dimensional human consciousness. With increasing numbers of triads, we connect to higher levels of third-dimensional consciousness, which can help us to master more aspects and qualities of this consciousness. The twelfth level gives the most access. We have to master the essence of each level before we are ready to move to the next dimension of consciousness represented by the thirteenth triad grid, the unity consciousness of the fourth dimension. This is a gradual process, allowing us to have fourth-dimensional experiences before the process is completed.

The twelve different triad grids show some variations. These variations make it easy to describe and understand each grid system. In the first seven triad grids, the energy is found mainly in the lines and the vortexes are small. In the other five grids the situation is reversed: The energy is mainly in the vortexes. This graph shows an estimate of the amount of energy in each of the twelve different triad lines as they were found naturally and after activating them with a crystal skull named Sam (see fig. 6.3). Crystal skulls are powerful tools that help in the activation of Earth energies as I discussed in my previous book *Crystal Skulls: Interacting with a Phenomenon*.[11] I calculated the estimated amount of energy in a line by multiplying the width by the total height of each line. This is called the intensity factor (IF). This is not an absolute measurement but is a good enough estimate

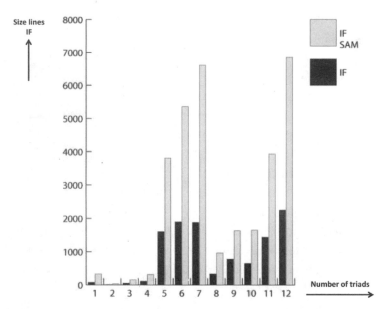

Fig. 6.3: Size of the twelve triad lines expressed as width x total height (IF). The black bars indicate the size as found in the field; the light bars indicate the size after placing an activated crystal skull (Sam) on the lines.

to see the general tendency. The graph shows that there is a dramatic drop in the amount of energy in lines with more than seven triads. The energy then moves from being more in the lines to being more in the vortexes. Slowly the amount of energy in the lines increases again, with a strong increase in the twelve triad lines.

Another difference found within the twelve grids is that there are grids with single lines and grids with double lines. A double line consists of two parallel lines of which one is a yin and the other is a yang. While single lines are either yin or yang, double lines always have both a yin and a yang line. We find single lines in grids with one to four and with eight to ten triads. The other grids have double lines. The differences in the lines help us to understand the way the grids represent aspects of our consciousness and how that is related to our chakras.

The One Triad Grid: A Tree Grid

The one triad grid stands on its own. It is a unique grid because it is the only grid that has a direct connection with trees. It has single lines and most of its energy is in the lines rather than in the vortexes. The grid does not seem to have a pattern other than that the lines move through trees. Every time the line goes through a particular type of tree, the line increases in size. Actually the trees on these lines *are* the vortexes. This is a unique phenomenon. Because the trees feed the one triad lines, they build up more energy than is found in the lines of the next two grids (see fig. 6.3).

The one triad lines have a beginning and an end. The beginning of a one triad line is always at a tree and the tree is always a deciduous tree, like a sycamore (see fig. 6.4), oak, beech, birch, linden, hawthorne, or alder. This is true for all areas I have checked: Western Europe, the United States, and Mexico. The line ends at a node that is formed by a combination of nodes of lines with two, three, and four triads, which means that one triad lines are the basis of the whole triad system and seem to feed it. This configuration has a parallel with the first chakra in that

Fig. 6.4: A sycamore tree.

the first chakra forms the basis of our whole system. Any disturbance in the first chakra will influence the whole system. When we cut too many deciduous trees, the number of one triad lines and/or the amount of energy in the one triad lines will decrease, which may weaken the whole triad system.

Many people feel attracted to trees, and we may subconsciously feel their importance. In many traditions, trees have been or still are sacred. Even in modern times, sacred trees are still known and revered all over the world. I do not fully understand the meaning of the energetic connections we have with trees, but their connection with the basic part of the grid system that holds our collective consciousness suggests that it is important to have a deep respect for trees. To ground ourselves we often imagine ourselves to be a tree. Our grounding chakra is chakra one. It is fascinating to see that the specific grid that has a connection with the first chakra is connected to trees.

The Two Triad, Three Triad, and Four Triad Grids

The grids of lines with two, three, and four triads are quite similar in construction. The lines are single lines, and the vortexes are small. The difference between the three grids is the distance between the lines. This distance increases with the increase in the number of triads. All three triad levels consist of two grids, both with lines that are perpendicular to each other. One set has lines almost to the magnetic north and almost east–west. The second set is turned about 45° in relation to the first set (see fig. 6.5).

To give you a better impression of these grids, here are some measurements. Measured in Sedona, the average distance between the nodes/cross points of the two triad grid is only 5 feet (1.5 m). The distance between the nodes of the three triad grid is larger: the average is 41 feet (12.5 m). The distance between the nodes of the four triad grid is again larger: 0.7 miles (1,127 m).

I also measured the distance between nodes of three triad lines in the Netherlands. The average distance between three triad lines in that country was 58 feet (17.6 m). The difference in distance between lines in Sedona and the Netherlands is over 40 percent. Based on other measurements, I believe that the distances between lines in the Sedona area are small and that those in the Netherlands are larger than normal. It seems that a country in which every square inch of its surface has been changed and worked with intensely is likely to diminish the energies available in the different grid systems. In chapter 13, we will see that human beings have indeed had a strong effect on the different grids.

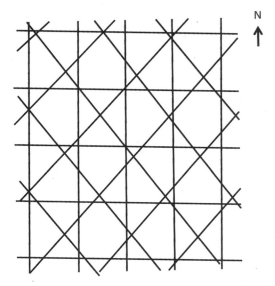

N
↑

Fig. 6.5: Layout of two, three, and four triad grids so that each consists of two overlapping grids that are turned 45° in relation to each other.

The four triad grid system is more similar to the lower levels than it is to the next three (higher) levels. When we relate this to our chakra systems, it suggests that only when we bring the heart in alignment with the lower chakras can we open ourselves to spirituality and unconditional love. And isn't that the essence of life in this third-dimensional reality?

The Five Triad Grid

This grid has double lines, thereby differing from the previous three grids. The similarity is that the lines with five triads also form two grids and that in each grid the lines are perpendicular to each other. However, the five triad grids are not oriented to the north. One of the grids has lines, which are about 30° from north with lines perpendicular to these lines. The second grid is turned 30° in relation to the first one (see fig. 6.6). The distance between the lines of these two grids is similar: on the average it is 3.25 miles (5,230 m).

The fifth chakra stands alone in our systems. It belongs to the spiritual chakras, but it is strongly affected by the condition of the lower four chakras and thus is more similar to the lower chakras than the more independent sixth and seventh chakras. We see a similar situation with the five triad lines. Their construction is closer to grids with fewer triads than to those with more triads.

Fig. 6.6: The five triad grid consisting of two grids that are turned 30° in relation to each other and are 30° turned away from the north.

The Six Triad and Seven Triad Grids

These two grids form one system that is inseparable. The lines of both grids are double lines. The six and seven triad systems can be understood by looking first at the seven triad grid. It took quite some time before I understood this pattern, because the nodes of this grid system are quite far apart. For example, if you start at a node in Sedona and follow the line that goes almost straight north, the next node of this system is 465 miles (748 km) away as the crow flies. The seven triad lines form an irregular pentagonal shape (see fig. 6.7). This means that there are five sides of different lengths and also five nodes. The six triad lines connect the nodes within the pentagonal shape and form an irregular pentagram. In this way, the six and seven triad lines form one system. In our chakra systems, the sixth and seventh chakras also work closely together. They are so close that there is confusion about which hormonal gland belongs to which chakra. In a sense, they form one integrated system that helps us to open up to spiritual truths and experiences.

It is interesting to note that the three grids that are related to the fifth, sixth, and seventh chakras all have double lines. These three chakras are considered the spiritual chakras in the physical system. The double lines seem to be characteristic for grids that are related to the more spiritual chakras.

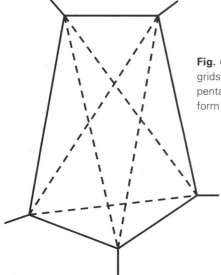

Fig. 6.7: The six and seven triad grids. The six triad lines form the pentagram and the seven triad lines form the pentagonal shape.

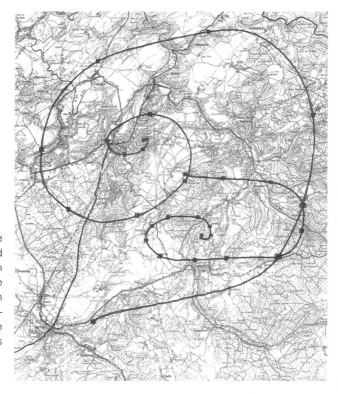

Fig. 6.8: Pictured are eight and nine triad lines spiraling through the landscape of the Ardennes (Belgium) in the area of the mega-liths around Wéris. The dots are the vortexes on the lines.

The Eight Triad, Nine Triad, and Ten Triad Grids

The grids with eight, nine, and ten triads are completely different from anything we have described so far or will describe in this or in any of the other chapters. This group has single lines and the vortexes are located on these lines. These vortexes are on lines, although they can be on nodes. The lines have a clear beginning and end. Most remarkable is the way they flow through the landscape. The lines of these three triad grids are laid out in spirals (see fig. 6.8). These lines can spiral clockwise or counterclockwise through the landscape. Both at the beginning and at the end there are vortexes. On a line are a number of vortexes separated by distances that increase the farther you move away from the beginning of the spiraling line.

The lines are not very long, although they seem to be long when you follow them through the landscape. The average length of the five nine-triad lines that we studied in the Sedona area is almost 34 miles (54 km). I studied a similar line in eastern Belgium (Ardennes), which had about the same length: 35.5 miles (57 km). In the Netherlands, however, in the most densely populated area of that country, the line that was studied had a length that was more than twice as long: almost 84 miles (135 km).

The spiraling lines cover quite a large area, and therefore it is not surprising that lines cross each other. When a line crosses another spiraling line, they may share a vortex. A nine triad line can share vortexes with other nine triad lines but it also can share vortexes with sight and ten triad lines (see Fig. 6.8). The only prerequisite seems to be that the vortexes on the lines spin in the same direction. When I looked in Western Europe at the number of shared vortexes versus the number of single vortexes, I found that only 13 percent of the 55 vortexes were "shared" vortexes. In Sedona, however, I found that from the 121 vortexes, more than 88 percent were shared. Most frequently there are two lines that share a vortex, but sometimes there are three lines and a few vortexes even have four lines. This finding seems to confirm previous observations that the systems in Europe are less dense than those in the Sedona area.

The Eleven Triad and Twelve Triad Grids

These grids again have double lines. Even though the vortexes are most important, the energy flowing through these lines is also considerable (see fig. 6.3). The research for the graph in figure 6.3 was done in 2000, and since then, the size of especially the lines of the eleven and twelve triad grids have increased considerably. Apparently our awarenesses increasingly express through the levels of the eleven and twelve triad grids.

The grids of both systems seem to go back to a simple basic form. Although the lines are not really straight, they form grids with lines that are roughly north–south and east–west, forming irregular squares. The nodes/cross points of the eleven triad lines are about roughly 4 miles (6.4 km) apart. There are no real differences between the north–south and east–west lines. The same is true for the twelve triad grid, although it seems that the lines are slightly closer to each other: about 3.75 miles (6 km).

Most people who visit vortexes of these two grids feel a strong effect, whereas they hardly notice an effect when they visit vortexes of grids with lower numbers of triads. The general reaction of people who visit vortexes of the eleven and twelve triad grids is that they like them. They are uplifting and, while meditating on these vortexes, people often receive wonderful experiences and images. The most common remark I hear is, "I like this place." Around 2006 there seemed to be a growing tendency to connect more with the twelve triad grid than with the eleven triad grid, as we will see at the end of this chapter and also in chapter 13.

Lines and Vortexes with One and Twelve Different Frequencies

I need to mention one final aspect of the twelve triad system. There is one more difference between the one to seven triad lines and vortexes and the eight to twelve triad ones that I have not yet mentioned. The one to seven triad lines and vortexes function within a single frequency range. However, the eight to twelve triad lines and vortexes each have twelve different frequency ranges. Each of these twelve frequency bands relates to one of the twelve chakras. For example, there is a twelve triad line and vortex that works mainly through the first chakra, one that works mainly with the second chakra, and so on. This creates a complex system with many different ways to connect with the collective consciousness. I brought many people to a twelve triad chakra, four-heart vortex. It has always amazed me how much information people receive and how many people actually feel their hearts.

Connecting with Triad Vortexes

I mentioned earlier that the collective consciousness contains a lot of information that helps us on our evolutionary journeys, but it also contains information that prevents us from evolving. Therefore, more than with any other type of vortex, it is important to prepare yourself for a positive experience by doing the meditation given in chapter 2. When you connect with these types of vortexes, it is very important that you are connected with love to the best of your ability and with a clear intent that you choose to connect only with those energies that are for your highest good. Only then can you use the collective consciousness for growth and expansion of awareness.

While observing people connecting with triad vortexes, I noticed that the effects are stronger when people are grounded. This is similar to what I observed with chakra vortexes. To be grounded optimally it is best to connect initially with Earth meridian energies. It does not matter what type of meridian energy you connect with, because all Earth meridian energies have a tendency to ground you. I still recommend meditating before you start your journey on any type of vortex.

When we do a meditation and connect with Earth energies, we move into the theta brain state. Especially when we meditate on a higher triad vortex, we may receive images, colors, and other information. This information can be factual, but most often the information is symbolic. The theta frequencies are the same as those of the dream state. Most of the information and images we receive when we are in a dream state comes from the subconsciousness and is therefore symbolic, which is true also for the theta meditation state. Therefore it is important to be careful with the interpretation of your experiences at such vortexes. Feel from the heart what your truth is. Do not get stuck in interpretations but allow and enjoy the experience. Although the lines are basically either yin or yang, through meditation the triad lines can become balanced. The parts of the lines above and below the surface of the earth become more equal (refer to C in fig. 6.1). This is true for both yin and yang lines. This seems to be unique for this triad grid system.

The triad grids represent the collective consciousness of all humankind, but there are local variations in the grids. In different parts of the world, the grids are colored by the experiences and perceptions of people who live and have lived in those areas. There are different energies, beliefs, ideas, and experiences when comparing China, Africa, Australia, North America, and South America. For example, people who visit eleven and twelve triad vortexes in the Sedona area frequently report receiving Native American symbols or seeing images of Native American people. There is no doubt that the triad vortexes can open us to interesting experiences.

While most of the grids we have described earlier have energies that cover the whole surface of the earth, this is not true for the triad grids. Only the eleven triad and twelve triad grids cover the earth. This seems to suggest that those two grids are indeed the most active and most important grids in the current expansion of human awareness. Following the development of these two systems may help us to understand the current changes in the collective consciousness and the overall development of consciousness in this dimension.

A Shift in Consciousness

Most of the research on the size of lines within the twelve triad system was done before and during 2000. I did not look at the size of these lines again until 2010. While I studied the grid of the twelve triad lines to check certain information, I also measured again the size of the twelve triad lines. I was in for a surprise. The size of the lines was much bigger than the size of the lines I measured in 2000. When I checked the size of the eleven triad lines, I saw that they had also increased in size, although less than the twelve triad grid. By gathering more data and also including other triad grids in the research, an interesting picture developed (see table 4).

Table 4 shows that over a period of ten years, the lines of the six, seven, and eight triad grids decreased in size while those of the nine to twelve triad grids increased. The increase in these lines is progressive; there is hardly an increase in the lines with nine triads while the strongest increase was found in the twelve triad lines. These results suggest that the energy in our collective consciousness is moving toward the higher aspects. We seem to be shifting our collective consciousness, which means that we are expanding in awareness. Many people hold the idea that we are living in a time in which a shift in consciousness is occurring and

Type of triad line	IF 2000	IF 2010	Factor of increase
six triad lines	1,913 (4)	764 (3)	0.40
seven triad lines	1,882 (3)	1645 (3)	0.87
eight triad lines	333 (4)	227 (6)	0.68
nine triad lines	780 (6)	900 (6)	1.15
ten triad lines	510 (4)	2,245 (6)	4.40
eleven triadone triad lines	1,402 (4)	8,137 (8)	5.80
twelve triad lines	2,323 (3)	25,122 (16)	10.80

Table 4: Size of triad lines six to twelve expressed as intensity factor (IF) (width X total height) in 2000 and 2010 with the number of measurements and the intensity factor indicating the increase in size of the lines.

this data supports this idea. More data supporting the idea of a shift is presented in detail in chapter 13.

Better Understanding of the
Relationship Between Chakras and Consciousness

The third-dimensional human collective consciousness on Earth is held in lines and vortexes of a rather complex system called the twelve triad system. This system has strong associations with our chakra systems. The number of triads in this grid system fluctuates from one to twelve, hence the name. The lines of the twelve triad grids differ quite a lot. These differences characterize the grids in a way that can help us to understand the relationship between chakras and consciousness on a deeper level.

The triad grids offer a vast amount of information that can help us to discover who we are. However, they also contain information that can strengthen the belief structures that prevent us from expanding in awareness. This means that triad grids can help us to evolve but they can also keep us locked in collective beliefs that no longer support us. Therefore it is important to prepare ourselves properly before connecting with these grids. Make sure to connect from your heart and to have a clear intent so that you can benefit optimally from the gifts these grids offer.

ENDNOTES

1. For more information about the holodgraphic universe, see 1. Michael Talbot, *The Holographic Universe* (New York: HarperPerrenial, 1992).

2. Drunvalo Melchizedek, *The Ancient Secret of the Flower of Life*, vol. 1 (Flagstaff, AZ: Light Technology Publishing, 1998), 43-47.

3. Talbot, *The Holographic Universe*. [Query: p #?]

4. Drunvalo Melchizedek, *The Ancient Secret of the Flower of Life*, vols. 1 and 2 (Flagstaff, AZ: Light Technology Publishing, 1999 and 2000).

5. This popular quote from Einstein is used often. If you type the sentence in a search engine, you will be provided with many references.

6. Rhonda Byrne, *The Secret* (Billsboro, OR: Beyond Words Publishing, 2006).

7. Lynne McTaggert, *The Field: The Quest for the Secret Force of the Universe* (New York: HarperCollins Publishers, 2001), 95.

8. Ibid., 118.

9. J. Havelock Fidler, *Earth Energies: A Dowser's Investigation of Ley Lines* (Northhampshire, UK: Aquarian Press, 1988), 25.

10. Guy Underwood, *The Pattern of the Past* (London: Sphere Books, 1972), 35.

11. Jaap van Etten, PhD, *Crystal Skulls: Interacting with a Phenomenon* (Flagstaff, AZ: Light Technology Publishing, 2007), 85-88.

CHRIST/UNITY
CONSCIOUSNESS GRIDS

MANY PEOPLE ON THEIR SPIRITUAL PATHS SEARCH FOR WAYS TO MOVE from third-dimensional consciousness, which is characterized by duality, to fourth-dimensional consciousness, which is characterized by oneness and unity. I believe that many of these seekers already move between third- and fourth-dimensional consciousness, often without knowing it. The challenge is to stay in fourth-dimensional consciousness for longer periods of time.

Because Earth provides us with everything we need, we can expect to find a system that supports the ability to stay in fourth-dimensional consciousness. This system is the second of the triad systems and is characterized by lines with thirteen triads. It gives us the opportunity to connect deeper with fourth-dimensional consciousness and ultimately helps us to stay in the fourth dimension permanently.

When we live fully in the fourth dimension, our thoughts seem to manifest immediately. In the third dimension there is quite a delay between thought and manifestation. This delay gives us time to consider our thoughts and to change them. When we are fully in fourth-dimensional consciousness, this delay does not exist anymore. Everything speeds up and manifests almost immediately. Many people have begun to experience fourth-dimensional reality, which is demonstrated by the fact that their thoughts become reality much sooner than they used to.

Because the length of time between thought and manifestation is so short, it is fortunate that humankind has not yet reached fourth-dimensional consciousness. Most people still have fear-based thoughts they would not like to see manifested, and definitely not immediately. Nonetheless, humankind is preparing for the move into fourth-dimensional reality, and we can choose to be part of that or not. If we choose this evolutionary step, we can use the energies of the thirteen triad grids to stimulate us to transform our limitations and expand in awareness in preparation for the move into this next level of consciousness.

Some believe that unity consciousness is or includes fifth-dimensional reality. However, it seems that the fifth dimension no longer supports physical forms and thus belongs to what is called the etheric realms. I believe that the unity consciousness can also be experienced in physical form, which means in the fourth dimension. This is our next step, and until we have taken this step, subsequent steps are irrelevant.

Many of the grids described in the previous and upcoming chapters are not found in literature with exception of the Christ consciousness grid, which is often mentioned. There is even a description of the form of the Christ consciousness grid. Authors like Drunvalo Melchizedek[1] mention a grid system that holds Christ consciousness and that this system is based on the combination of two Platonic solids: the dodecahedron and the icosahedron. These Platonic solids basically form the grid system that holds Christ consciousness.

I believe that there is often a confusion of terms in the research about grid systems. When Drunvalo Melchizedek talks about the grid formed by the two Platonic solids, he is not talking about lines and vortexes on Earth but rather about an energy field. I have mentioned that these fields exist as layers around Earth. Melchizedek suggests that these fields may have a certain structure and describes that structure as a matrix and the Christ consciousness field as a combination of the two above-mentioned Platonic solids.

I can fully support the idea that the Christ consciousness field is held in a matrix that is formed by the two Platonic solids. The basic form is the Platonic solid called a dodecahedron (see fig. 7.1). Each of the sides of this geometric form is equal in length. Imagine that you pull the center of each of the five-sided faces up until the length of the point to each of the corners of the pentagon is equal in length and has the same length as all the sides of the dodecahedron. In this way you create twelve icosahedron caps (see fig. 7.2). The end result of this is a stellated dodecahedron (see fig. 7.3). If you connect the twelve points of the stellated dodecahedron to each other, you get an icosahedron. This explains why it is said that that the matrix was formed by a combination of the dodecahedron and the icosahedron.

Looking for a grid system that holds Christ consciousness, I remembered that I had found vortexes that were of a high frequency that I could not place in any

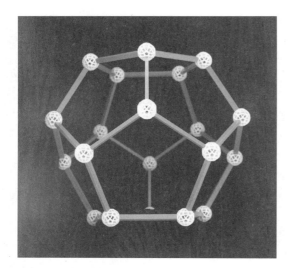

Fig. 7.1: Dodecahedron.

Fig. 7.2: Icosahedral cap.

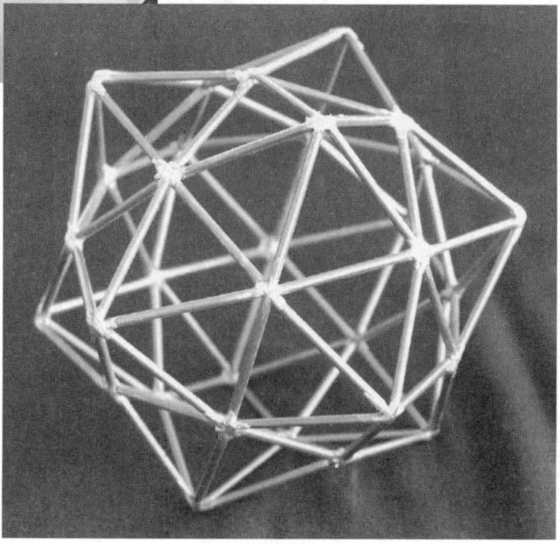

Fig. 7.3: Stellated dodecahedron, the matrix of the Christ consciousness field.

system. These vortexes were found on lines that had thirteen triads. Thirteen is a transcendental number. Seen from the human perspective, we reach Christ consciousness after we transcend the twelve levels of third-dimensional consciousness, and therefore it is not surprising to find that the lines of the Christ consciousness grid have thirteen triads.

My research into this grid started in Sedona. I looked for thirteen triad vortexes and from there I followed the lines. Initially I found two types of thirteen triad/Christ consciousness vortexes, which I called the primary and the secondary vortexes. These vortexes differ in size: the size of a primary vortex was about twice that of a secondary vortex (about 14–16 miles [23–26 km] versus about 6–8 miles, [10–13 km]).

Melchizedek also described the shape of the matrix that holds the Christ consciousness field and gave information on the Christ consciousness grid itself.[2] According to Melchizedek, there was a unity consciousness grid in existence during the time of Atlantis. Due to a failed experiment, this grid was destroyed. However, at this time, we need this grid to allow human consciousness to evolve or we risk stagnation.

Melchizedek even believes that due to possible pole shifts that could induce a temporary collapse of Earth's magnetic fields, we could even lose our consciousness, and this could mean the end of human civilization. Therefore the ascended masters looked for a solution, and with the help of higher-dimensional beings, they started to rebuild the grid. According to Melchizedek, the grid was rebuilt by three men: Thoth, Ra, and Araragat. They started at the axis of the old grid and used that axis to build the new grid. The north pole of this axis is in what is now the Giza plateau. There is a hole that is the starting point of a spiral that is the basis of the grid. Nearby is a second hole, and there a second spiral was created. These two spirals cross over each other, and at these cross points/nodes, 83,000 sacred sites were created. Thoth, Ra, and Araragat created fourth-dimensional structures at these places. Over time physical third-dimensional structures needed to be built at those places.

Melchizedek mentions that the north pole of the unity consciousness grid is located in the Giza area and its south pole in the South Pacific on the Tahitian Islands. It is found on a small island called Moorea. This island has the shape of a heart. The mountains form a ring with a specific phallic mountain in the center. All sacred sites are connected to the Egyptian pole and they are interlinked through the central axis leading to Moorea.

According to Melchizedek, there are three components of the grid: the masculine (father), the feminine (mother), and the child (neutral). The masculine aspect of the grid is in Egypt, and the feminine is in South America, especially in Peru, Central America, parts of Mexico, and even the southern part of North America. The child is found in Tibet. By now most of the sacred sites have third-dimensional structures. Melchizedek believes that there are still important sacred sites that have only fourth-dimensional structures. He says that those fourth-dimensional pyramids (it is interesting that here he uses the word "pyramid" rather than "structures") mainly belong to the child aspect of the unity grid. The data I have gathered give a different perspective. On some level, Melchizedek and I seem to agree, but we differ in terms of the way the grid is laid out in the landscape.

Research Results

My research on the thirteen triad grid has been limited to Arizona in the U.S. I found three different lines that have thirteen triads. The fact that I found three Christ consciousness lines seems to be in alignment with what Drunvalo Melchizedek has said about Christ consciousness lines, as he mentions three different lines: male, female, and neutral. Although Drunvalo mentions that the three lines are found in different parts of the world, I found all three lines in Arizona. My definition of female, male, and neutral was again based on the amount of energy above and below the surface of the earth. In this system, the female lines have energy mainly below the surface of the earth (yin), male lines have energy mainly above the surface (yang), and neutral lines had more or less the same amount of energy above as below. This is the only system I have found that has stable neutral lines and is characterized by three different lines that form a unit.

In third-dimensional reality, we work with opposing forces. This polarity creates opposites, like male and female, positive and negative, and so on. In fourth-dimensional reality, or Christ consciousness, we overcome this duality by adding a third aspect, the child or the neutral line, creating a triad that is an important aspect of unity consciousness. The grids of third-dimensional consciousness have lines that are either male (yang) or female (yin). However, our consciousness holds the potential to move into unity. This unity, symbolized by the triad, is hidden within the lines of the twelve triad system reflecting to us that hidden in third-dimensional reality is the potential for unity. The Christ consciousness grid system still has internal unity (the triads in the lines) but also has three visible lines making the three aspects of unity visible for all to see and understand.

As I followed the lines through the Sedona area I found that these lines run through many sacred sites. With the exception of some small ruins, all sacred sites in the Sedona area are on the thirteen triad Christ consciousness lines. Also, new sacred sites like the Chapel of the Holy Cross (see fig. 7.4) are found on these lines. Following these three thirteen triad lines gave me the answer to a riddle I had been trying to solve since I'd first visited Sedona in 1994. In Sedona, four vortexes are usually mentioned as "the" vortexes of Sedona. The idea that these are the important vortexes is based on a channeling done by Page Bryant in 1980.[3] These four vortexes are Cathedral Rock (considered feminine), Bell Rock and Airport Mesa (both considered masculine), and Boynton Canyon (considered neutral). I have never been able to figure out why they were given these qualities. At these locations, I always found more than one vortex, and they were both yin (female) and yang (male), which made it difficult to understand why in the channeling they were called masculine, feminine, or neutral. Following the thirteen triad lines brought the answer. At these four locations, only the thirteen triad lines have vortexes that are in alignment with the information given in the channeling. The female Christ consciousness line goes through Cathedral Rock. The masculine Christ consciousness line goes through Bell Rock and through the small hill near Airport Mesa (the airport vortex). At both locations, there is a vortex on this masculine line. The neutral line goes through the saddle at Kachina Rock at the entrance to Boynton Canyon. The vortex at Kachina Rock is neutral.

Two other locations in Sedona are increasingly mentioned as having vortexes: the Chapel of the Holy Cross and Schnebly Hill Road. The Chapel of the Holy Cross is visited by an increasing number of people. This chapel is located on a vortex that is at a cross point of a male and female thirteen triad line. I found a similar situation at Schnebly Hill Road. At a red rock knoll that is called the Merry-Go-'Round there is a vortex located at a cross point of a female and a neutral line.

When I followed the three lines through the Sedona area to Prescott to the west and to Chavez Pass (located about 18 miles south/southwest of Meteor Crater near Winslow, Arizona) to the east, I thought I understood the principle of the thirteen triad Christ consciousness lines, but I was wrong. I am always grateful to Spirit, who gives me a sign when needed—in one way or another! As I was writing this chapter, I kept feeling like I had missed something. I have learned to recognize this signal as an indication that I need to go back to the beginning, which means that I have to let go of all my ideas and start my research again. After all, I was influenced by Melchizedek's information that there are three Christ consciousness lines moving across the earth. Once I let go of this idea, I was able to find my mistakes. That resulted in a surprisingly different pattern.

Fig. 7.4: Chapel of the Holy Cross in Sedona, Arizona.

The pattern that emerged was rather simple. In the first place, there are always three lines: the female, male, and neutral lines that cross over each other at the different vortexes or sacred sites while flowing through the landscape. As mentioned, these three lines form an external triad and are inseparable from each other, like the triads within the lines. However, there is not one set of three lines but many. These different sets of three lines form a grid. This grid has sets of three lines that are more or less oriented north–south and east–west. Where the sets of three lines cross, there is a node of six lines and a rather large vortex, which in Arizona has a radius of between 50–55 miles (80–88 km). See figure 7.5.

These nodes are far apart. There is a distance of about 110 miles (177 km) between the north–south nodes, and the distance between the east-west nodes is close to 125 miles (201 km). In between the nodes, each of the three lines meanders, sometimes over quite a distance, separating the lines from each other while going through different sacred sites. Sometimes the line goes through sacred sites that are about 15 miles (24 km) away from a hypothetical straight line between nodes. This can happen with each of the three lines separately (see

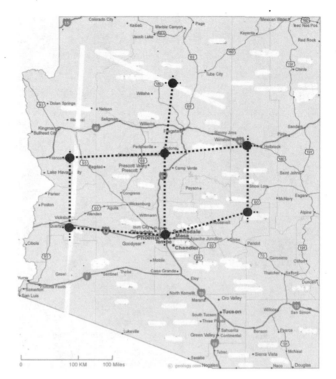

Fig. 7.5: The basic shape of the Christ consciousness grid in Northern Arizona indicated through six nodes. The round dots are the vortexes on the nodes.

fig. 7.6). However, they always come back and pass through the nodes together as a threesome.

The energy of the Christ consciousness grid does not seem to cover Earth. In Arizona, about 40 percent of the surface is not yet covered. I believe that when we live more completely in unity consciousness, these vortexes will expand and the energies will begin to cover the whole Earth. This may be part of the shift in human consciousness.

The Christ consciousness grid has another interesting phenomenon. I mentioned earlier that I had found two types of vortexes on the Christ consciousness lines. One type of vortex is about twice as large as the second type. They are independent from the vortexes at the nodes. At the nodes, the vortexes are even larger—about twice as large as the largest of the other two. Although many of the two smaller vortexes are located on sacred places and ruins, there are also vortexes at locations where there are no visible remnants of structures. This is true for vortexes of all three types of lines. In general, only one of the three types of Christ consciousness lines goes through a particular site to make it feminine, masculine, or neutral like in the Sedona area. However, sometimes there are two lines going

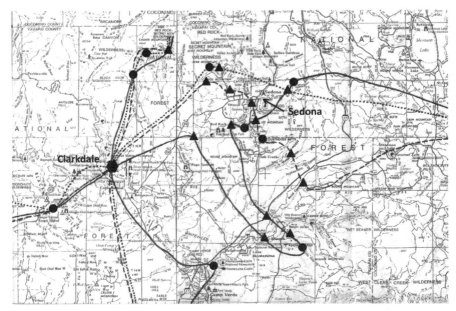

Fig. 7.6: Lines of the Christ consciousness grid in the Sedona area with a node in Clarkdale. The hexagon is the node, the black round dots are the larger vortexes on the lines, and the black triangles the smaller one. The solid lines are the feminine lines, the broken lines and the masculine, and the dotted lines are the neutral lines.

through a site, and I even found sites where all three lines pass through, crossing over each other at such points.

The nodes where the three north–south and east–west lines cross seem to be independent of sites that we know of as sacred sites. A sacred site is a place where an ancient structure exists or a place that has been used for ceremonies over long periods of time, like caves, springs, and mountains. The nodes of the Christ consciousness grids are not on such sites.

The distance between two smaller vortexes is variable and it seems to be determined more by the presence of special places than by a certain distance. I have seen distances between vortexes of less than 1 mile (1.6 km) and have also found distances of more than 40 miles (64 km) (see fig. 7.6). The thirteen triad Christ consciousness lines belong to the largest lines I have found so far. Their width is almost 0.33 miles (531 m) and the total height is about 1.25 miles (2,012 m).

I have brought people to the center of Christ consciousness vortexes. People always have profound experiences, although they often have difficulty describing what these experiences are. Experiences seem to differ greatly depending on the spiritual development of the individual. I also noticed that the experience at this type of vortex is deeper when people have first visited meridians or chakra vortexes. I have visited the Christ consciousness vortex at Bell Rock in Sedona often enough to know that visiting a meridian or chakra vortex first will help to deepen the experience at a Christ consciousness vortex. The experiences people have at Christ consciousness vortexes show that they are ideal places to help people who are on a spiritual journey to shift their consciousnesses more toward unity/Christ consciousness.

The Christ consciousness vortexes have been one of my favorite places to meditate. They always give me deep peace and they help me to feel connected to all that is around me. I always feel uplifted after visiting such vortexes. I have often wondered what makes a place sacred enough to become part of a Christ consciousness grid. I have not been able to find the answer. I can only conclude that there is still much to learn about this grid.

The Evolution of Human Consciousness

Christ consciousness is the next step in the evolution of human awareness/consciousness. An increasing number of people move with increasing frequency from third-dimensional to fourth-dimensional consciousness (Christ or unity consciousness). However this process is incomplete. Earth supports this process by providing a Christ consciousness grid. This grid consists of lines that appear always in a set of three: feminine, masculine, and neutral/child line. These lines belong together, forming a unit, an external triad, but the lines also move separately through sacred sites, creating feminine, masculine, and neutral Christ consciousness vortexes and sites. There are two types of vortexes at these sites, which differ in size by a factor two.

These three lines form a grid. The lines of this grid run roughly north–south and east–west. At the nodes of this grid the three north–south and the three east–west lines cross, creating a vortex that is larger than the vortexes on the individual lines. Connecting with this grid, especially through the different vortexes, helps us to shift from third- to fourth-dimensional consciousness, supporting human spiritual evolution.

ENDNOTES

1.   Drunvalo Melchizedek, *The Ancient Secret of the Flower of Life*, vols. 1 and 2 (Flagstaff, AZ: Light Technology Publishing, 1998 and 2000). Drunvalo refers several times in both volumes to the Christ consciousness grid. On page 35, he gives information on the Platonic solids that form this grid.
2.   Drunvalo Melchizedek, *The Ancient Secret of the Flower of Life*, vol. 1 (Flagstaff, AZ: Light Technology Publishing, 2000), 104-118.
3.   Page Bryant, "Sacred Sedona," in *Sedona Vortex Guide Book*, Light Technology Research (Flagstaff, AZ: Light Technology Publishing, 1991), 3-15.

COMMUNICATION LINES

EVERY TYPE OF ENERGY LINE, GRID, AND VORTEX IS IMPORTANT. THESE grids would not exist if they did not support an aspect of the whole that we call Gaia. Human beings seem to interact with all these different Earth energy systems. Within the different systems, the lines that I term "communication lines" have a special place. They give information about our current activities but also about activities from the past, the activities of our ancestors. The energies and information in communication lines help us to understand the energies of the past and the present and help us to embrace, transform, and integrate them as a basis for our evolutionary journeys. We do not connect with energies of communication lines in the same way as with vortexes of other systems. However, these lines are present at every sacred site and have an effect on people, mostly unconscious. Because communication lines are so important, attention will be given to them, both in this chapter as well as in the final chapter.

Communication lines form the third group of triad lines. They are different from the previous two groups because the lines are completely above the surface of the earth (as seen in chapter 6, fig. 6.1). They are anchored to the surface of the earth at vortexes of the three triad grids of our collective consciousness. That may be the reason why there are no communication lines with fewer than three triads; the number of triads in communication lines varies from three to twelve. The anchoring of communication lines on vortexes of the three triad grid is independent of the number of triads a communication line has. It seems that the three triad grid forms the basis and source of the whole communication line system.

Communication Lines Appear Between Similar Structures

I discovered communication lines when I tried to understand the characteristics of church lines. This term was mentioned in Wigholt Vleer's *Leylijnen en Leycentra in de Lage Landen* and was defined as: lines that exist between churches.[1] These lines are easy to find. In Europe, each church has many such lines, connecting a church with the many churches found in the nearby villages and cities. Initially I was surprised that these lines did have triads, as these lines seemed so different from other lines, but I came to understand that these lines are created by us, which means that they are part of human consciousness.

When human beings create two similar types of structures, preferably from natural materials (many types of concrete contain natural materials), and the distance is not too far, a communication line may appear. There are no communication lines between modern houses and apartment buildings, so it seems that the structures have to be developed with a certain type of energy in order to create communication lines. When this energy is not available during construction, subsequent use of the building may energetically charge a building in such a way that communication lines appear in a later phase. For example, modern churches are often built by people who have no connection with the church, like a contractor and his workers. Consequently, the building may not have the energies to connect it with other churches. However, as soon as the church is initiated and used for services, the energy of the building will change. This may allow for the development of communication lines between churches.

Another important factor is distance. The strength of the energy field created during construction or subsequent use creates a vortex. The strength of the vortex determines the distance that can be bridged. In order to create a communication line, a certain amount of energy is needed. The energy for the line may come from the vortexes and the three triad grid it is anchored on. I still do not know all the factors that play roles in the creation of communication lines. At the moment, I am aware of communication lines that exist between churches, temples, and mosques but also between banks. They exist between megalithic sites (including pyramids) and standing stones. I have not found any other type of modern building that has communication lines other than the ones mentioned.

It is easy to create a three triad communication line over short distances. Anyone can do this, and you may already have done it without knowing. The easiest way to create communication lines is with stones. Select three reasonably sized stones and handle them with attention. When you place these stones in a row in the landscape within a 100 yard (91 m) distance, there will be three triad communication lines connecting the three stones. In a sense, you have created a ley line, an alignment in the landscape. You can do this with many stones to create longer lines. The stones do not have to be placed in a straight line. You can create circles, squares—any shape you would like. As long as you give the stones enough attention/energy, lines will appear between them. You can even check that maximum distance between stones that will still allow you to create a communication line. This experiment assumes that you can dowse or sense these communication lines. You can also allow someone else to do it.

Havelock Fidler has done extensive research on this phenomenon.[2] He charged stones in different ways and studied the charge and the lines that appeared between them. In his studies, he describes that the lines always have three triads. When I repeated this research, I also found lines with three triads, and you will be able to do the same. However, when my wife Jeanne and I used three crystal skulls, activated them, and then placed them in a line in the landscape at a total distance of about 200 yards (183 m), we were able to create lines with five triads. Whatever we tried, we were unable to create lines with more than five triads. That result was surprising because I have found lines with up to twelve triads in the field.

Both human consciousness triad grid lines and communication lines have up to twelve triads. Therefore it is tempting to think that there is a parallel between these two systems. However, this does not seem to be true. Although the communication lines draw energy from the three triad consciousness grid, the energetic meaning of the number of triads in the two systems is quite different. If they were the same, it would be much easier to create communication lines with a higher number of triads. But in reality, it is not easy to create lines with more than five triads, at least not for individuals.

The number of triads in a line seems to be determined by four major factors: intent, the level of consciousness with which the structures are created, the number of people involved, and the distance between the stones and structures.

When the Ancients Built Sacred Spaces

Intent and the level of consciousness—which are two related aspects—are important. They determine the basic frequencies of the materials people work with and, consequently, those of the construction. It makes a difference whether you just place stones in a landscape or you do so with love, respect, and intent, or even work in a ceremonial way. Depending on intent and level of consciousness, you will create lines with three triads (created without much intent or focus) or lines with four or five triads (created with specific intent and attention).

After construction and initiation, most modern churches have three triad communication lines between them and other churches. Looking at older churches and especially the European cathedrals, we see a different picture. These cathedrals have lines with a higher number of triads. A beautiful example is the Cathedral of Chartres in France, which has four nine-triad communication lines connecting this cathedral to other structures with similar types of energies. The fact that the construction of this cathedral is based on sacred geometry[3] may have contributed to these higher frequencies.

Ancient people built their constructions in alignment with Earth and the cosmos. They looked for supportive Earth energies (vortexes) and looked at the sun and moon phases. We do not build our churches and important buildings that way anymore, let alone our houses—although there are a few exceptions. The ancients' selection of location for their constructions and their alignment with the cosmos all may have contributed to the number of triads in the communication lines.

Not all knowledge about the sacredness of place has been lost. Even in modern times I have seen some beautiful examples of temples and statues that are connected by communication lines with higher numbers of triads. All of the examples I present are from Taiwan because they are the most illustrative. The first one is the Chung Tai Chan Buddhist Monastery in Nantou County, which has a very special temple. The building was designed by the same architect who designed the Taipei 101 building, which has been the highest building in the world for a while. Above the temple is a tower designed to gather cosmic energies. This newly constructed building has a number of nine triad communication lines.

Another example of working with energies in modern times was found in the gardens of the I Ching University, which is also located in Nantou County, Taiwan. Here, one of the four recognized masters in Taiwan teaches feng shui based on the I Ching. I understand that it is a complex system but it seems to work very well. There is unfortunately little to no information in English about this system. In the gardens, each tree, plant, stone, and statue has been placed according to the teachings of this master, creating a wonderful feeling of peace and harmony. This also resulted in communication lines with twelve triads between the three main statues in the garden: the statues of Quan Yin (see fig. 8.1), Buddha, and the Longevity Buddha. It is a place with very special energies. In my opinion, this master has truly mastered the material world and is able to bring it into a state of pure harmony. It is one of the most special and harmonious places I have ever visited.

Over time, I have found networks of communication lines of every number of triad between three and twelve. The number of lines with three triads is most

Fig. 8.1: Statue of Quan Yin at the I Ching University in Taiwan.

common, but communication lines with twelve triads are far from rare. At many nodes where communication lines come together, we find physical structures, but there are also many nodes that do not have any sign of a physical structure. Structures may have been there in the past but there is currently nothing visible. These nodes are always located at vortexes of one of the types described in this book. However, the higher the number of triads, the more likely it is that the vortex is one of the four chakra types.

There is another factor that contributes to the number of triads in a communication line. To help to understand this factor, let me start with sharing some observations made in Taiwan. In 1999 there was a big earthquake in Taiwan that destroyed many buildings. One of these buildings was a temple located near Wufong. It had the largest Buddha statue on the island. Visiting the place where the temple used to be, we discovered that this temple had been part of a nine triad communication line network.

They had not yet rebuilt the temple, and the monastery moved to two temporary buildings, one for ceremonies (the temple), and one for monks of the monastery to live in. When I checked the communication lines of these buildings, I found that the building where the ceremonies were held had lines with only five triads. This observation raised an important question. Could it be that we can create lines up to a maximum of five triads only and that higher numbers need to be built up over time through conscious use of the place? In other words, do prayers and ceremonies increase the number of triads? To answer this question, we did an experiment in the Sedona area. This experiment was carried out in phases, the description of which will help you to understand communication lines and their developments.

The Sedona Landscape Temple

The story of this experiment with communication lines started in Sedona in 2004. In that year I read *Sedona Sacred Earth* written by Nicholas Mann.[4] He described several interesting energy structures in the Sedona landscape. He called the combination of these structures the Sedona Landscape Temple. As part of the Temple, he defined a six-pointed and a five-pointed star. His book intrigued me and I went out into the field to see whether I could dowse any energy lines that delineated the structures in the landscape he described.

It was not difficult to find lines that formed the six-pointed star, but I could not find lines that formed the five-pointed star. The lines that formed the six-pointed star were indeed located very close to where Nicholas Mann described them in his book (see fig. 8.2). Each of the points of the six-pointed star was anchored on a chakra vortex. The lines that formed the six-pointed star were twelve triad communication lines. Because he was so accurate in his description of the six-pointed star, it was amazing that I could not find any indication of lines of the five-pointed star.

In 2005 Adam Yellowbird, director of the Institute of Cultural Awareness[5] (ICA), organized an event around Earth Day. His purpose was to activate through ceremonies the Sedona Landscape Temple as described by Nicholas Mann. My goal was to support the event and, in particular, see what happened with Nicholas Mann's five-pointed star when a couple hundred people were creating a lot of energy focused on the Temple.

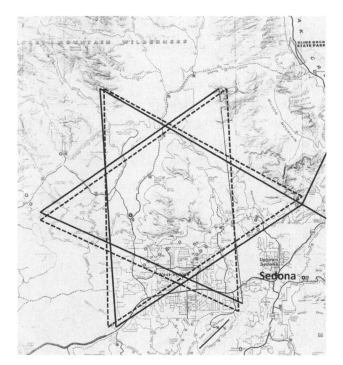

Fig. 8.2: The six-pointed star in the Sedona area as described by Nicholas Mann (solid lines) and as found formed by twelve triad communication lines (broken lines).

While the majority of the people were contributing to ceremonies in a location in Sedona, we placed four groups of eight to ten people at different places in the so-called Sedona Temple. Of the four groups, one was placed in the center of the six-pointed star and one in the center of the five-pointed star as described by Nicholas Mann. The purpose of these groups was to be connected both with the energy of the main group and with the location to which they were guided.

The results were impressive. Besides the fact that all of the energy systems, vortexes, and lines expanded in size, energy lines appeared that delineated the five-pointed star. These lines were communication lines and they all had five triads. Again we see that initially lines with a maximum of five triads are created. The lines were close to the five-pointed star Nicholas Mann indicated in his book, although they were a bit more off than those of the six-pointed star (see fig. 8.3).

The next year Adam Yellowbird organized another event around Earth Day. The focus was again on the energies of Sedona with a special focus to see whether ceremonies could change the number of triads in the lines of the five-pointed star. As in the previous year, a large group of several hundred people gathered. There were no special groups placed anywhere. Again we saw an increase in the size of vortexes and lines in the area. I observed that the number of triads in the lines of the five-pointed star shifted from five to six. It seems that repeatedly adding energy to a system of communication lines will allow the energy in these lines to change their frequency and add triads.

In 2009 another large event with many ceremonies was organized in the Sedona area. This event was called the "return of the ancestors" event and many elders from the Americas and other parts of the world gathered. I did not do any monitoring around that time. Almost a year later I visited one of the points of the five-pointed star, and I realized that again a shift had taken place: Now the lines were showing seven triads!

In summary, it seems that we can easily create communication lines with three to five triads. However, creation of communication lines with more than five triads requires powerful additional energy impulses. It seems that this requires groups of people with a common goal.

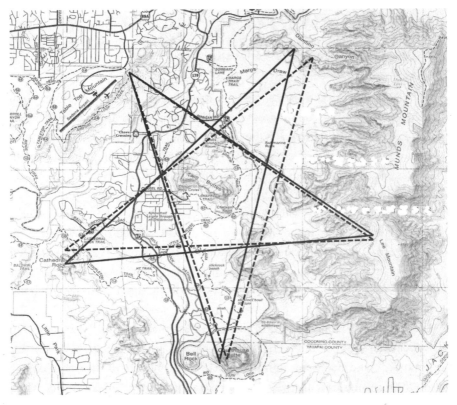

Fig. 8.3: The five-pointed star as it appeared in 2005 after ceremonies (broken lines), and how these lines relate to the findings of Nicholas Mann (solid lines).

Communication Lines Are a Source of Information

Over time a dense network of communication lines has been created. The number of triads in these lines reflects levels of consciousness. When we study sites and structures, the number of triads in the communication lines present makes it possible to get an idea of the level of consciousness of people who have used these sites. However, there are some confusing aspects. Over time many sites have been used by different peoples, and consequently there are different layers of energy. However, we can learn to recognize these layers through training, using either feeling/sensing or dowsing. Studying the different communication line systems can give us information about the people who created these lines: those who lived before us in the area where we now live, our ancestors. This is important because these energies have an effect on our daily lives.

In my initial research phase into communication lines, the different energies seemed complex and often confusing. After many years of study, certain patterns have emerged to provide insights about the energies of place. My results show that the energies of place are actually a combination of the energies of current times and ancestral energies. Communication lines help us to create a better understanding of the energies present at a specific location. We will focus especially on the ancestral energies of a place because of their importance for us in terms of our daily lives and our evolution.

Ancestral Energies

We can separate ancestral energies into two distinct types. One type is what we normally refer to when we talk about ancestral energies. These are the energies of our forbears, the grandmothers and grandfathers of our lineage. It is our genealogy.

The second type is a different type of ancestral energy. These are the energies of the people who lived before us in the location where we are now living. They are the ones who created sacred places over time in the area where we live. They also created communication lines between sites. It is these energies and these communication lines that form the ancestral energies of a place. These energies can have quite an effect on us and may even be the reason why we are attracted to certain areas or sacred sites to live in or visit. In this chapter, we look at these ancestral energies of place.

When we live in or visit a certain area, we consciously or unconsciously experience the effects of the ancestral energies of that area. This does not mean that all people resonate with all layers of energy existing at a place. It may be that a person needs only one specific layer of ancestral energies because these energies are important for that person in that phase of life. Each area has its own history and, consequently, its own energies. It is therefore impossible to describe the ancestral energies of our world. I will offer a number of examples that will enable you to get an impression of what ancestral energies are. I have examples from different places, although the most extensive data in the U.S. comes from Arizona, especially in the area around Sedona. This area is visited by millions of people annually, and thus many people experience the ancestral and other energies of this place. For me, looking at ancestral energies is one of the most exciting aspects of the study of the energies of a location. Recognizing different energies is like seeing the unfolding of the story of a location, often in a totally different way.

Ancestral Energies and
Communication Lines of Atlantis and Lemuria

The study of communication lines makes it possible to recognize the energies of those people who created these lines. Some of the lines were created by peoples known by archeology. However, there are also grids of communication lines that were created by peoples that are not known or recognized by archeology. These are the grids of the people of legends and stories. Of these, the best known are the peoples of Atlantis and Lemuria. Once I could recognize the energies of these two grids, I became very excited. I know that many people feel connected with these energies, and therefore I have included them in this chapter.

The legends of Atlantis and Lemuria (or Mu) can be a rather touchy subject. There is no real proof of their existence. At the same time there are many stories about sunken lands, both in the Pacific, where it is believed that Lemuria was located, and in the Atlantic Ocean, where Atlantis is believed to have existed. However, besides legends and channelings, there is no firm proof. The only description of Atlantis is found in two of Plato's Dialogues: "Timaeus" and "Critias." These dialogues have been the basis of many books on the subject of Atlantis. In all of them, the location of Atlantis has been described. I am not sure about the official number of locations mentioned in these books, but there are more than twenty. This could mean that Atlantis was spread over a wide area. However, it could also mean that there is no physical evidence and that many of the places called Atlantis were built by descendants of Atlantis who tried to reconstruct Atlantis based on memories of their homeland. It is also possible that Atlantis is a consciousness that exists on Earth in a different reality or vibration than ours and therefore does not exist in physical reality. I strongly believe in this possibility. I also believe that the energy grids from the reality we call Atlantis are detectable in this reality. After all, subtle energies are not bound by space and time. In other words, we can find Atlantis by studying the communication lines that belong to Atlantis. A similar story may be true for Lemuria.

In the mid-1990s I did a lot of dowsing. At that time, I worked with many people, and one of these people was a friend who also made the dowsing rods that I have used in my research since 1995. These dowsing rods, which are rather heavy, have been my most important tool in gathering the information you are reading in this book. He made a similar pair for himself, and together we did much dowsing. He was with me when I finally came to understand the basics of the triad lines. While working on a project in the southwest of the Netherlands near the North Sea, he called me and told me that he had found a pyramid, or at least the energetic imprint of a pyramid. If I had not have known him so well, I would have shrugged my shoulders and left it alone. But I knew that he was good at dowsing archeological sites, so I decided to check it out.

With the critical presence of a third person to compare our results, I dowsed a pyramid with a base of the same size as the one he'd uncovered. What was even more exciting is that there were communication lines connected with this imprint, and these lines had nine triads. Following these lines became the focus of our research for a number of weeks. Although we never completed the study, we made some interesting discoveries. There were several of these lines, and when these lines formed a node, we found the imprint of a structure. We found three types of structures: a pyramid, as we found the first time; a tetrahedron, which is a pyramid with a triangle as a base of which the size of all lines, all sides, and all angles is the same; and a dome. All were connected by nine triad communication lines. At least three lines converge in the North Sea. This node is far from the coast, estimated to be 20 miles (32 km) away from the coastline. It is believed that the North Sea was dry during the Ice Age. They find remnants of mammoths at the bottom of the Sea, an indication that mammals once roamed there. Even during Roman times the Sea was lower'than it is today. A Roman castle called Lugdunum Batavorum existed near the town of Katwijk, and the ruins of that castle have since disappeared under water as cited by Wigholt Vleer's *Leylijnen en Leycentra in de Lage Landen.*[6] Increasingly we believed that we were dealing with the energetic imprints of Atlantis, and therefore we called these communication lines "Atlantis lines."

As intriguing as these results were, research stopped after a couple of months for diverse personal reasons. It took until 2001 before I again connected with this

subject. In that year, Jeanne and I visited Gran Canaria. Many Atlantis researchers believe that the Canary Islands were once a part of Atlantis.[7] On the island we
soon found some interesting sites that are considered places of power. At these
sites we found energetic imprints of pyramids, tetrahedrons, and domes (see
fig. 8.4) connected by communication lines with nine triads. It brought back
memories of my earlier research in the Netherlands. Jeanne and I both strongly
felt the energy of Atlantis in Gran Canaria. If I had had any doubts as to whether
these systems had anything to do with Atlantis, those doubts evaporated while
we were there.

Fig. 8.4: Site with an Atlantean energy dome at the base of the large rock called Roque
Nublo in Gran Canaria (Canary Islands).

This is not the end of the story. In fact, this is where the story really begins. By the end of 2001 Jeanne showed me a place in Colorado that she believed had an energetic imprint similar to the ones we'd found in Gran Canaria. She was right. There was a tetrahedron with nine triad communication lines in the area. However, it felt energetically different. It was softer, more feminine. People believe that the western part of the U.S. may have been part of Lemuria, MU, or the Motherland. These people believe that Mount Shasta and Sedona were Lemurian.[8] We felt that the energies were soft and feminine, similar to the energies we had felt at Mount Shasta and Sedona. We also believed that this node had a Lemurian etheric structure.

"United States" of Lemuria

The discovery of this node brought up the question as to what network this Lemurian site was part of. We decided to look at the nine triad communication lines in more detail to get an answer to this question. We discovered that there was an irregular pattern of nodes where several of the nine triad communication lines came together. Several of these nodes had ruins, but most of them had no visible human structures. All of them had an energetic imprint of a pyramid, a tetrahedron, or a dome. Another phenomenon we noticed was that there were lines that seemed to form the edge of an area within which these Lemurian lines and nodes were found. Were we discovering a Lemurian area in the United States?

This question set Jeanne and me on a journey of more than 10,000 miles (16,093 km) to find and define the edges of this area. This journey resulted in the discovery of a large area with Lemurian energies in the west of the United States (see fig. 8.5). The most northwestern point is in Oregon, near Newport. The most southwestern point is in San Diego. At these two places, the lines that form the edge of the Lemurian area disappear into the ocean. Toward the east the area narrows and ends up in a kind of point in Colorado/New Mexico, between Alamosa and Santa Fe. There are fifty-four nodes connected by lines that form the edge of this area. Some of these nodes had interesting structures—for example Casa Malpais near Springerville in east Arizona (see fig. 8.6).

There is only limited information to support our findings. A few authors have produced maps that indicate that some part of Lemuria, was located in the western part of the United States. In his book *The Lost Continent of the Pacific* on Lemuria, Cerve indicates that it mainly California and the northern coastal part of Mexico were part of Lemuria.[9] Although this is different from what we found, California is included in both maps of Lemuria.

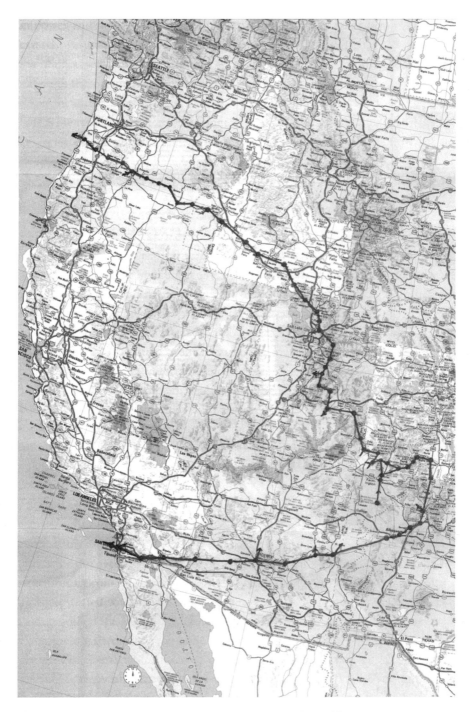

Fig. 8.5: Map showing the area of Lemuria in the western United States.

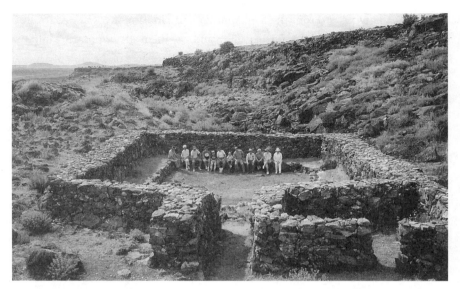

Fig. 8.6: Kiva in Casa Malpais, Arizona, is one of the Lemurian nodes at the edge of the Lemurian area.

Another map can be found in *Home of the Ancients*, a book on Mount Shasta edited by Bruce Walton.[10] The same map can be found in a booklet called *Into the Sun* about the Lemurian Fellowship.[11] This map shows Lemuria covering a larger part of the United States, including California, Nevada, Utah, Oregon, and Washington State. The map has many similarities to our findings, although it indicates a larger area in the north and includes Baja California in the south.

The map that shows most similarities with our findings is the map of William Scott-Elliot.[12] He was a member of the Theosophical Society, and he made many maps of both Atlantis and Lemuria during different phases of their existence. The one that he called the "later period of Lemuria" has the most similarities with what we found.

It seems that Atlantis covered a much larger area. At this moment, I have found Atlantis lines in Holland, Belgium, France, Spain (Mallorca), Gran Canaria, Mexico, and Puerto Rico. In Mexico I found Atlantis lines south of Durango, around Mexico City, and around Mazatlan. From Mazatlan, we followed the lines of the western edge of the Atlantis energies north along the Pacific coast. There are no lines moving into the Pacific Ocean and going into the west. At San Carlos, the lines that form the edge of the Atlantean area bend northeast. They enter the United States at El Paso. Almost immediately they bend east and head almost straight east. The last point I have checked is at Centerville, about 130 miles north of Houston, Texas. I know that lines continue further east, but I do not know their path after Centerville. From the San Antonio and Houston areas and Galveston Island I followed Atlantis lines further south and saw them all disappearing into the waters of the Gulf of Mexico. It seems that at least a large area of the Gulf of Mexico is part of Atlantis. As I mentioned, we found Atlantis lines in Puerto Rico.

There is no doubt that the study of communication lines can give us information about past civilizations and the areas in which these civilizations were active. It also helps to understand these lines' relationships with Earth energies and how ancient peoples blended the energies of their civilization with those of the earth. A beautiful example of Atlantean energies and how they were used by later civilizations is found in Mallorca.

Atlantis in Mallorca

Mallorca is one of the Balearic Islands located east of Spain in the Mediterranean. On this island, we found an interesting layout of communication lines. These lines were all connected to Atlantean energies. I have mentioned that there are pyramids, tetrahedrons, and domes both at the Lemurian nodes and the Atlantean nodes. These three forms indicate the energies of the masculine (the pyramid), the feminine (the tetrahedron), and the child/neutral (the dome). I call these three energies the three universal principal energies. We find also these energies in Christianity under the names of the Father, the Son, and the Holy Spirit (Shekinah). As we have seen, we also find these three energies in the three lines of the Christ consciousness grid and more are hidden in the triads of the twelve triad system. Apparently these three energies were very important for both the Lemurians and the Atlanteans. It is not easy to understand why they created these sites and how they used the energies in these locations. There is, however, no doubt that they are important because we find these sites, representing the three energies, in every area where Atlantean and Lemurian energies are found.

In Mallorca, it became very clear that these three energies were very important for the Atlanteans. The Atlantean energies, as expressed in the three universal principal energies, are organized in such a way that there is a perfect balance between these three types of energies. Maybe also this balance exists on a larger scale, but it may take lifetimes of work to collect all the information necessary to confirm this idea. On Mallorca, the area is small and therefore is easy to oversee.

On Mallorca, Jeanne and I found seven Atlantean nodes where communication lines came together and also where one of the three etheric structures could be found (see figs. 8.7 and 8.8). With the exception of one site, all of these sites

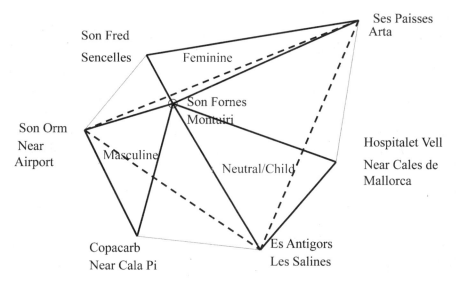

Fig. 8.7: The seven Atlantean nodes on Mallorca with the different communication lines that connect these sites. There are three triangles with solid lines (nine triad communication lines) forming a masculine, feminine, and neutral triangle. The broken lines form a triangle of ten triad communication lines.

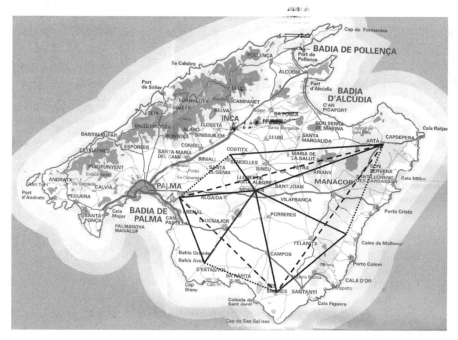

Fig. 8.8: Location of the seven Atlantean nodes and the different connecting lines on the Mallorca map. For explanation, see fig. 8.7

also have talaiotic structures. Talaiots are megalithic structures of the Balearic Islands that were built 3,000 to 4,000 years ago.[13] (see fig. 8.9). This means that the people who built the talaiotic structures were capable of finding Atlantean sites and used them for their own ceremonial purposes. While the Atlantean sites were connected with communication lines of nine, ten, or eleven triads, the talaiotic structures were connected by lines with seven triads or less. Obviously the talaiotic people worked at a lower level of consciousness than the Atlanteans. This is a beautiful example of the use of different sites by people from different times, forming different layers of ancestral energies. This is similar to the situation in the American southwest where at the Lemurian sites, kivas and other structures of the Pueblo people are found.

The center of the Atlantean system in Mallorca is in Son Fornes (see fig. 8.10), a talaiotic settlement just north of Montuïri (see figs. 8.7 and 8.8). This is a very special place. Much restoration is going on and two of the major talaiots have been mostly restored. It is the only site on the island of Mallorca that has a pyramid, a tetrahedron, and a dome in close proximity. At this site all three principal cosmic energies are represented. This means that there are three nodes. They form a triangle with communication lines that have eleven

Fig. 8.9: The author's wife Jeanne at the Talaiot near Son Fred on Mallorca (Spain).

triads. The Atlantean people obviously worked with high levels of conscious-ness at this center.

Each of the three nodes is also part of a larger triangle that is laid out in the landscape (see figs. 8.7 and 8.8). These triangles are formed by nine triad com-munication lines. Each of these triangles holds the energy of one of the three prin-cipal cosmic energies. The feminine triangle is formed by Son Fornes, Son Fred (near Sencelles), and Ses Paisses (near Arta). The masculine triangle is formed by Son Fornes, Son Oms (near the Palma airport; the only place without a talaiotic structure), and Copacarb Vell (about 5 km north of Cala Pi in the south). Finally the neutral/child triangle is formed by Son Fornes, Ets Antigors (near Ses Salines), and Hospitalet Vell (near Cales de Mallorca).

This is not the whole story. We found two systems that worked with the three cosmic principal energies. One system, found in Son Fornes, has communica-tion lines with eleven triads, and the other system has nine triads and is formed by three triangles. There is yet another level at which three sites, each represent-ing one of the three cosmic principal energies, are connected. This connection is with ten triad communication lines and consists of a triangle formed by Son Oms (masculine), Ses Paisses (feminine), and Ets Antigors (neutral/child). Looking at

Fig. 8.10: Talaiot at Son Fornes that forms the masculine aspect in the center of the Atlantean energies in Mallorca.

the different systems that were created, there is no doubt that they were created with a clear purpose in mind: to help people experience these three cosmic principal energies at different levels of awareness.

The Communication Lines of the Sacred Geometry People

While studying the different grids of communication lines, I came across another system that does not seem to be created by people that are known by archeology. This grid of communication lines has a distinct vibration that is even higher than that of Atlantis or Lemuria. The people connected with these energies have been referred to as the "techno people." However, I do not like this name and started to call them the "sacred geometry people." I have no way to prove whether or not they had knowledge of sacred geometry; however, feeling their energy brings up such images. You will not be able to find the name sacred geometry people anywhere. I created that name to describe a grid system that has communication lines with eleven and twelve triads. I found these lines first in the Sedona area and later in a large part of Arizona, in Texas, in Mexico, and also in Peru. I have no doubt that such grids exist in other places as well.

Like the Atlantean and Lemurian grids, this grid system has at each of its nodes one of the three etheric structures of pyramid, tetrahedron, or dome. In ancient times, these communication lines must have been key to working with cosmic principal energies.

Earlier in this chapter, I mentioned the Sedona Landscape Temple. In this Temple, there is a six-pointed star (see fig. 8.2). This six-pointed star is part of the energy system of the sacred geometry people. Besides the two lines of the star, the most eastern point of the star has two additional twelve triad communication lines. About a year later, I decided to follow these lines. These two lines turned out to be the start of two sides of a square (see fig. 8.11). The sides of this square are about 40 miles (64 km) long. At each of the corners of the square, I found a six-pointed star. These four six-pointed stars are linked to the four directions: the one in the southeast corner points south, the one at the southwest corner (Sedona) points west, the one at the northwest corner points north, and the one in the northeast corner points east. The northeast corner has the smallest six-pointed star. Going counterclockwise, the size of the six-pointed stars increases. One wonders about the purpose of this structure.

Initially I thought that the square with the four six-pointed stars was an isolated structure. However, I later found eleven and twelve triad communication

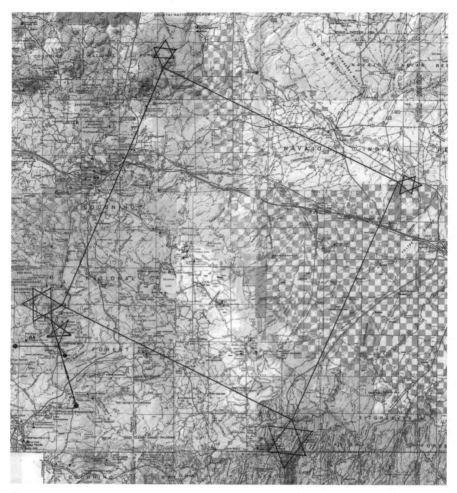

Fig. 8.11: Map of the square in Arizona with four six-pointed stars formed by twelve triad communication lines. This is part of the grid of the sacred geometry people (see fig. 8.10). Also shown is the five-pointed star in Sedona with lines that were created when the five-pointed star was formed.

lines connected with this structure, forming a whole network. The area that is covered by the eleven and twelve triad networks is about the same for both systems, and the area covered by the twelve triad system is slightly larger. The twelve triad system goes from the Phoenix area in the south to Hopi land in the north, Lake Havasu in the west, and central Arizona in the east. This system is totally restricted to Arizona (see fig. 8.12). There are many sacred sites involved, although not all the nodes are found at sacred sites. A very powerful point in the twelve triad system is Prophecy Rock on the Third Mesa in the Hopi Reservation.

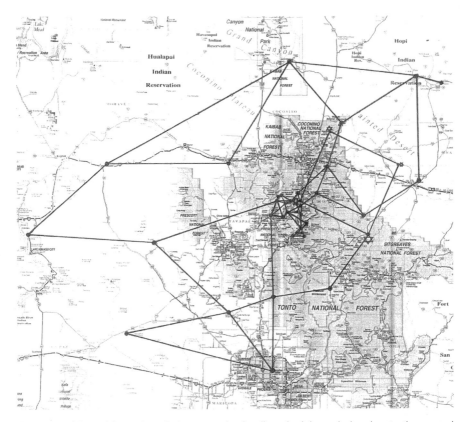

Fig. 8.12: Map with twelve triad communication lines in Arizona belonging to the sacred geometry people.

That point is anchored on a seventh chakra level one vortex with a radius of over 250 miles (402 km). While the eleven triad communication lines system covers more or less the same area, in the north it does not go farther than the I-40, the Interstate from Los Angeles to Albuquerque.

Communication Lines and the White-Robed People

One day I went out with a woman to one of the ruins located in Lost Canyon in the Sedona area. This ruin is located in a cave-like part of a rock wall. We sat and meditated for a while and then she said to me, "This is a dome." My reaction was to confirm that the cave-like part of the wall indeed looked like a dome. "No," she said, "It *is* a dome." Again I confirmed, wondering why she was so insistent. With her South-American intensity she almost yelled at me: "It is a dome!" Finally I wondered if she meant an etheric dome structure as I'd seen from Lemurian and Atlantean sites. That turned out to be exactly what she meant, and she was right. Initially I thought this was another Lemurian site. It was, but we also found twelve triad communication lines. She brought my attention to yet another system of eleven and twelve triad communication lines. Energetically these grids were different from anything I had found before. At each of the nodes of this grid, I found one of the three etheric structures representing the three cosmic principal energies.

The energy of these eleven and twelve triad communication lines are found in different areas of the world. The lines I found in the Sedona area are part of a larger area that stretches from southern Arizona to the Four Corners area (where Arizona, New Mexico, Colorado, and Utah meet). The southern edge is very close to the Mexican border. To the north it stretches out into the southeast corner of Utah and the southwest corner of Colorado. To the east it includes Chaco Canyon (see fig. 8.13).

I also have found lines with these energies in the Netherlands and in Peru and Bolivia, mainly around Lake Titicaca. The study of these areas is still incomplete. In the Netherlands, I found a southern edge close to the border of Belgium. The eastern border is slightly east of the middle of the country, but I do not know how far the area stretches to the north. To the west the lines disappear into the North Sea. The direction of the lines indicates that there is a node in the North Sea, about 20 miles (32 km) from the coast. This is the same point I mentioned in the previous section about Atlantis; it is a place where the nodes of the two systems are in the same location. This is a normal phenomenon. In the Netherlands, all of the nodes of the system of communication lines that I am describing are also nodes of the Atlantis grid, although the Atlantis grid is more extensive and spreads over a much larger area, going south into Spain and beyond. In Peru and Bolivia, the lines of these energies stretch from Machu Picchu in the north to Tiwanaku in northern Bolivia in the south. I do not know how far the area stretches in the western and eastern directions.

I named these grids of eleven and twelve triad communication lines the "grids of the white-robed people" and, like the name "sacred geometry people," you will not find this title anywhere. I'd like to share a story that may help you to understand this name and make a deeper connection with the energies of these grids.

One day I was sitting in Chaco Canyon, the famous Anasazi ruins in northwest New Mexico, U.S. My back was against Casa Rinconada, which is one of the largest kivas in the southwest United States (see fig. 8.14). I was meditating and feeling into the energies of the place. Suddenly I felt the urge to open my eyes. I

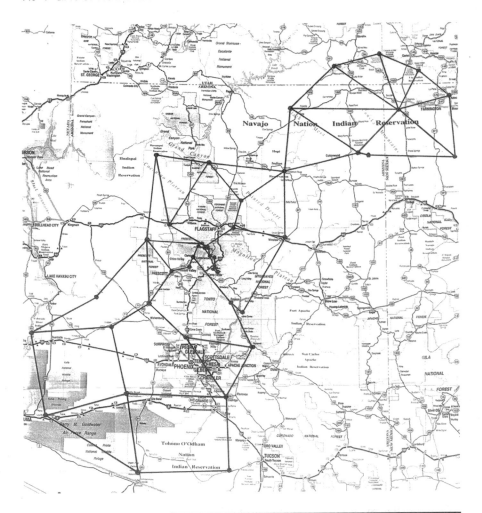

Fig. 8.13: Map with the twelve triad communication lines in Arizona and the Four Corners area belonging to the white-robed people.

Fig. 8.14: The large kiva in Chaco Canyon, New Mexico called Casa Rinconada. Note the T-shaped "doors" (see text, under heading "The Sinagua").

was unprepared for what I saw. I was literally in a different world. I saw people, buildings, and even a pyramid, but it was not the world I knew. Everything contributed to an impression of white: all was clean, bright, and very pleasant. I saw adults and children walking down what seemed to be a street, but there were no vehicles. Then I realized that the people could see me too. They looked at me and asked me something I could not hear. When I tried to say something back, I suddenly was back at Casa Rinconada. Never before had I experienced anything like this and I did not know what to make of it. It was not so much the images but the energies of the experience that made a deep impression on me, especially the energy of peace that I felt.

Later in the day when I was on my way to the petroglyphs near Una Vida (still in Chaco Canyon), I met a mother and her son of eleven years old or so. The mother saw my dowsing rod and asked me what I was doing. When I explained it to her, she obviously gathered her courage and then asked me what she should do with a story that her son had told her. Earlier in the day, he'd told her that he'd seen people and a city. The boy was sitting a bit farther away and looked as if he'd been accused of doing something wrong. When I said to him, matter-of-factly: "They were all dressed in white, weren't they," his eyes lit up. He nodded his head and began to tell me that he had seen a kind of town with white buildings and people wearing white clothes. They were only walking, and there were no cars. He was so excited that he'd told his mother. She had not seen anything and did not believe him. When I left, the boy was happy and the mother was more accepting. I was left wondering: What is going on in this place? Was this how Chaco Canyon had looked in the past?

About a year later I had a similar experience in Boynton Canyon (near Sedona). The experience was weaker, but I undoubtedly looked into the same world as the one I had seen in Chaco Canyon. Although the experience was weaker, it was actually more important. I felt that I had to let go of the idea that I was looking into the past. It is unlikely that a city has ever been situated in the place where I was in Boynton Canyon. Later I heard from two more people that they had similar experiences in Boynton Canyon, although our experiences happened at three different locations in the Canyon. Then I forgot about the experiences.

When I studied the grid system of the eleven and twelve triad communication lines I'd found that held different energy from that of the sacred geometry people, I became aware of the similarity in energies to those that I'd experienced in Chaco Canyon and Boynton Canyon. I realized that the people of Atlantis and Lemuria have their own grid, and so do the white-robed people. It seems that the nodes of these grids are access points into that reality, which may explain the experiences I had.

The three areas of the white-robed people (Arizona and the Four Corners area, Lake Titicaca, and the Netherlands) have a distinctly different quality. They hold different aspects of the white-robed peoples' energies. These three different qualities reflect again the three cosmic principal energies of feminine, masculine, and neutral/child, but instead of finding these qualities in a specific location, we now find them over a large area. The Lake Titicaca area represents the feminine energies, Arizona and the Four Corners area represent the masculine energies, and the Netherlands and the North Sea area represent the neutral or child energies. There is still much to learn from these areas. I believe that there are other areas holding the white-robed peoples' energies, but so far I have not found them.

Ancestral Energies in the Sedona Area

Anywhere in the world we can look at the different energy layers created by the ancestors of that place, although it requires a lot of time and patience. I have looked at a few areas like the Netherlands, Lake Titicaca, and the area around Teotihuacan (close to Mexico City) but none of these areas have I studied as extensively as the area around Sedona, because that is where I live. Therefore I will use the Sedona area as an example to describe the idea of layers of ancestral energies as I understand them to function. When I talk about the Sedona area, I am referring to an area that stretches between Mingus Mountain and the Black Mountains in the West and the Mogollon Rim to the north, west, and south. This area includes Sedona and the Verde Valley area.

Like most places on Earth, the Sedona area has quite a history. Different groups have lived here and each of these peoples left their physical and/or energetic imprints on the area. Although the list may not be complete, I am aware that the following peoples live or lived in this area. Moving from recent to ancient times:

- Modern settlers
- Yavapai Apaches
- Sinagua
- Paleo-Indians
- Archaic hunter-gatherers
- People of the land of Mu (Lemurians)
- Sacred geometry and white-robed peoples

Each of these peoples left their energetic imprints on the area, sometimes combined with structures that are still visible.

The Modern Settlers

No other group of people has had such a noticeable impact on the world as the modern human, especially during the past century. This is true all over the world, and human impact only increases. We see the same phenomenon in the Sedona area. An ever-expanding population takes up more and more land, and this has a strong impact on the environment. In the area, several smaller and larger towns have been developed in the past hundred years: Sedona, Cottonwood, Camp Verde, Clarkdale, Rimrock, Lake Montezuma, Cornville, Page Springs, and some smaller communities. Our modern constructions have been built without consideration for the energies of the land, except in a few rare cases. Some of the largest environmental impacts include artificial electromagnetic energies and human fear-based emotions. Fortunately many people in the area have an increasing awareness of the importance of Mother Earth, which has led to many meditations and ceremonies. This has created necessary compensation for these accumulated disturbances and has made the Sedona area at large one of the better areas to live in, from a subtle-energy point of view.

In these modern times, communication lines have been created, but almost all the lines have only three triads, sometimes four, and very rarely five. In other words, in general we are creating structures at a lower vibrational level. Earlier we mentioned that we are able to create communication lines with more triads. This has happened in the Sedona Landscape Temple, where the lines of a five-pointed star now have seven triads.

The Yavapai Apaches

The Yavapai Apaches form a nation of two tribes. The Yavapai are a Yuman tribe that has often mistakenly been referred to as the Mohave Apache tribe. The Tonto or Dilzhe'e Apache belong to the group of the Western Apache. Both tribes were living in the area when white settlers came. They were removed forcibly from the area in 1875. The survivors came back toward the beginning of the twentieth century and established the Yavapai Nation. It seems that these tribes did not make permanent structures in the past, and from an energy point of view, their impact on the area was limited. It seems that they did not add communication lines to the area and instead used the sacred sites of those who came before them.

The Sinagua

Of all the people who lived in the area before white settlers came, the Sinagua seem to have had the most visible impact on the land. There are many ruins in the area attributed to them (see fig. 8.15). It is believed that they lived in this area from around A.D. 700 to A.D. 1425. For unknown reasons, they left the area and there is no formal agreement as to what happened to them.

The name Sinagua means without (*sin*) water (*agua*). The early Spaniards who came to the area wondered how these people could have lived without water. However, it seems that the Sinagua had water when they lived here. They lived near streams, rivers, or springs and their agriculture was always located near places with water. Many of the smaller ruins indicate places of worship or of ceremony, and water could likely have been brought to these places when needed.

The Sinagua were surrounded by three other tribes: the Hohokam in the south, the Mogollon in the east, and the Anasazi (or Hisatsinom, as the Hopi tribe calls them) in the north. If we look at the different Sinagua ruins it is not difficult to see that their culture was influenced by these surrounding tribes. For example, they learned irrigation from the Hohokam and the method for constructing cliff dwellings from the Anasazi (see fig. 8.15).

I have looked at many ruins from all four tribes. Every ruin, whether small or large, has a vortex that formed the energy center of the pueblo or the structure. The vortex is also a place where all the communication lines come together. There is a wide variation in the number of triads in these lines. However, lines with a higher number of triads (nine and higher) were already there before the Sinagua came. They were obviously able to recognize the energies created by their ancestors and preferred to use these places to support their daily and spiritual lives.

Contrary to their neighbors, the Sinagua hardly ever created kivas. Kivas are round (see fig. 8.14) or sometimes square (see fig. 8.6), almost always are underground dwellings, and are usually covered by a roof. In the roof is a hole through which people can enter and exit the kiva. It is a place for ceremonies and gatherings. These sacred places are still used by the Hopi people today. It is believed that all Pueblo people—from the Anasazi in the north to the Paquime in the south (Chihuahua, Mexico)—have the same origins. Although there are many local differences, there are strong similarities, as seen in the cliff dwellings, T-shaped doors, and kivas.[14] In ancient times, kivas were located on vortexes, mostly on chakra vortexes, but also on meridian and triad (eleven or twelve triad) vortexes.

Most of the sacred sites of the Sinagua are located on a plaza and very rarely in one of the rooms of the structures. Vortexes can be found at these plazas, and

Fig. 8.15: Montezuma Castle, a cliff dwelling attributed to the Sinagua people.

these vortexes are the nodes of the communication lines. It seems that the Sinagua were creating communication lines of up to seven triads. There are communication lines with a lower number of triads that connect other structures in the area with the node at the plaza. There is no doubt that the Sinagua have strongly contributed to the energies of the Sedona area.

Archaic Hunter-Gatherers

These people used the area from 2,000 to 6,000 years ago until about A.D. 300. They created rock art, some of which has been found in the Sedona area. Most of this rock art has a scratched design. Although they had a culture, I have not been able to find a detectable grid of communication lines that hold their energies. Most likely they did not construct permanent structures, and therefore it is unlikely that they created any communication lines.

Paleo-Americans and Paleo-Indians

Archeologists believe that people have lived in the southwest since about 11,500 BC. These people were mainly hunters of megafauna like mastodons, mammoths, saber-toothed tigers, bison, giant sloths, and camels. The remnants of their culture have been found all over the southwest. However, not much is known of their spiritual activities, and as far as I can determine, they have not left a strong energetic imprint on the land. In the Sedona area, I have not been able to find any energetic sign of their presence.

Lemurians

We mentioned earlier that Lemuria covered a large part of the western and southwestern part of the United States. The Sedona area is located within this area, and consequently we can find several nodes of their communication lines with one of the three types of structures: the pyramid, the tetrahedron, and the dome. Many of these sites have been used by people who came later, which in the Sedona area is mainly the Sinagua. The Lemurians primarily created communication lines with nine triads. I have not yet found lines with a higher number.

Sacred Geometry People and the White-Robed People

Both of these peoples have created communication lines with eleven and twelve triads, and therefore they created lines that hold the highest vibrations in the area. This means that they must have been highly conscious people. The grids of these peoples are independent, but there are nodes where their grids coincide. Both peoples created a higher number of nodes in the Sedona area than anywhere else I have researched. It seems that already in ancient times Sedona was seen as special.

The people who came after these cultures were apparently still aware of the energies of their ancestors and used the energy nodes they created as a basis for their own energy systems. This is evident with the energies of the Lemurians, who created a more extensive system than the eleven and twelve triad communication line grids of their ancestors. They were unable to create lines with the same high frequencies and created their own system existing of mainly, if not solely, nine triad communication lines. The Sinagua people were still connected to all of these energies and also to their structures are on the nodes of their ancestors. It is only in recent times that we have lost these connections and built at locations that were selected for practical reasons, discarding considerations of the energies of a place. Slowly we are finding our way back.

The Energies of Our Ancestors

Communication lines are created through human activities. These lines have triads, like all systems connected with human consciousness. There is a relationship between the level of awareness of the people who created the lines and the number of triads in the lines. However, we seem to be unable to create lines with more than five triads unless we repeat the activation of these lines until it reaches the maximum level we can achieve. Communication lines have been created for as long as the human race has existed and for as long as stone structures have been created. Therefore all sites that we recognize as sacred have communication lines independent of the time in which they have been created.

Both the number of triads in the lines and the quality of the energies in the lines can help us to understand the energies that our ancestors created. At sacred sites, it can often be observed that different layers of energy were created by different peoples. We can connect with these ancestral energies and they may help us to integrate the past and the present. Such integration will enable us to create a new future in which we can live with expanded awareness and create balance, joy, happiness, and love.

ENDNOTES

1. Wigholt Vleer, *Leylijnen en Leycentra in de Lage Landen* (Deventer, NL: Ankh-Hermes, 1992), 27-31.

2. J. Havelock Fidler, *Earth Energies: A Dowser's Investigation of Ley Lines* (Northhampshire, UK: Aquarian Press, 1988), 76-88.

3. Louis Charpentier, *The Mysteries of Chartres Cathedral*, translated by Sir Ronald Fraser, Research into Lost Knowledge Organisation (Suffolk, UK: Rilko Books, 1966).

4. Nicholas R. Mann, *Sedona Sacred Earth: A Guide to the Red Rock Country*, rev. ed. (Flagstaff, AZ: Light Technology Publishing, 2004).

5. The website for the Institute of Cultural Awareness is http://www.ica8.org.

6. Vleer, *Leylijnen en Leycentra in de Lage Landen*, 331.

7. Islands in the Atlantic Ocean such as Cape Verde and the Canary Islands are most frequently mentioned as remnants of Atlantis. See, for example, the *Wikipedia* entry "Location Hypotheses of Atlantis," last modified January 30, 2011, http://en.wikipedia.org/wiki/Location_hypotheses_of_Atlantis. There are even some online travel resources about the history of the Canary Islands that mention Atlantis (see for example http://www.ctspanish.com/communities/canary/canary.htm and http://spain-grancanaria.com/uk/history.html).

8. There are several books that talk about Lemuria at Mount Shasta. A few examples are Bruce Walton's *Mount Shasta: Home of the Ancients* (Pomeroy, WA: Health Research, 1985), Wishar S. Cerve's *Lemuria: The Lost Continent of the Pacific* (San Jose, CA: Supreme Grand Lodge of AMORC, 1931 and 1982), and Susan Isabelle's *On Assignment with Adama* (Bloomington, IN: Author House, 2005) and *8. Return The Goddess, The Lemurians Shall Come* (Bloomington, IN: Author House, 2007).

9. Many people who live in Sedona see it as normal to talk about Sedona as a "Lemurian" place.

10. Cerve, *Lemuria: The Lost Continent of the Pacific*, 9. i.

11. Bruce Walton, ed., *Mount Shasta: Home of the Ancients* (Pomeroy, WA: Health Research, 1985).

12. Lemurian Fellowship, *Into the Sun* (Ramona, CA: Lemurian Fellowship, 2006), 14-15.

13. William Scott-Elliot, *The Lost Lemuria* (London: The Theosophical Publishing House, 1904), available in its entirety at http://www.erbzine.com/mag11/1122.html. The book was reprinted as W. Scott-Elliot's *Legends of Atlantis and Lost Lemuria* (Wheaton, IL: The Theosophical Publishing House, 1972). In this later edition, the map that indicates "Lemuria at a Later Date" (map 6) is no longer available.

14. "Talaiot," *Wikipedia*, last modified August 12, 2010, http://en.wikipedia.org/wiki/Talaiot.

15. Carlos Lazcano Sahag'n, *Exploring a Forgotten World: Lost Sites of the PaquimÈ Culture*, (Mexico City: Grupo Cementos de Chihuahua, 1999), 55.

9.

OTHER CONSCIOUSNESS GRIDS:
DOLPHIN, WHALE, AND
WHITE BUFFALO

THE TRIAD GRID SYSTEMS ARE NOT THE ONLY GRIDS THAT HOLD CONSCIOUSNESS. Triad grids hold the consciousness of human beings, but awareness is not limited to human beings. Actually, every species of plant and animal holds some aspect of consciousness. As soon as more than two of one species exist, there will be a field and a grid system for that species.[1] The field makes it possible for that species to exist and the grid holds the information that reflects what aspects of the field have been expressed in the physical reality. Rupert Sheldrake calls these fields "morphogenetic fields."[2] By now we know that when a species exists, there will also be a grid on Earth. I call these grids "morphogenetic grids," and I will discuss them in more depth in chapter 11. These grids hold information that determines what a species looks like, but they also hold the consciousness of that species. Awareness/consciousness determines behavior, so these grids also determine behavior. For almost all species, the morphogenetic grid is a single grid. This is different for human beings. We have a twelve-layered system, the triad system that holds the information of both form and behavior, along with our consciousness. In addition there are the communication lines and there is the unity, or Christ, consciousness system. At this moment I am aware of three other species that have more than one consciousness grid: dolphins, whales, and white buffalo.

Human beings seem to feel a strong attraction to dolphins and whales. This may be the reason why we train dolphins and killer whales. It may also be the reason why people go whale watching and swim with dolphins. We may subconsciously know that these beings are more than just animals. The idea of looking down on animals as lesser creatures in creation is in and of itself a misunderstanding of the importance of all of creation. It is the consequence of our lack of awareness that we are all children of Earth—we are all supported, nurtured, and fed by Mother Earth, and we are all part of the same morphogenetic grid. In regard to dolphins and whales, the misunderstanding of their level of consciousness is even greater. Slowly we begin to understand that these wonderful beings contribute to the evolution of human awareness. It is shocking to see that we revere dogs and cats and slaughter dolphins and whales—although isn't the human species the only species that slaughters individuals of their own kind on a large scale? The white buffalo is a creature of legend. Native Americans see its appearance in these times as an important signal. The white buffalo's energetic contribution to Gaia and to the development of awareness of the human race may be more important than most humans are willing to realize.

Dolphins

Most people find it difficult to believe that dolphins have a high consciousness. Fortunately, with growing awareness and sensitivity, an increasing number of people are becoming aware that dolphins are special creatures. The size of a dolphin's brain is larger than a human's, although the size of its brain in proportion to its body is smaller than a humans.[3] While some people believe that the intelligence of dolphins is less than that of humans, others believe they could be our equals.[4] However, there is a difference between intelligence as measured by human standards and consciousness/awareness. Spiritual awareness is more important for our development and understanding of physical reality as compared to how easy it is for a species to learn tricks. Within the context of this book I focus only on consciousness and the energies that support us in our personal and collective spiritual evolution.

Once you have made a connection with the dolphin consciousness through their grid system and its vortexes, it becomes easier to accept that dolphins have a high level of consciousness. Personally, I believe that the highest level of dolphin consciousness surpasses the highest level of human consciousness as it is held in the twelve triad system. In other words, dolphins experience aspects of unity, or Christ, consciousness. While scientists believe that dolphins have a lower intelligence than humans (as seen from a human perspective), dolphins are nonetheless able to include unity consciousness in their lives. What a lesson they teach us: It is not intelligence that determines the ability to experience and live in unity consciousness.

When we studied the grid systems that hold dolphin consciousness, we found four levels, each with its own grid. The two highest levels of dolphin consciousness have aspects that are similar to unity, or Christ, consciousness. This does not mean that these levels are identical to the Christ consciousness as human beings experience it. Dolphins have a very unique way of expressing consciousness, just as we have our own way of expressing ours. This is true for the third- and fourth-dimensional consciousness.

When we connect with dolphins, we are connecting with the energies of love, joy, playfulness, and a sense of unity and family (the pod). We can experience this through a direct connection with dolphins but also when we connect with the vortexes and lines of their grids. The lines of the four dolphin grids basically form triangles. Each vortex has five lines that make the triangles rather irregular. In the lowest level, incidentally, a line is missing, thus creating a diamond shape. However, this does not happen in the higher grid levels. The vortexes come in the usual two forms, spinning predominantly clockwise (yin) or counterclockwise (yang). Each level has a yin and yang version, but these two systems do not differ much. They display the usual features of these grid systems in that the lines connected to the clockwise spinning vortexes are mainly under the surface of the earth, whereas the lines with predominantly counterclockwise spinning vortexes are mainly above the surface of the earth.

The study of the dolphin grids has mainly been focused on understanding the basic pattern of the grids and the size of the lines. The lines of the grids of the first three levels of dolphin consciousness are similar in size (height and width) while those of the highest level are about 30 percent larger. The size of the vortexes increases with increasing levels of consciousness, as does the length of the lines between the vortexes. Based on the size of the vortexes and the distance between vortexes, we noticed that the three highest levels (at least in the Sedona area) cover every square inch of the earth while the lowest level almost does. Therefore we are permanently in contact with dolphin consciousness. However, most people are not aware of this and without awareness we most likely do not connect with these energies. Consequently we do not experience the wonderful joyful, playful, and loving energies of dolphin consciousness. When I bring people to dolphin consciousness vortexes, they love the energies and a surprising number of people are even able to recognize the energies.

When I finished the study of the four levels of dolphin consciousness, I thought that it was complete. My friend Kristina, with whom I have dowsed many systems, helped me to see that I had missed something. I'd missed two levels of dolphin consciousness. One was the level below the lowest level I had found. We felt that these were remnants of a frequency level that was no longer used, one that will likely disappear even more as time goes on. We also found a level above the highest level. It seems that this level is under construction. Apparently we are not the only species expanding in awareness. This discovery brought up several questions. Are dolphins expanding in consciousness as a consequence of the shift toward higher energy frequencies on Earth? Or are dolphins aware of our shift toward Christ consciousness and are supporting us by bringing higher aspects of unity consciousness into our world? Further studies may provide us with answers to these questions.

The Different Dolphin Species and Their Roles

I am sometimes asked about the role of the different dolphin species in the general dolphin consciousness grids and field. This is a very valid question, because the idea of a general dolphin consciousness seems to contradict the idea that each species has its own morphogenetic grid (chapter 11). I believe that each species does have its own morphogenetic grid but in addition there is a collective dolphin consciousness grid.

Dolphins are in many ways different from other animals. They have a higher consciousness and their consciousness is held in more than one grid. Many people believe that their origin is not on Earth but is in Sirius. Whether this is true or not, the fact is that their consciousness feels different to most people who connect with them. I believe that all dolphin species together created a field that is a summation of the consciousness of all dolphin species and individuals from the moment when they came to Earth. This consciousness field is again a layer around Earth, while the grids hold that aspect of the field that dolphins have brought into the Earth realms. The dolphin consciousness field and grids contain information that supports humankind to evolve from beings with a third-dimensional consciousness into beings with a fourth-dimensional consciousness.

Each dolphin species brings different aspects of the collective dolphin consciousness into the grids on Earth to allow humans to connect with it and to learn from it. Each of the dolphin species is equally important, although they each have a different task. In my opinion the bottlenose dolphin as a species functions as a kind of guardian of the grids and is the species that determines when a new grid needs to be developed to allow new information to become available to the human species.

Whales

Much that has been said about dolphins can also be said about whales. However, looking at the frequencies of the different whale consciousness grids, it becomes clear that whales surpass dolphins in their levels of consciousness. The energies in the grid systems suggest that whales hold the highest consciousness in a physical form on Earth. Sitting on one of the vortexes of the higher levels of the whale consciousness grids makes it easy to believe the truth of this statement. There are six grids holding six different levels of whale consciousness. In general, all six levels are of a rather high level of consciousness. When visiting a vortex of the highest level of whale consciousness, many people can hardly experience the energies. These levels of consciousness are, for them, out of reach.

Whales are seen as the record keepers of Earth.[5] It is believed that they hold records that go beyond the akashic records. Connecting with whale consciousness can open a doorway into these expansive records. The six consciousness grids of the whales are similar to those of the dolphins in the sense that they are also based on triangles created by five lines that radiate from each vortex of the grids. They differ from the dolphin grids because the six grids have lines that increase in size with increasing levels of consciousness. This is also true for the size of the vortexes and for the distances between the vortexes.

The energies of the vortexes of the whale grids cover every place on Earth (based on observations in the Sedona area), which is similar to the vortexes of the dolphin grids. Also we see that the lowest level has the least coverage. There seems to be an expansion of whale consciousness. Besides the six levels, my friend Kristina and I found a seventh level that is under construction. Whether this is a true expansion of whale consciousness or the development of another morphogenetic grid needs further investigation.

Whale Species and Their Roles

When we look at the role of the different whale species in this Earth reality, we notice a parallel with the dolphins. Each whale species has its own morphogenetic field, while all whale species together form a collective field. This field forms a layer around Earth. On Earth, the six grids hold the information of all that the whale species brought into Earth reality. It is believed by indigenous peoples that whales hold the ancient records of Earth,[6] and this collective whale energy field may contain these records or give access to it. Connecting with the whale grids may allow us to connect with these ancient records and these records may hold a key to humankind's future. We need to integrate this information into our current knowledge and understanding in order to move to the next level of consciousness, the Christ consciousness. Like with the dolphins, each of the whale species holds an aspect of the total collective field, and they bring energies and information into the grids on Earth whenever appropriate. I believe that the coordinating species of the whales is the humpback whale.

White Buffalo

The idea that whales and dolphins may hold levels of consciousness higher than humans is a stretch for many people. It is even more of a stretch to believe that an animal like the white buffalo may hold aspects of a higher consciousness. Although their consciousness is not as high as that of dolphins and whales, it is supportive for the expansion of our consciousness. In the past I would have doubted this to be possible with an animal like the white buffalo. This perspective changed in 2003 when we connected with a woman who had made a spiritual extract of the white buffalo.[7] The energy of this essence is so strong that I was immediately interested in exploring the energy further. My wife Jeanne and I have meditated many times with other people after taking this essence orally or after it was sprayed in our aura. There was little doubt that this essence was special and had high frequency energies.

In several Native American traditions, the white buffalo is connected to White Buffalo Calf Woman, who is believed to have come from the Pleiades.[8] According to legend, about 2,000 years ago, she taught the Lakota people many things and brought them the sacred peace pipe. She taught them seven sacred ceremonies, of which the sweat lodge is one. When she left, she promised to return. The birth of a white buffalo calf would be a sign that it would be near the time when she would return.[9] Several white buffalo calves have been born since 1997, and we have been fortunate enough to have seen them many times. According to legend, this heralds not only the time when White Buffalo Calf Woman will return but also the coming of a time of peace.

A white buffalo is not an albino and it is also not snow white. It has some coloration, although the color gets lighter as the calf gets older (see fig. 9.1). It has been genetically proven that the white buffalo is pure buffalo and not a hybrid.[10] When I met the white buffalo in Flagstaff, it confirmed my feeling that the white buffalo is energetically very different from its brown relative. I feel that the white buffalo expresses an aspect of the Pleiadian consciousness that is in alignment with what many Native Americans believe.

Fig. 9.1: A White Buffalo. Photo taken in Flagstaff at the ranch of Jim and Dena Riley.

The white buffalo consciousness grid forms a system of lines and vortexes with six levels. These levels do not reach as high as the dolphin and whale consciousness levels do. Only the highest level of the white buffalo consciousness is supporting us on our journey toward unity, or Christ, consciousness. The other levels help us to find peace and harmony in our lives. In my opinion, this is the function of the white buffalo consciousness: to support us in finding peace and harmony and to help us feel connected to all living beings on Earth. The white buffalo also teaches us the true quality of abundance. When we are in a state of love, we will always have abundance, meaning that we always have what we need to live a happy and healthy life. Abundance does not mean having more than we need. This is one confusion in our modern times: We believe that abundance requires having far more than we actually need; therefore, we can never have enough.

Visiting the vortexes of these grids gives us a sense of the consciousness of the white buffalo and helps us to connect to aspects of the Pleiadian consciousness. The white buffalo grids also make us aware of the support that these wonderful beings give us on the path of learning to live in harmony with our environment. Once we live in harmony, we will never again take more than we need.

The white buffalo/Pleiadian grids are based on pentagonal shapes, like the seven triad grids (as seen in fig. 6.7). There are six frequency levels, and as the levels increase, so do the size of the lines, the size of the vortexes, and the distance between vortexes. As with the grids we described earlier, there are yin and yang lines. Only the energy of the four higher levels covers Earth completely while the two lowest levels cover it to a large degree.

I really enjoy connecting with the vortexes of the white buffalo grids and so do all who I have brought to these places. The information in the grids is at an early stage since there are only a few white buffalo. Many Native Americans have connected with these grids and even recognize them as being connected to the White Buffalo Calf Woman of their legends. I hope that this sharing will stimulate more people to connect with the white buffalo and also with the prophecy of peace that is connected to them. Connecting with them directly or through the grids will stimulate the flow of information and energy from the field into the grids so that these energies can become more easily available to all.

Many Animals Offer Energy Consciousness Now

Whales, dolphins, and white buffalo support us on our spiritual journeys. The energies of the grids that hold their consciousnesses are spread all over the world and are therefore easily available to those who are willing to open themselves to these energies. Whales offer the possibility to connect with ancient records; dolphins offer the possibility to connect with the energies of playfulness, joy, happiness, and the feeling of community; and the white buffalo offers the possibility to connect with peace and an awareness of abundance. They all also support us in shifting from third- to fourth-dimensional consciousness.

ENDNOTES

1. Drunvalo Melchizedek, *The Ancient Secret of the Flower of Life*, vol. 1 (Flagstaff, AZ: Light Technology Publishing, 2000), 106.
2. Rupert Sheldrake, *A New Science of Life: The Hypothesis of Morphic Resonance* (Rochester, VT: Park Street Press, 1995), 76-91.
3. "Cetacean Intelligence," *Wikipedia*, last modified January 19, 2011, http://en.wikipedia.org/wiki/Cetacean_intelligence.
4. Regina Blackstock, "Dolphins and Man.....Equals?" *Little Townmart* (2004), accessed February 2, 2011, http://www.littletownmart.com/dolphins/.
5. Jamie Sams and David Carson, *Medicine Cards: The Discovery of Power through the Ways of Animals* (Santa Fe, NM: Bear and Company, 1988), 201.
6. Ibid., 201.6.
7. The essence of the white buffalo, called "White Buffalo Bliss," was created by Jana Shiloh. Several stores in Sedona offer this essence for sale. For more information, visit *HealthRays* at http://www.healthrays.com and click on "Sedona Sacred Essences."
8. Tom Gannon, "White Buffalo (Calf) Woman: (Ptesan Winyan) (Wohpe)," *TGC* (February 23, 2009), http://incolor.inebraska.com/tgannon/WhBuffWoman.html.
9. Paula Giese, ed., "White Buffalo Calf Woman Brings the First Pipe: As Told by Joseph Chasing Horse," *Native American Indian: Art, Culture, Education, History, Science* (1995), http://www.kstrom.net/isk/arvol/buffpipe.html.
10. At the moment of the writing of this book, Dena Riley is the caretaker of eleven white buffalo that were genetically tested as buffalo and not hybrids. They are temporarily in Oregon. For more information, visit *Spirit Mountain Ranch* at http://www.sacredwhitebuffalo.org.

CRYSTALLINE GRIDS

AFTER HEALING AND BALANCING OUR PHYSICAL AND SUBTLE ENERGY systems and expanding our awareness, we are ready to work with the energies described in this and the next two chapters. These energies include crystalline grids, morphogenetic grids, and portals. I have been studying Earth energies for almost two decades, but only in the past couple of years was I able to include the subject of crystalline grids. I found the subject too confusing and I did not have the proper information to start. Whenever people spoke about crystalline grids and I asked them what these grids were and where I could find them, I never received a clear answer. I do not consider "layers around Earth" to be a clear answer because there are many layers around Earth. All these layers have their counterpart on Earth in the form of energy lines and vortexes/grids. Being unable to obtain any information about crystalline energy lines and vortexes, I did not include this topic in my studies for a long time.

In 2004 Jeanne and I bought the house we now live in. We checked all energy lines and vortexes connected with the house and the property. Over time the energies changed, but we attributed these changes to all the work we'd done with crystal skulls in our house (see fig. 10.1). We hold weekly crystal skull meditations, and a vortex was created at the very beginning of these meditations. The energies in this vortex changed due to the contributions of all of the people who have participated in these meditations over the years.

A couple of years later I felt the need to again check all the energy lines connected to our house and property. To my surprise, I found lines I had never seen

Fig. 10.1: The crystal skull circle in our house.

before. They felt different and were all connected to the center of the circle of our crystal skulls. I'd found my first crystalline grid lines!

The excitement was great, and I started a new chapter in my study of Earth energies. As we have seen, there are many systems of lines and vortexes that have twelve levels. Through dowsing and intuition, I learned that the crystalline grid system also has twelve levels. When I first discovered the crystalline lines connected to our house, they were of levels six, seven, and eight. Following the lines, I discovered that they connect our house to other places where people were or have been working with stones, crystals, or crystal skulls.

A Dynamic and Incomplete System

In the years following the initial discovery, it became clear that the system as a whole changes rapidly. An exception is levels one to five, which form a stable system that is spread all over the world. These five levels seem to be a characteristic of Earth. Connecting deeper with these first five levels, it seems that these levels are needed to allow Earth to function at a basic level. Earth, being crystalline in nature herself, has these levels as a base in the same way that a crystal always has at least four energy layers.[1] It seems that a system needs a minimum level of energy to be functional.

The above observations raised some interesting questions. These questions became even more important when I discovered that I could find only nine of the twelve levels of the crystalline grid system. Could it be that Earth was active only to a certain degree? Could it also be that human beings have a certain responsibility in this process of activation or, better, expression of the potential of Earth? Is the expansion of awareness of human beings key to the expansion of the awareness of Earth as expressed and held in the crystalline grids? Are we really moving into a shift of consciousness as one superorganism we call Gaia? The more I followed the dynamics of the crystalline grid lines, the more it seemed that the answer to all these questions was yes.

I noticed that when the energies of a location that is connected to our crystal skull circle lower the skulls' vibration, the line from our circle to that location decreased in level as well. I observed this phenomenon a couple of times. In the same way, as soon as a connection between two places increased in vibration, the level of the connecting lines increased as well. This was truly fascinating. I have seen some dynamic activity in consciousness grids, like in our triad grids and in the dolphin and whale consciousness grids, but here I could actually see a system in development. Here are some observations and ideas that I have developed during the past few years of studying the crystalline grid system.

Development of the Crystalline Grid

We are only in a beginning phase of understanding the crystalline grid. There are twelve levels, the first five of which are fully developed. These five levels seem to hold the basic energy for the functioning of Earth. When I discovered the crystalline grid, there were already some lines of level six, seven, and eight. However, it was not clear what exactly induced the forming of these lines. There is no doubt that working with crystals and crystal skulls was important but equally, if not more, important was working with structures of natural stones, like stone circles, standing stones, dolmens, pyramids, and so on.

This grid has a characteristic I have not seen with other grids. It needs constant activation to maintain what has been created. This is only true for levels higher than five. The need for permanent activation may explain why stone structures from the past no longer contribute to the creation of the higher levels of this crystalline grid. My impression is that the crystalline grid began to diminish both in power and in frequency when the ancient knowledge of activating stones and crystals was to a large degree lost. The remaining knowledge was insufficient to maintain a well-developed crystalline grid. We are now able to rebuild this grid, although there is still much to learn.

In the creation of the crystalline grid lines, two factors seem to be important. One is the intensity and frequency of the energies created at a certain location, usually a vortex. The other one is the distance between the vortexes. The larger the distance, the more powerful the created energy/vortex needs to be to enable the creation of a line. It seems that the creation of lines is possible through the energy of the vortexes; the energy needed for the creation of the line is literally taken out of the vortexes. The level of a line between two vortexes is determined by the vortex with the lowest frequency. Once the line is created, it seems that the vortexes need to stay active; otherwise, the line disappears. This is a very important point. People need to work actively with crystalline energies; otherwise, the energies disappear. First the frequencies go down and the level of the lines decreases, then the line disappears, and finally so does the vortex. This grid system is quite different from any of the other systems we have described due to this phenomenon.

The crystalline vortex in our house, created predominantly by the circle of our crystal skulls, increased rapidly in frequency when Sherry Whitfield and an ancient crystal skull named Synergy,[2] visited our vortex a couple of times. The higher frequencies of this ancient crystal skull activated our crystal skulls. The meditations stimulated this process of activation even further, and as a consequence, the frequencies of the vortex increased.

Etheric Crystalline Structures

The increase in frequencies and levels of the lines allowed me to follow the process of change in the system. The most interesting change was the shift from level nine to ten. Because this shift is important, I will discuss it in greater detail. An important aspect of it is the discovering of what we now call the etheric crystalline structures. These structures are connected with crystalline vortexes of levels ten to twelve.

It all started with a fairy ring. Sherry Whitfield felt guided to create a circle that she called the fairy ring. She gave it this name because she'd been inspired when she'd visited a fairy ring in Scotland. Key in this Scottish fairy ring was its stones. For Sherry and those who visited the place with her, there was no doubt that many elemental and devic beings were present, and therefore she called it a fairy ring.

Once back in Arizona she started to build her own fairy ring. When we visited her fairy ring for the first time, I was very impressed. She had created a place where lines and vortexes of different systems came together. One of these systems was the morphogenetic Earth elemental grid (see chapter 11). Over time the energy built up and there could be no doubt that the energy of Synergy played an important role. One day Sherry told me that she'd observed the development of an etheric structure over the fairy ring. We concluded that this structure was an aspect of the crystalline grid. This structure was based on a pentagonal shape and had developed over time into a more complex fractal structure. It had a point at the top that seemed to function as an antenna for receiving and sending energies.

After awhile we perceived that the crystalline vortex at our house had also begun to develop a crystalline structure. However, this structure was based on a triangle instead of the pentagonal shape found at Sherry Whitfield's place. Also, this structure had an antenna and became more complex in a fractal-like way. Once the structure felt complete, a shift occurred and the vortex connected to this structure shifted to level ten. Although both Sherry's fairy ring and our place had a vortex of level ten, there was not yet a level ten line between the two places. The distance was about 220 miles (354 km), as the crow flies, and apparently the vortexes were not yet powerful enough to create a connection. It took a couple of months before the line between the two places appeared.

This is not the end of the story. Thanks to all of the people who have come to the crystal skull meditations in our house, our crystalline vortex has now been activated to the optimal level of twelve. While level ten created an etheric structure based on a triangular shape like an elongated pyramid, levels eleven and twelve added a similar but larger etheric structure—of which the structure of level twelve is the largest. This means that there are three etheric structures at our house, and they look similar but are different in size. Together they developed into a complex energetic structure. A similar situation has developed at Sherry Whitfield's fairy ring. Not everyone can see or sense these structures; however, people perceive aspects of these structures during meditations at our house.

Meanwhile, vortexes of level twelve have developed at other sites. We see that as soon as a vortex on the crystalline grid reaches level ten, an etheric crystalline structure begins to develop. At this moment, the grid has a very irregular pattern and is continuously changing. Although some basic understanding exists, there is still much to discover about this grid system. After all, this grid is still in the early stages of its development.

Crystalline Grids as Mentioned by Others

Nowadays many people talk about crystalline grids. I mentioned earlier that it is often difficult to understand their meaning. In many instances, it seems that their information could be a reference to the structure of a crystalline field above Earth. This crystalline field could be similar to what I like to call the collective crystal field and the collective crystal skull field. Others are clearly referring to grids on Earth. I'd like to mention a few descriptions of crystalline grids as used by other people. This may help to better understand discussions and opinions about this subject.

A lot of information about crystalline grids that can be found on the Internet comes from channeling. I am always careful about accepting channeled information as truth. Nevertheless, channeled information can help us to look at a subject in a different way and may help us to connect to information we have not yet been able to access ourselves. This does not mean that we should accept all information that is channeled. The best way is always to feel if you resonate with the presented information. If you do, you can include it in your model of reality and test its value.

Kryon, as channeled through Lee Carroll, discussed grids in a channeling from 2002, one that he conducted in Newport Beach, California.[3] This channeling identifies three grids: the magnetic grid, the crystalline grid, and the human consciousness grid. He mentions that each of these grids has many aspects. I like his classification system. The magnetic grid is what I have called the lower and higher subtle energy grids. The human consciousness grid refers to the three triad systems and includes the twelve triad system, communication lines, and the Christ/unity consciousness grid. And then there is the crystalline grid.

According to Kryon, the crystalline grid is a stable grid, one that he invites grid workers to start working with. It is not clear from this session what "working with" means exactly. Kryon mentions that part of the crystalline structures of this planet are in the most sacred places that you can imagine and that they will remain there. He does not mention the names or locations of these in this channeling, though.

Kryon identifies the creators of the crystalline grid as a type of dragon energy—not the dragons from mythology, which are monsters, but different dragons, those that are beyond our current understanding. It is metaphoric, and it means strength and stability. The Chinese call many Earth energy lines dragon lines. The link is that in both cases, dragons are associated with energy lines, although it seems that Kryon and the Chinese are talking about different energies. The dragon lines of the Chinese seem to be comparable to the systems that I call the higher subtle energy grid systems. Kryon talks about grids that are called the grid of light or the grid of stability. These grids are the spiritual foundation of the planet. Kryon says that a part of the crystalline grid's energy is responsible for the storehouse of the knowledge of the planet. All that ever was—all that exists, all the potentials of what can be—are located in the crystalline grid. When it is formulated like this, it sounds as if this crystalline grid is similar to the morphogenetic grid of Earth (see chapter 11). So it seems that Kryon and I are describing different crystalline grids.

Kryon states another interesting aspect. He says that a section of the crystalline grid is alive and is a mammal. It contains the planet's storehouse of knowledge of everything within its DNA. Although I doubt that such information is stored in the DNA, it is interesting that he mentions the whales as holders of the ancient knowledge of the world. Many Native American tribes see the whales as record keepers (see chapter 9). As Jamie Sams put it in her famous book *Medicine Cards*, the whale is very much like a swimming library. The whale carries the history of Mother Earth.[4] I have always felt a deep connection between whales and the crystal skulls because both hold ancient knowledge. I never understood this connection but it may be possible that the connection is made through the crystalline grids.

Many Internet sites on the subject of crystalline grids are based on Kryon's channeling. It appears to be difficult to have some original ideas about the subject of crystalline grids. An exception is Soluntra King, author of several books. I refer here to her article "Earth's Grids and Portals."[5] She talks about three major grids, but besides the crystalline grid, there is no relation to any other system I have mentioned in this book. According to her, the crystalline grid links the crystals in the earth. She makes some bold statements: "The Dragon people, who are part of the Reptilian story on Earth, along with the Snake and Lizard people, worked with the Crystals within the Earth to create the crystalline grid. This created life on the planet as we know it."[6] She continues by saying that at major junctions in the grid, we have dragon lairs or serpent vortexes. Later she mentions that the crystalline grid is also called by names such as dragon lines or "lay" [*sic*] lines. According to her, this grid works on different dimensions. It links all the major portals of the earth through the grid to the light grid on higher planes. On this crystalline grid, pyramids, temples, standing stones, and stone circles have been built. The pyramids once kept harmonious resonance between Earth and the universe.

I do not resonate with everything that she says, but I mention her ideas because there are some interesting aspects to them. It seems that several sources combine a number of elements into one system, which is also the case with Soluntra King:

the crystalline grid is basically everything. Many of the systems I have mentioned are summarized in this one term: crystalline grids. All vortexes and all sacred sites are placed by her into this one grid. Even lines are included in it.

Another interesting aspect is that she relates the grid to the reptilian, dragon, lizard, and snake people. Remember that Kryon mentions that the dragon energy created the crystalline grids. King and Kryon are not alone. Mark Amaru Pinkham[7] dedicated the subject matter of his book *The Return of the Serpents of Wisdom* to serpent energy, which includes the snake and the dragon. He believes that all important civilizations have been created by masters called the Serpents of Wisdom, who were originally extraterrestrials. In his book he states that the preserving power of the serpent, the life force, is projected to Earth via the stars and planets of the cosmos, with the Sun being the most important. When the serpent life force has reached Earth, it enters dragon lairs or vortex points and circumnavigates the planet within a network of subtle channels. Collectively these vortexes and channels comprise the Earth's etheric grid,[8] and here Pinkham uses terminology similar to Soluntra King's.

Pinkham does not say that the dragons created the grid, but the grid is a consequence of the dragon/serpent energy entering the earth in vortexes numbering 1,746.[9] Pinkham, like Soluntra King, mentions that ancient peoples built pyramids, stone circles, standing stones, and mounds over the dragon layers to facilitate the movement of life force in and out of the Earth's dragon body, which is also the Earth's etheric body.[10]

In conclusion we can say that the subject of crystalline grids is quite confusing. Some authors describe the crystalline grid as being the more general grid on the earth. As we have seen in this book, there are many different grids. It seems attractive to see the crystalline grid as the main grid, but that is not what I have found. I do not know what to think about dragons and dragon energy.

Stone Structures

I believe that stone structures can be and have been used in the creation and maintenance of the crystalline grid. Unfortunately most ancient stone structures have been at least partly destroyed and may no longer be functional. This is an area that requires more study. Most megalithic sites, and other sites that use stone structures, have lain dormant for long periods of time. As a consequence, the frequency levels of the lines have diminished, and sometimes lines have disappeared completely. In contrast to communication lines (see chapter 8), the crystalline lines and vortexes lose their power and disappear when they are no longer activated. Many sites have been destroyed to such a degree that they can no longer be revived. However, some places may have the potential to be activated again. Places like Stonehenge and Avebury in England; Mayan pyramids and temples; sites in the Andes like Machu Picchu; the pyramids in Egypt, China, Bosnia, Italy and other places—all still may have the potential to be part of the crystalline grid. Due to ceremonial activities at these sites, it is already happening to a certain degree.

We need a deeper connection with stones to be able to activate these ancient sites and their stone structures in an optimal way. Once we know how to use stone structures in the creation of crystalline grids, we also will be able to create new sites to allow the development of an optimal crystalline grid. At the moment, we do not yet know what "optimal" means. Only through experience and activities guided by love and respect for All That Is will we be able to accomplish the creation of such an optimal grid.

The Crystalline Grid Must Be Activated through Human Activities

The crystalline grid is a grid in development. It needs to be activated and used continuously in order to be stable and grow. The grid has twelve levels of which five are stable and fully developed. The development of the remaining seven levels seems to depend completely on human activities related to stones, crystals, and crystal skulls. The three highest levels of the grid induce the creation of etheric structures. There is still much to learn about this grid. However, we seem to be invited to work with this grid once again in an active way. We can do this by working with stones, crystals, and crystal skulls to develop this grid to an optimal level. An optimal crystalline grid will contribute to the shift of Gaia into higher vibrational states, supporting the shift in consciousness of the human species.

ENDNOTES

1. Jaap van Etten, PhD, *Crystal Skulls: Interacting with a Phenomenon* (Flagstaff, AZ: Light Technology Publishing, 2007), 76.
2. For more information about Synergy, see Sherry Whitfield's "The Ancient Crystal Skull Synergy," *Blue Star Traders*, accessed February 2, 2011, http://www.crystalskull.net/Crystal_Skull_Synergy. html.
3. Kryon through Lee Carroll, "The Celebration! What's next?" *Kryon* (December 8, 2002), accessed February 2, 2011, http://www.kryon.com/k_chanelnewport02.html.
4. Jamie Sams and David Carson, *Medicine Cards: The Discovery of Power through the Ways of Animals* (Santa Fe, NM: Bear and Company, 1988), 201.
5. Soluntra King, *Crystals: Gateways of Light and Unity* (Gisborne, NZ: Evenstar Creations, n.d.), chapter excerpt "Earth's Grids and Portals" published at *Evenstar Creations* (2001), http://www. evenstarcreations.com/index.php?option=com_content&view=article&id=118&Itemid=93, 2001.
6. Ibid.
7. Mark Amaru Pinkham, *The Return of the Serpents of Wisdom* (Kempton, IL: Adventures Unlimited Press, 1997).
8. Ibid., 335.
9. Ibid.
10. Ibid., 337.

MORPHOGENETIC FIELDS
AND GRIDS

IN PREVIOUS CHAPTERS, I REFERENCED THE VERY IMPORTANT MORPHOGENETIC grids, or morphogenetic fields. The terms have been used over the past twenty years with increasingly more information becoming available on this rather new subject. By sharing my research, I hope to demonstrate the importance of these grids for life on this planet in general and for human evolution in particular.

In the mid-1990s I took a Flower of Life course, which is based on the teachings of Drunvalo Melchizedek. During this course I heard Melchizedek say that each species has its own grid. This information can be found in his text *The Ancient Secret of the Flower of Life*.[1] He defined a grid as a planetary grid with an etheric crystalline structure enveloping Earth that holds the consciousness of a particular species. He said that there were initially 30 million grids. Now there are only 13 to 15 million left, and the number is decreasing rapidly.

These grids are not known by science, but at least one scientist came up with two terms that seem to refer to what these fields do: morphic resonance and morphogenetic fields. This scientist is Rupert Sheldrake, and he has written many articles and several books on the subject. My favorite is *A New Science of Life: The Hypothesis of Morphic Resonance*.[2] Some researchers claim that it was the hundredth-monkey concept that formed the basis for Sheldrake's hypothesis. In fact, the hundredth-monkey effect is a great example of how morphogenetic grids work.

Sheldrake's hypothesis is an attempt to resolve other unresolved issues in biology. Although many people know the story of the hundredth monkey, it is worth repeating because it helps us to understand the essence of the idea of morphogenetic fields and grids.

This story is best described by Lyall Watson and Ken Keyes, Jr.[3] The story may not be completely true, but it beautifully illustrates the principle of the working of the morphogenetic fields and grids. The story describes a scientific research project that was solely focused on *Macaca fuscata*, the Japanese monkey. The behavior of this monkey was studied on several islands simultaneously. The island of Koshima near Japan was the starting point. Scientists studied a wild colony and fed them sweet potatoes. They dropped these potatoes in the sand. It seemed that the monkeys did not like the sand on the sweet potatoes. At a certain moment an eighteen-month-old female named Imo started to wash the potato in water. That clearly resolved an unpleasant problem and she taught her mother and her playmates to do the same.

These playmates taught it to their mothers and to others and soon the behavior spread throughout the colony. These behaviors were recorded between 1952 and 1958. In the year 1958 something interesting happened. By now a large amount of monkeys washed their potatoes, and then suddenly almost all the monkeys on the island started to wash their potatoes. The behavior was not limited to monkeys on the island of Koshima, as monkeys on other islands were observed to be doing the same action—even monkeys on the mainland of Japan. The number at which this sudden expansion occurred was not exactly one hundred, but that was the number Watson mentioned, which led to the expression of the hundredth-monkey concept, or effect. The basic principle is that when a certain number of animals shows a certain behavior, that behavior unexpectedly expands at a surprisingly fast rate. That certain number is sometimes referred to as critical mass.

The general idea is that every monkey is tapping into or is connected with a field called a morphogenetic field. All information about a species is in that field, even behavior that is very uncommon. If it is information from only one individual, its effect will most likely go unnoticed. However, when more individuals share information creating a coherent field, the signal can be picked up far more easily.

It may seem that the idea of morphogenetic fields applies only to animals, but there are sufficient indications to claim that it is also applicable to human beings. Rupert Sheldrake[4] calls the hypothesis "formative causation," which is the idea that the form and the behavior of organisms are influenced by morphic resonance with energies emanating from past events. I believe that these energies and information are available in energy lines (grids), and that through vortexes these energies are connected with the main field. In this way, there is a continuous exchange between the grids and the field. It seems that every species is able to tap into its own grid. Through experiences the grids change continuously—although they change within the parameters of form and behavior set in the fields.

Sheldrake used two terms: "morphic field" and "morphogenetic field." He used the term "field" as he was not aware of the idea of grids. According to him, the term "morphic field" is more general in its meaning than "morphogenetic fields," and the term includes other kinds of organizing fields in addition to those of morphogenesis. The organizing fields of animal and human behavior, of social and cultural systems, and of mental activity can all be regarded as morphic fields that contain an inherent memory. I prefer to use the term "morphogenetic fields and grids," because this term is used generally and can easily include all aspects that Sheldrake covers with the term "morphic field."

An important aspect of the morphogenetic fields and grids is that they work beyond time and space. In the story about the Macaca monkeys, no direct contact between the monkeys of the islands and the mainland occurred; nonetheless, information was transferred. In that sense, we cannot say that the characteristic was inherited, because there was no direct contact. This obviously goes beyond normal biological explanations. The morphogenetic field and grids work across time and space and are apparently accessible by every individual of a species that is connected with that field or grid. By now there is much more proof that Sheldrake's hypothesis may be true. Many experiments were done with laboratory rats, all confirming the existence of morphogenetic fields.

Rupert Sheldrake did several experiments with humans to prove that people are also connected through a morphogenetic field. He tested people's abilities to recognize a form in what appears to be a blob. He also asked how many faces a people could see in a given image. The blob or image was shown to a number of test people. Both the meaning of the blob and the number of faces in the image were shown on television. Next, a group of people were tested in a country in which the images and information had not been shown. Compared to the original test, there was always a significant increase in the number of people who saw the same images or faces.[5] From a scientific point of view, formative causation is still not proven, but there is much information to support Sheldrake's hypothesis.

Melchizedek mentions that the American and Russian governments are aware of the Christ consciousness grid.[6] My feeling is that they are also aware of the morphogenetic grids. People like Peter Moon and Preston Nichols believe that the American government was studying and manipulating the morphogenetic grid in a project called Montauk. That project's purpose was to influence mass through the morphogenetic grid.[7] Peter Moon describes the grid as follows. "As a species, we create a matrix of energy known as the "human wave form" and are fed as one body by the "sleeping collective Unconscious." This is why people in different locations can adopt the same habits, patterns, or speech. And on a deeper level, it is the morphogenetic grid which feeds the sleeping collective unconscious.[8]

In his book *Pyramids of Montauk*, Peter Moon brings up another interesting point. He believes that the pharaohs of Egypt were the guardians of the ancient wisdom that trafficked the grids.[9] The place that the pharaoh used to bring new information into the morphogenetic grids was the Great Pyramids of Giza. If the pharaoh was attuned properly to both the physical and spiritual realms, this would create harmony and prosperity for his people. According to Peter Moon, the pyramid directly taps into the morphogenetic grid.[10]

Based on experiments with animals, particularly rats, it is becoming clear that rats can develop abilities that can be passed on through the morphogenetic fields. Based on early research, this seems to be true for people as well. If Peter Moon is right and the pharaohs of the past and the American government in the present are influencing the grid, it brings up the question of freedom. It would appear that our freedom to develop our potential in an undisturbed way is at stake.

According to Drunvalo Melchizedek, the governments of Russia and the United States were aware of these grids as far back as the 1940s. That means that they knew about the grids before the hundredth-monkey effect was known. Because of World War II, governments were beginning to place military bases everywhere in the world. Interestingly, their locations were often at places that were grid nodes or close to grid nodes of the morphogenetic grid. There are too many of these locations to be a coincidence.[11] I am not really surprised. During my research on this grid in the Netherlands, I heard from psychic people that when they connected with these lines, they felt the energy of Nazis. Apparently the Nazis also tried to influence people on a larger scale through the morphogenetic grid.

Research into the Morphogenetic Grid

It is important to state clearly that when I am discussing the morphogenetic grid of Earth, this grid includes the earth and all species living on her. I sometimes call this grid the supermatrix. In addition each species has its own grid or grids, and in previous chapters we've already looked at the grids of the human species (the triad systems) and at those of dolphins, whales, and white buffalo.

The morphogenetic grids of Earth are very important, and therefore we need information to help us understand these grids. It may be that certain groups, like governments and secret societies, know these grids very well, but this information has not been made available to us. It is important that we gather information about this system and collectively connect to these grids with love. Love will have a harmonizing effect on the grids and prevents others from influencing this grid in a way that could have an impact on our free will, evolution, and the evolution of Gaia as a whole.

Like many other systems, the morphogenetic grid system has twelve different levels. The basic structure of the first eleven levels is an irregular pentagon, much like that of the seven triad grid of our consciousness system (see fig. 6.7). Within this pentagonal shape there are lines that connect the five nodes, creating an irregular pentagram similar to the six triad grid. Above level five, the grids become more complex and more lines are added.

Moving from level one to twelve, the grids of the different levels increase in size. The average distance between the nodes of the pentagonal shape of level one is only 1.7 yards (1.6 m) while that of level eleven is about 116 miles (187 km). In the south of France, a pentagonal shape of level nine had an average length of 18.2 miles (29.1 km) for the five sides. Level twelve is based on the dodecahedron. This grid has been described by William Becker and Bethe Hagens in *Antigravity and the World Grid*.[12] It is the grid that is most frequently described as the Earth grid (see fig. 11.1).

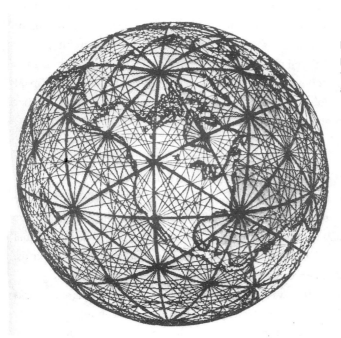

Fig. 11.1: The morphogenetic grid level twelve. William Becker and Bethe Hagens.[13]

Fig. 11.2: The Burcht in Leiden, The Netherlands; a node of the level eleven morphogenetic grid.

There are many interesting structures located either on the nodes or on the lines of these grids. The nodes of a level nine pentagonal shape in France were typically located on either a church or the ruins of a castle. In the Netherlands, a node of the level ten grid was found at the center of the building where the Dutch government meets in the Hague (the Ridderzaal, or the Knight's Hall, is the main building at the Binnenhof). A level eleven node was found in the center of a fortress in Leiden (see fig. 11.2). When I followed a level ten and a level eleven grid line in Europe, I found many churches, mansions, and castles on these lines. There is no doubt that studying this grid can reveal many interesting aspects.

The Morphogenetic Grid of Mother Nature

At a certain phase in my research, I became aware of the morphogenetic grid, the grid of Mother Earth and all that lives on her. I called the grid the morphogenetic grid of Gaia. I was already aware of the morphogenetic grids for each individual species, so I thought that this was all there was to know about morphogenetic grids. That turned out to be incorrect, as there are still more morphogenetic grids.

In the beginning of 2010, I was in Peru and Bolivia. One of the elders who was also a member of an important Andean spiritual group talked about "a doorway to Mother Nature." Initially I thought it was a different name for Pachamama,

Mother Earth. However, when I asked, I heard that Mother Nature was different. It was not clear to me what exactly her role on Earth was, let alone what the doorway was. According to Andean teachings, Mother Nature has been dormant for about 5,000 years. It is believed that she awoke recently to again assume her role. According to the stories, she even appeared in person. This apparition reminded me of Mother Mary. It was interesting to hear that one of the doorways of Mother Nature was protected and was located in a chapel of the Black Madonna in the Basilica in Copacabana on the shores of Lake Titicaca.

Returning home I could not forget Mother Nature. If she is the mother of what we call nature, she has to be either part of the morphogenetic grid of Gaia or possessed of her own morphogenetic grid. Checking on whether or not there was another grid, I was surprised to find the vortex of a grid system that was new to me. It was the morphogenetic grid of Mother Nature. The Mother Nature grid holds information about interactions between species. It helps to establish balance in the different ecosystems. It helps to create harmony in order to allow every species to be supported, nourished, and unconditionally loved. This means that Mother Nature functions in between the level of Gaia and that of the many species existing on Earth. In my experience the essence of the energies of the Mother Nature grid feel like paradise. However, this grid also holds the energies of current chaos and pain due to the disturbance of nature by humans. The fact that Mother Nature has been dormant has moved nature out of balance, instead of nature being a balanced, loving system. The human species is currently not functioning in harmony with nature. For our species, nature is something we control and use, not something we live in harmony with. Will this change with the awakening of Mother Nature?

The Mother Nature grid has only one level. Its shape is different from that of the morphogenetic grid of Gaia in that it has four sides and each node has four lines. The form is best described as irregular rectangles with shapes that are close to diamonds (see fig. 11.3). The grid is small; the average length of the lines is close to 5 miles (8 km). Compared to the length of the grid lines, the vortexes are large, a radius of 4.5 miles (7.2 km) and the lines are large, about 100 yards (91 m) wide with a total height of 360 yards (329 m). The amount of the line that is under the surface of the earth is about equal to the amount above the surface of the earth. In that sense, this grid is different from most of the other grids we have reviewed. Based on this research obtained in Sedona, the surface of Earth seems to be totally covered by the energy of this grid system.

Working with this grid, I had the impression that it was dormant. We saw a change in the lines when we visited the vortexes and meditated on them. After a

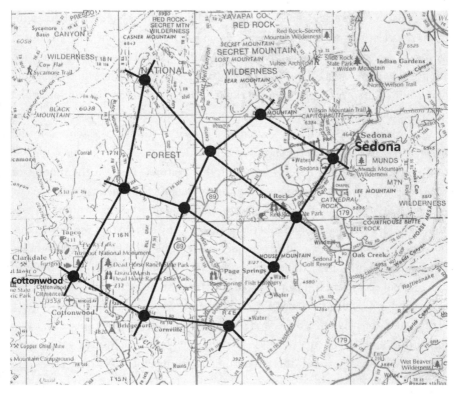

Fig. 11.3: A part of the morphogenetic grid of "Mother Nature" in the area between Sedona and Cottonwood.

couple of weeks, the lines became wider and their total height shorter. The total volume of the line did not change, however. When I multiplied the total height with the width, the initial number (IF) and the number after activating remained the same. The feeling is that with the awakening of Mother Nature, the grid is also awakening. Human beings seem to contribute to this awakening. The grid adjusts itself to align to the situation of a diminishing number of species and ecosystems. Our contribution in supporting Mother Nature is to love her and support her process of rebalancing and restoring herself. It is a process of supporting, not of guiding and directing. After all, we are unable to completely oversee nature and should leave that to a higher consciousness.

While Mother Nature can be seen as information in the grid or field, my feeling is that there is also an overseeing being. Some people call her a deva or an angel. She appears to people, choosing a form that resonates with the people present. This being is known in the Andean tradition. The Andean people see it as their task to make other people aware of her presence so we can learn to work with her instead of against her.

Everything I have shared does not explain the term "doorway to Mother Nature." When doing research on the Mother Nature grids, I came across vortexes that were more resonant than the vortexes I normally find in this grid. These vortexes were indeed doorways or portals. It seems that this doorway is the entrance into the energies of the divine feminine and that Mother Nature is an aspect of this divine feminine. This may explain why the Andean people could accept Mother Mary so easily, since she is an aspect of the same energy. I will explain the concept of portals or doorways in the next chapter (chapter 12).

Morphogenetic Grids of Elementals, Fairies, and Devas

One day I was asked: "Do you think that devas and fairies have grids like plants and animals that make their existence possible?" The question implies that such beings exist. I believe in their existence but never thought about the fact that if they exist, there must be a grid that holds the information that makes their existence possible. Elementals, fairies, and devas seem to be involved in the creation and maintenance of the different physical beings, objects, and energy systems that exist in this reality. I have always wondered how energy systems come into being, who is maintaining them, and who their guardians might be. I believe that elementals contribute to all creation processes. From a universal point of view, angels fulfill the role of guardians of systems. In this physical reality, Earth angels, devas, and fairies fulfill that role. In no way do I want to suggest that fairies look the way they are depicted in many books. I see them as energy forms, and that may translate for some people into often-depicted forms, because to their minds, those are acceptable images.

The initial discovery of the grids of the devas and fairies was based more on a joke than on a serious research approach. I was in an area where people often sense the presence of fairies and devas when I was asked a question about the existence of morphogenetic grids for devas and fairies. I did not take the question seriously, but I wanted to play along. I was more than surprised when it turned out that I could dowse such grids. After my initial skepticism, I became very excited.

Many people equate fairies with elementals, but I do not agree. I see fairies as part of the devic realm while elementals are tiny beings who are responsible for the energy aspects of creative processes. While elementals focus on processes, fairies and devas have the task of guarding, protecting, and maintaining the results of creative processes: the different aspects of our physical world. Within the physical world, fairies work with the manifested physical aspects of the four elements: earth, water, air, and fire. Devas work with stones, plants, animals, human beings, areas, landscapes, mountain ranges, and oceans. Therefore fairies and devas have similar functions, and I see fairies as small devas. Larger devas are often seen as angels. There are some beautiful images of such beings in *The Kingdom of the Gods* by Geoffrey Hodson.[14]

Elemental Grids

There are four elemental forces and thus four types of elemental beings, each responsible for one of these four forces. Each of these four types of elemental beings has their own grid. These four grids are actually similar in all aspects: in the size of their vortexes, in the size of their lines, and in the distance between the lines. They form square grids, although they are a bit irregular in shape. They have alternating yin and yang lines. The only difference between the four grids is that they are energetically different and turned roughly 23° in relation to one another. Because the grids are irregular, the angle could only be determined at a point where all four grids share a node at the same location. So far I have found only one such point (see fig. 11.4), but it helped me to understand the layout of the four grids (see fig. 11.5).

These grids hold information that makes the presence of elemental beings in this reality possible. The importance of elementals is beyond words. They are involved in every process, particularly in all creative processes. In other words: Without elemental beings, there would be no creation. Let me describe their function and their qualities as far as I understand them.

- **Fire elementals** support the energies that belong to intent, the spark of the creation process, the birth of something new. Intent can be conscious or unconscious and can be made on any level. Intent forms the basis of creation in physical reality. Elementals do not pass judgment about the possible consequences of an intent. They support any intent, even when it leads to something that is harmful for the one who set the intent or for others.
- **Air elementals** are involved in all thoughts and ideas. Thoughts and ideas create a matrix that forms the basis for any creation. Air elementals, like fire elementals, never judge a thought or idea. They simply fulfill their tasks by creating the thought forms and matrices that consciousness on Earth chooses to create.

Fig. 11.4: The location of the node where all four elemental grids coincide: a small knoll north of the Airport Mesa in Sedona, Arizona.

Fig. 11.5: A cell of each of the four elemental morphogenetic grids with a common node at a knoll near the Airport Mesa in Sedona, Arizona. (Solid line: air elemental; broken line: fire elemental; dotted line: earth elemental; broken and dotted line: water elemental.)

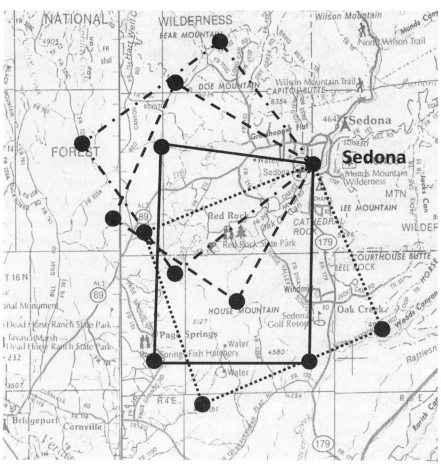

- **Water elementals** are involved in all emotional energies. They add this quality to the matrix created by air elementals. They work with emotions, independent of how we feel about those emotions. For these elementals, emotions are energies to work with independent of their qualities. Like the other elementals they do not judge; they simply carry out their tasks.
- **Earth elementals** assist in the creation of form. This is true not only for natural forms like stones, plants, and animals but also for all forms created by us. Earth elementals are always involved in the creation of any form. They also play a role in giving form based on the morphogenetic grids.

In summary, fire elementals are responsible for supporting the energetic development of intent, air elementals for supporting the creation of the matrix to realize this intent, water elementals for adding an emotional quality to the intent, and earth elementals for bringing intent into form. This means that all four elementals are needed in every creative process. Therefore we are working with elemental beings all of the time, even though most of us are unaware of it. Let us honor elemental beings with gratitude from our hearts for all the support they unconditionally give to us in every moment of our lives.

The Devic Grids

I include fairies in the devic grids, because in my opinion, they form an inherent part of the devic realm. I found twelve different devic grids. Of these, the first couple of grids are the grids that belong to the devas who are called fairies. The fairies are the little devas who oversee the physical aspects of earth, water, air, and fire. In other words, they oversee that which has been created already. The devas, or fairies, who belong to these physical elements are ordered as follows: gnomes, who are overseers of earthly aspects; undines, who are overseers of water; sylphs, who are connected with air; and salamanders, who are connected with fire in all forms. During the creation of each of these four physical elements, all four elementals were needed. We often also call flower devas "fairies." It would be easier to skip the name fairies completely and call them all devas, but the name and the idea of the fairies is deeply anchored in our consciousness. Once a creative process is completed, the fairies and devas become guardians and make sure that these systems remain in an optimal condition. They need help from elementals to repair or change systems.

The study of the devic grids is far from complete, and I am still in the process of understanding the function of the devas of all of the twelve different grids. Basically the devic grids form a hierarchical system. The highest level, level twelve, belongs to devas who are responsible for large systems, like mountain ranges and oceans. These systems contain many smaller parts including stones, crystals, plants, trees, animals, streams, meadows, forests, lakes, and so on. Each of these smaller parts within these large systems has its own deva of one of the lower levels. Devas of a higher level are not more important than devas of one of the lower levels; they only have different responsibilities. We can learn a lot from devas and how their hierarchical system works. If we could change the idea of "being more important in our society" into just having different responsibilities, we would honor each person in her function equally, and the world would look completely different.

The grids of the twelve levels are all based on triangles. At each node we find six lines that radiate out like spokes, creating hexagonal shapes (see fig. 11.6). In general the size of the vortexes, the size of the lines, and the distance between vortexes increases with increasing levels. However, this increase is not

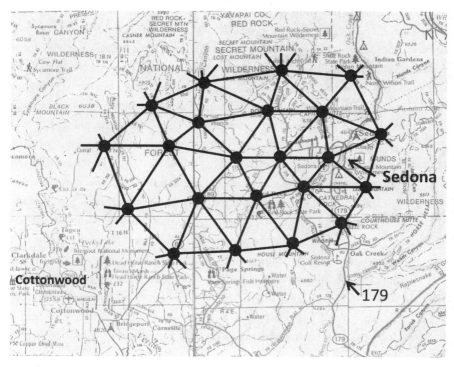

Fig. 11.6: A part of a deva morphogenetic grid of level four in the area between Sedona and Cottonwood.

linear. The increase is very slow for the first seven levels. From level eight on, the increase speeds up and is very high for the last two levels.

Devas are the guardians of different systems. They direct other devas of smaller systems and ultimately the elementals to make sure that each system stays in optimal condition. I have no idea how devas look at human beings, who have the tendency to disturb systems continuously. My feeling is that they are open if not even longing for a connection with us in order to find a way to work together.

There are many books on fairies and devas. However, our studies of the morphogenetic grids of devas indicate that we still have a lot to learn. In my opinion it is time to leave the fairytale approach behind and study in more detail the different grids in order to learn how to connect directly with devas. This will allow a better understanding of devas, which may result in a collaboration that leads to the re-creation of harmony and balance on planet Earth.

The Importance of Morphogenetic Fields and Grids

There is little doubt that morphogenetic fields are important. According to Rupert Sheldrake, each atom has its own morphogenetic (morphic) field, and this is true for each molecule, cell, tissue, organ, and organism,[15] and consequently also for Mother Nature, Gaia, the solar system, the galaxy, and the universe. Each of these units has to have a morphogenetic field that is in alignment with the next higher unit. This means that if something is changing in a morphogenetic field, it may have an effect on the fields that are hierarchically below that particular field.

Morphogenetic grids hold the information of those aspects of the morphogenetic field that have been realized and experienced. Their function is based on morphic resonance, which means resonating with information that has been created through the past experiences of that species. As mentioned earlier, each species has its own morphogenetic grid or grids, and that of the human species is the triad grid system. Therefore our form and behavior is determined through morphic resonance, which means that it is based on the history of our species. For example, the recent increase in cancer could lead to information entering the grid that could lead to even higher incidence of cancer. Unfortunately, we see that this is indeed happening.[16] Therefore it is important to maintain a lifestyle that promotes health instead of a lifestyle that promotes dysfunction and dis-ease.

Fortunately, human beings are not completely dependent on formative causation. They also have what Rupert Sheldrake calls "conscious causation."[17] This means that consciousness can overrule passive connection to the morphogenetic fields and grids, and therefore consciousness can free us from physical limitation. This is the most important aspect of human evolution.

The morphogenetic grids mentioned in the beginning of this chapter are the grids of Gaia, the superorganism. These grids hold information for Earth and all species and beings who live in and on her. Without this grid, Earth and the many species living on her could not exist, because Gaia could not maintain the conditions needed for life to exist. James Lovelock mentions in his books the importance of maintaining the conditions of life and the fact that there is something that makes this possible.[18] However, he does not mention that this "something" is the morphogenetic grid, the grids that allow life to be possible. The maintenance of the conditions for life is so important that it can be said that these grids are the key of life.

These grids change when circumstances surrounding different species change. Every time a species disappears, the amount of information in the Gaia grid diminishes. There are estimates that about half of all species are extinct, which has a large impact on the morphogenetic grids of Gaia. To state it more bluntly: Gaia is weakening. A weakened Gaia may still be able to maintain conditions for life, but not necessarily for all life. It may be that the human species ultimately becomes endangered. Therefore it is in our best interest for these grids and the information they contain to remain in optimal condition in order to guarantee the continuation of human life.

As more species disappear, nature becomes less complex with fewer variations. Humankind's effect on the environment has had a deep impact on Mother Nature. Although the field may still hold the same potential, the information in the grids has diminished considerably. Consequently the possibilities for Gaia and Mother Nature to support the continuation of our species are also diminishing.

I am unable to see the effects we have on the world of the devas and elementals. The elementals will do their work independent of the quality of the energy that induces their activities. In other words, they create harmony as easily as chaos. This may differ for the devas, as their task is to maintain systems. This includes all of the morphogenetic grids and the other grids mentioned in this book. Therefore if we understand these grids, it will be easier to work together with the devas toward the creation of a beautifully balanced and healthy system in which everything and everyone can thrive.

ENDNOTES

1. Drunvalo Melchizedek, *The Ancient Secret of the Flower of Life*, vol. 1 (Flagstaff, AZ: Light Technology Publishing, 2000), 106.
2. Rupert Sheldrake, *A New Science of Life: The Hypothesis of Morphic Resonance* (Rochester, VT: Park Street Press, 1995).
3. Ken Keyes Jr: *The Hundredth Monkey* (Devorss & Co Txp, second edition, June 1984). Available electronically: http://www.wowzone.com/monkey.htm. This website also shares the story of Lyall Watson with critical notes on the story of the 100th monkey.
4. Sheldrake, *A New Science of Life*, 249-256.
5. Ibid., 249-256.
6. Melchizedek, *The Ancient Secret of the Flower of Life*, vol. 1, 107-108.
7. Peter Moon has written many books on the Montauk project. Here I refer mainly to Preston B. Nichols and Peter Moon's *Pyramids of Montauk: Explorations in Consciousness* (Westbury, NY: Sky Books, 1998). In many chapters of that work, the authors talk about the influence on the grid, and they describe the grid in great detail in Chapter 13, 97-102.
8. Ibid., 102.
9. Ibid., 107.
10. Ibid., 203-204.
11. Melchizedek, *The Ancient Secret of the Flower of Life*, vol. 1, 108.
12. William Becker and Bethe Hagens, "The Planetary Grid: A New Synthesis," in *Anti-Gravity and the World Grid*, edited by David Hatcher Childress, (Kempton, IL: Adventures Unlimited Press, 1992), 27-50. The grid system described here is based on a synthesis of all five Platonic solids.
13. Ibid., 27.
14. Geoffrey Hodson, *The Kingdom of the Gods* (Adyar: Theosophical Publishing House, 1980).
15. Rupert Sheldrake, *A New Science of Life*, 83 and 88.
16. David Rose, "Cancer Cases 'to Increase a Third by 2020,'" *The Times*, December 4, 2007, accessed February 2, 2011, http://www.timesonline.co.uk/tol/life_and_style/health/article2994698.ece.
17. Rupert Sheldrake, *A New Science of Life*, 202-206.
18. James Lovelock has written a few books on the subject of the Gaia hypothesis. I recommend *Gaia: A New Look at Life on Earth* (Oxford: Oxford University Press, 1979) and *The Ages of Gaia: A Biography of Our Living Earth* (New York: W.W. Norton, 1988).

12

PORTALS

IN ORDER TO COMPLETE THE DESCRIPTION OF THE DIFFERENT EARTH ENERGY systems we can work with, one last topic needs to be included: the subject of portals, or doorways. The term "portal" is commonly used in science fiction and New Age texts, but the word is also used to mean an access point for information systems. For example, USA.gov is the U.S. Government's official web Portal.[1] The Library of Congress website has "portals to the world" that contain selective links providing authoritative, in-depth information about other areas of the world.[2]

The term "portal" is most frequently used to mean a "doorway into another dimension." A portal is also a vortex [**Author's Note:** Remember that earlier a vortex was defined as a place where energy, in whatever form, is exchanged between two systems]. Therefore we can also call a portal a vortex between this and other realities. The Library of Congress and the U.S. Government use the term portal to mean a doorway or access point into an information system so that information between the user and the information system can be exchanged.

In most cases, a portal is a doorway that is experienced in a certain state of consciousness and not an actual door through which we physically move. This we know from science fiction. There are sci-fi television shows built on this phenomenon, such as *Stargate*—and yes, I am a fan![3] On the show, the stargate is a door through which people travel to other planets and star systems in this galaxy, and even to other galaxies. In these situations, a vortex is called a wormhole. I have heard people claiming that such a stargate actually exists, and there are many theories that agree with this claim.[4] However, this is not the type of portal that most people will connect with, and maybe we should say that this is fortunate, as too many people may mysteriously disappear.

In stories, other objects are seen as possible doorways: for example, mirrors. We see examples of mirrors as doorways in a couple of episodes of *Stargate*.[5] Another example of a fictional portal is the wardrobe mentioned in the books and movies of the *Chronicles of Narnia*.[6]

Within the framework of this book, the portals we will talk about do not produce such dramatic results. In general, portals are places through which information and/or energy is exchanged between this reality and others. Because a portal is a vortex, the energy spirals either clockwise, counterclockwise, or in both directions. When the portal is spiraling clockwise, the information that goes through the portal comes into human reality from the outside, from other realities. When it is spinning counterclockwise, information goes from Earth to other realities. Most portals have energy that is spinning in both direction and thus allows information and energy to flow both in and out. This means that portals give us a permanent possibility for exchange with aspects of consciousness that are located in other dimensions, realities, or star systems.

From my perspective, there is no doubt that portals exist. They are actually pretty common. Nonetheless it is not so easy to describe a portal such that they can be easily found and recognized. As we will see, that is a good thing. The phenomenon of portals is far more complex than most people realize. There are wonderful and challenging aspects connected with them. Therefore it may take some time before we know how to use them in a way that assists us on our personal and collective journeys. I separate portals into two main groups: those that we create, whether temporarily or permanently, and those that already exist.

We Create Portals

Many people will be amazed to hear that we are able to open new portals and often do so unconsciously. In a sense, we are walking, moving portals, because we have the ability to open a doorway or doorways into other realities and dimensions at any time. After all, we are multidimensional beings; we have connections with many dimensions. Although we are able to create portals, most people who do so are not aware that they are doing so and under what circumstances. Nonetheless, during ceremonies, meditations, and circle gatherings, portals are opened regularly. Often this is all right, but not always, because it depends on the quality of the energies that induced the opening of a portal. If these energies have been created from unconditional love, the opened portal will allow energies to come through that will be supportive. However, when the energies that induced the opening of the portal were created from ego, this will not necessarily lead to something positive. The same is true when people consciously open a portal. Only when intent has been created with unconditional love will the effect be positive.

I believe that it is not advisable to open portals. This conclusion is based on my personal experiences and those of others. A few examples will demonstrate that the opening of portals can have unwanted consequences. One example is the opening of a portal that is believed to have had and still does have a dramatic impact on human life. Another example is personal and less dramatic but still illustrative.

The first example is rumored to be the most powerful magical act in history. An article that summarizes the event more extensively than I do here is "Did Magicians Cause UFO Sightings" by Whitley Strieber.[7] It is not possible to prove whether this is true, although many in occult circles believe that it actually happened.

In 1918 a most controversial and powerful magician named Aleister Crowley made a drawing showing an alien intelligence with whom he'd come in contact with during a series of invocations he called the Amalantrah workings, carried out in New York over a three-month period. Crowley was in the practice of sketching the beings he encountered during his invocations to add to the detailed written records that he kept of all his "magickal" [sic] workings. The Amalantrah workings were part of what Crowley called the "great work," the intentional cultivation of spiritual growth. According to Crowley, part of the great work involved the "establishment of contact with nonhuman intelligences"—in other words, extraterrestrials.

The purpose of the Amalantrah invocations, by Crowley's own admission, was to open an interdimensional portal that would allow him access to beings from other dimensions. One of the beings who came through this portal was Lam, the one that Crowley sketched. Lam is regarded by occultists as a generic entity rather than an individual being. The drawing bears a startling resemblance to the popular conception of a Gray.[8] The picture of Lam can certainly be considered genuine, as it has a verifiable history. Crowley actually included the portrait of Lam in his Dead Souls exhibition, held in Greenwich Village, New York, in 1919. It was also used as an illustration in H.P. Blavatsky's book *The Voice of the Silence*, written at around the same time. According to Blavatsky, Lam in Tibetan means "way" or "path."[9]

When the Amalantrah workings were complete, Crowley ensured that the portal he had used to grant Lam access to the human world was sealed. This would have completed the story of the portal if there had not been two people who were very close to Crowley during that period. Two of Crowley's unofficial students during his final years were L. Ron Hubbard, who later founded the Scientology movement, and Jack Parsons, who founded Jet Propulsion Laboratories. The pair of them studied Crowley's work at length, especially in relation to the interdimensional portal Crowley had created using his extensive occult knowledge.

Crowley was concerned about what he viewed to be the pair's recklessness when dealing with higher energies. Having spent a lifetime mastering supernatural forces, he considered his students overconfident and inexperienced and told them as much, finally ceasing all communication with them. This did not change their minds, and Hubbard and Parsons proceeded to work with the dormant portal that Crowley had created years earlier.

Thus in 1946 they began what is known in occult circles as the "Babalon workings."[10] The intention was to use "sex magick" [sic] to create a child in the spiritual realms. They would then call down the spiritual baby and direct it into the womb of a female volunteer (thought to be Marjorie Cameron, whom Parsons later married), where it would manifest as human after the usual nine-month period of gestation. When born, this child would incarnate the forces of Babalon—the Scarlet Woman of Revelations that in occult circles symbolizes the dawning of the Age of Horus, the new age. The Babalon workings not only reopened the portal but also increased its intensity and made it highly unstable. The Babalon workings were well documented and many seem to highlight Parson's and Hubbard's inability to close the portal they had reopened and which seemed to slip from their control.

It is interesting to consider the time frame between Hubbard's and Parsons' reopening of the interdimensional portal, or what could be called a stargate, and the wave of extraterrestrial activity and UFO sightings that began with Kenneth Arnold's sighting of nine flying silver discs over Mount Rainier in June of 1947, not long after the Roswell incident. During this incident it was alleged that aliens, possibly Grays, had crashed in a flying saucer. Such UFO activity has held steady since then.

The stargate, or stellar rift, in space and time created by Crowley's Amalantrah workings created a portal through which Lam and other extraterrestrial influences could enter our known universe. Although Crowley himself was careful to seal this portal on the completion of his workings, subsequent magical operations have served to reopen the portal and leave it in a state whereby extraterrestrial beings could use it to access our world.

Although I cannot vouch for the truth of this story, certain occultists warn us that playing with portals without mastering their workings is a dangerous undertaking and could have large-scale effects. When we open portals unconsciously, this has an effect that is usually less dramatic, although it still can be quite harmful to people. Let me give another example of the opening of a portal.

During a training I did in the mid-1990s we did a ceremony for two women to support the deep connection they felt existed between them. During the ceremony, I was drumming to hold the space and maintain the most optimal energy, and I could feel that the energy had changed. I did the best I could, but I could feel that we as a group had lost it. The person leading the ceremony stopped it rather abruptly. I was very upset. At that time, I did not know what had happened, but I noticed all kinds of lower astral beings affecting the people in the group. I blamed the person leading the ceremony for not creating the right conditions. It took me many years to understand that a power struggle during the ceremony induced the opening of a portal that allowed astral beings to come through into this reality. As I mentioned earlier, when a portal is spontaneously opened, the quality of the energies that induced the opening of the portal also determine the quality of the energies that come through it. The egos of the people involved obviously created a portal through which unpleasant energies and beings entered. Several times I went back to close the portal and deal with the beings and energies. At that time, I was less trained and inexperienced. It was a very unpleasant experience and it made me decide to stay away from opening portals. Subsequent unpleasant experiences with portals that were opened during ceremonies only strengthened my decision.

I can offer more examples, but I hope that my caution is clear: Do not open portals unless you have been trained and know on every level what you are doing. Because often portals are opened unconsciously, it is important to do every ceremony, meditation, or other activity from the heart with unconditional love and respect. If you then open a portal, whatever comes through will most likely be of the same positive vibration.

There are many portals all over the planet. These portals can be separated into different groups. For each type of portal, the risk of working with them will be indicated.

Portals to Parallel Realities or Other Dimensions of Earth

Although there are many theories about parallel realities or universes their existence is still hypothetical. Nevertheless, scientists are beginning to make an increasingly strong case for the existence of such portals.[11] Considering portals to be parallel realities, there is the possibility that people or objects may disappear. Unsolved disappearances of people may be attributed to an event where someone unknowingly goes through a portal and so disappears.[12] I have no doubt that these incidences occur but I do not know how common they are. Although I believe that there are many portals, doorways into other dimensions, other realities, and other space-time continuums, most of these doorways are not of such a nature that people can physically pass through them. Most of these portals are places where the veil between the dimensions and other realities is so thin that information can more easily be accessed, images can be received, and sometimes communications can be established. It is a subject about which another whole book could be written.

Over time I have learned about several of such portals. None, however, are as dramatic as the one that is described by Tom Dongo and Linda Bradshaw in their book *Merging Dimensions*.[13] This is one of the doorways that allows the passage of physical beings. They describe many strange incidents and give examples of beings who seemed to pass through this portal. This portal is not so much a defined location but rather an area that is dimensionally unstable, allowing different beings to come through. Sometimes it is even possible to look into another reality. The book describes many strange beings seen through the portal, including dinosaurs and Big Foot. However, there is no report of a human disappearing into these other realities. I have had several experiences in which I looked into other realities. In two instances, I perceived these other realities in a very clear and even challenging way (see chapter 8).

Portals that Lead to Other Places and Dimensions in the Universe

When people talk about portals, they mostly talk about portals leading to other dimensions or places in the universe. People believe that it is safe to work with these portals without any limitations. The question arises whether that is true. Let us look at the different types of portals and describe their characteristics.

- In the first place, there are portals that I call the "safe" portals. These portals allow through only energies that have a beneficial effect on us. We can use these energies for personal expansion and awareness. A beautiful example of this type of portal is the Andromeda portal. We have encountered these portals at several different locations, among others in Sedona. As people experience these portals, they feel that the energies coming through are always connected with love and always come from the dimensions of light and love.

    Another beautiful example is the Mother Nature doorways that I mentioned in chapter 11. These portals give us access to the divine feminine. It is not easy to describe, but it seems to be an aspect of consciousness that exists in many dimensions. The dimension with which these doorways/portals connect holds the presence of many beings who we associate with the divine feminine, like Mother Mary, Quan Yin, Isis, Inanna, and many others. These portals are safe and a pleasure to connect with.

- The second group of portals is formed by portals that can only be accessed when we are able to fully connect with all aspects of that portal. I call them the "all-or-nothing" portals. In a sense, these are also safe portals, because you have to be able to resonate with the whole energy/information system before energy or information can come through. Although the energies can be of different levels, the ones that I have encountered are all from such a high vibration that I feel them to be safe. To this group belong the portals through which the original crystal skulls came to Earth. I have described these portals in my book *Crystal Skulls: Interacting with a Phenomenon*[14] (see fig. 12.1). The location of one of these portals is also the center of the six-pointed star in the Sedona Landscape Temple (see fig. 8.2).

- The third group of portals is the majority of portals, and I call them "Pandora's box" portals. You never know what you will encounter when you connect or activate such a portal—when you open Pandora's box. These portals may connect with one system, but often there are many levels of energy in that system, and unless you are sensitive enough to know the level you are connecting with

Fig. 12.1: A portal of the "all or nothing" type in Sedona. This portal is the center of the six-pointed star in Sedona (chapter 8) and is one of the crystal skull portals.

and the impact of the energies, you risk connecting with energies that, instead of supporting you on your journey, could create more challenges. Most people have enough issues to deal with and prefer not to add more than they already are handling or can handle.

- I call the fourth group the "multipurpose" portals. Such portals give us access to different dimensions or systems or realities. Most of the multipurpose portals also fall into the category of Pandora's box portals. I have found portals that give access to two completely different systems, but I am also aware of a portal that gives access to six different systems. Not all of these systems are supportive. Therefore it is important to know with which system you are connecting. I find these portals a challenge to work with, because it is not easy to separate the energies of the different systems and be certain with which part you are connecting.

- The last type of portal is what I call an "induction" portal. This is an existing portal that needs to be activated through intent. Again, if you do not know what type of portal it is or do not sufficiently understand its energies, please stay away from activating it. For almost everyone, this is the best advice I can give.

To summarize, we can say that connecting with portals can be a risky undertaking, and it is better not to try to actively open a portal. Trust that when you come from a place of unconditional love, the result of your actions will be for the highest good of everyone involved. If a portal is then opened, it will always be in alignment with your journey. Alternatively, to open a portal based just on an idea most likely arises from ego and may create challenging situations.

Portal Networks and Single Portals

My wife Jeanne is very good at finding portals. Her sensitivity for them is far greater than mine. Thanks to her ability, we have gathered quite a lot of information over time. After looking at all of the research we have collected, we see that some portals are common and others are rare. Most common are the portals that connect to other star systems, the other-dimensional portals. These portals are all Pandora's box portals. Of this group, a few are very common. These include portals to the Pleiades, Sirius, Arcturus, Orion, Alpha Centauri, and Tau Ceti. It sounds as if these portals are safe, and they are when you connect with them from a place of unconditional love, because you are connecting with the higher aspects of these portals. However, when you are in fear or come from ego, even on a subtle or unconditional level, you may connect with lower-dimensional aspects that may not be beneficial. The safe Andromeda portals also belong to the group of common interdimensional portals.

The portals that are very common are connected with each other and form grids. I have not studied these grids in detail. We know that they are irregular in shape and pattern and that the density of the portals varies by area/country. The grid system of portals is also dynamic, meaning that the grid system is continuously changing. It seems that the number of portals is still increasing, but I have no actual data to demonstrate this. Maybe in this time of expanding awareness, people invite consciously or unconsciously the energies of other-dimensional or extraterrestrial beings and consequently more portals are opening. This seems to be especially true for Pleiadian and Sirian portals. These are also the two systems with which people feel most connected. Indigenous people all over the world, including the Maya, North American indigenous peoples, the Taiwanese indigenous people, and the Maoris of New Zealand all believe that their ancestors came from the Pleiades, and consequently there is a deep connection with this star system.

In addition to the portals that form grids, there are portals that are rare, and they do not form grids. Examples are portals to Venus. I found three portals in the Sedona area, yet I have never found another Venus portal anywhere else.

The study of portals is in an initial phase, as we never conducted a systematic study but rather collected data as we studied other Earth energies. The energies of portals appear to differ from energies described in the previous chapters. However, they are part of the energies on Earth, and as such, they deserve a place in this book. I also believe that portals deserve more attention, because we can bring new information through portals and into this reality and also into the different grid systems. Portals are, in a sense, options for renewing the way we look at reality. Nonetheless, I like to repeat the warning that playing with portals without a proper understanding of their energies, of your own intent, and of an awareness of your state of being is not a wise action.

ENDNOTES

1. *USA.gov*, http://www.usa.gov/.
2. "Portals to the World," *The Library of Congress*, http://www.loc.gov/rr/international/portals. html.
3. *Stargate* is a very successful science-fiction television series that actually started with a movie. *Stargate* went through ten seasons. Successful spinoffs of the show include *Stargate Atlantis* (five seasons) and more recently *Stargate Universe*. All stories are based on the concept of gigantic, ring-shaped gates that have the ability to create a wormhole through which people can travel throughout the universe. For more information, visit http://en.wikipedia.org/wiki/Stargate, http://stargate.mgm.com/ and http://www.gateworld.net.
4. A good example of one of these articles would be Karen Lyster's "Stargate: The Real One?" *UFOs: The Beginning of a New World*, accessed February 2, 2011, http://www.karenlyster.com/stargate. html.
5. Brad Wright and Jonathan Glassner, *Stargate SG-1* (Century City, CA: Metro-Goldwyn-Meyer, 1997-2007).
6. C.S. Lewis, *The Chronicles of Narnia*, (New York: HarperCollins Publishers, 2001). The seven chronicles were originally published between 1950 and 1956.
7. Whitley Strieber, "Did Magicians Cause UFO Sightings," *Unknown Country: The Edge of the World* (July 20, 2005), http://www.unknowncountry.com/insight/did-magicians-cause-ufo-sightings.
8. For an image of the drawing of Lam see Daniel V. Boudillion's article "Aleister Crowley's Lam and the Little Grey Men," *boudillion.com* (August 15, 2003), accessed February 2, 2011, http://www.boudillion.com/lam/lam.htm, or Ian Blake's "Aleister Crowley and the Lam Statement," *The Excluded Middle* (1996), accessed February 2, 2011, http://www.excludedmiddle.com/LAMstatement.html.
9. Helena Petrovna Blavatsky, *The Voice of the Silence* (London: The Theosophical Publishing Company, 1889), quoted in Whitley Strieber's "Did Magicians Cause UFO Sightings."
10. Strieber, "Did Magicians Cause UFO Sightings."
11. Fred Alan Wolf, *Parallel Universes: The Search for Other Worlds* (New York: Touchstone, 1988).
12. There are many references on the Internet about unexplained disappearances and the possibility that portals could be involved. The Wikipedia entry "Unexplained Disappearances," last modified January 2, 2011, http://en.wikipedia.org/wiki/Unexplained_disappearances, includes many of these.
13. Tom Dongo and Linda Bradshaw, *Merging Dimensions: The Opening Portals of Sedona* (Sedona, AZ: Hummingbird Publishing, 1995).
14. Jaap van Etten, PhD, *Crystal Skulls: Interacting with a Phenomenon* (Flagstaff, AZ: Light Technology Publishing, 2007), 126-132.

13

EFFECTS OF HUMAN
ACTIVITIES ON THE
DIFFERENT GRID SYSTEMS

THROUGHOUT THE BOOK I HAVE MENTIONED HOW HUMAN BEINGS HAVE a powerful effect on the different Earth energy systems. This chapter will expand our discussion about human effects on these energies. Most of the grids have not been studied quantitatively. However, those grids that are most important for our well-being and spiritual development have been studied, and data is available. This does not include research on the lower subtle Earth energies. We mentioned in chapter 3 that the lower subtle Earth energy grids only change qualitatively, and therefore it is not possible to add more data.

Our Effects on Earth Meridian, Earth Chakra, and Triad Grids

Our effects on the Earth chakra and meridian grids can be measured quantitatively, both positively and negatively. There are also qualitative effects, but they are not measurable. The same is true for the twelve triad system. We have already seen the effect that the activation with a crystal skull has on the size of lines of this system (see fig. 6.3). Most of my quantitative research has been focused on these three grid systems because firstly, these grids are important to us; secondly, I was curious why I'd found such differences in size between the vortexes of these three systems in different locations, and thirdly, I was curious why these vortexes changed over time.

Every time we meditate in the energy field of a vortex we receive energies and we also bring more energy into the vortex. It seems that we function as a kind of acupuncture needle while sitting in a vortex area. With the right attitude, which is

Type of vortex	Optimum size in miles and meters
Meridian vortex	3.78 miles (6,083 m)
Chakra vortex level four	12.97 miles (20,873 m)
eleven triad vortex	4.27 miles (6,872 m)
twelve triad vortex	5.59 miles (8,996 m)

Table 5: Optimum size of four types of vortexes expressed as the size of the radius in miles and meters.

most easily achieved through meditation, we bring information/energy from the fields into the grids through the vortex we are sitting on. I do not understand all of the factors involved, but we have observed that meditating on a vortex leads to an expansion of that vortex.

Let us look first at the size of vortexes in different parts of the world. Over time I learned that vortexes of these three types (Earth meridians, Earth chakras, and triad systems) have a certain optimum size that seems to be quite constant (see table 5).

I express the size of a vortex as the length of the radius of the area that a vortex covers. The optimum size of the smaller vortexes of all twelve Earth meridians is on average the same. This is also true for all twelve different chakra vortexes of the level four type. The triad vortexes, however, differ in size depending on the number of triads. Initially I studied the sizes of the vortexes of the eight to twelve triad grids, but later I restricted my focus to the vortexes of grids with eleven and twelve triads, because they seemed to have become the most important triad grids. Therefore only data for vortexes of the eleven and twelve triad grids has been included. Although eleven and twelve triad grids have twelve different chakra frequencies, the size of the vortexes of these twelve different frequencies do not differ in size, and therefore there is one optimum size of all the vortexes of the eleven and twelve triad grids.

In table 6, the size of vortexes is expressed at a percentage of the optimum size. This makes it possible to compare changes in different systems against one another. Although for some data sets the number of measurements is low, we nonetheless can see a clear pattern. It seems that level four chakra vortexes are most sensitive to human activities. They are always the ones that have the largest reduction in size. This is especially striking when we look at data from two countries in northwestern Europe: the Netherlands and Denmark. Here the size of the level four chakra vortexes is reduced to just below 15 percent. There is no doubt that intense human activity in these countries has had a strong negative, or

Location	Meridian %	Chakra level four	Consciousness eleven triads	Consciousness twelve triads
The Netherlands 2006	41.4 (8)	14.9 (11)	29.5 (4)	23.9 (5)
Denmark 2006	52.2 (2)	14.1 (4)	37.3 (3)	38.2 (2)
Mallorca, Spain 2008	71.7 (11)	70.8 (15)	?	?
Sedona, U.S. before 2002	81.8 (24)	44.1 (18)	57.5 (7)	52.2 (11)
Taiwan (nature) 2005	88.7 (13)	74.9 (22)	89.1 (3)	82.9 (8)
Taiwan (city parks) 2005	77.0 (13)	48.6 (11)	64.4 (3)	64.4 (7)
Taiwan (city) 2005		40.9 (3)	47.1 (1)	58.8 (2)

Table 6: The size of four types of vortexes measured in different parts of the world, expressed as percent of the optimum size (with number of measurements).

reducing, influence on these vortexes. Of all countries and situations measured, the size of all four measured types of vortexes was the smallest in the Netherlands and Denmark.

The meridian chakras seem to withstand human influence best. In all situations, they are the ones with the highest percentage, meaning that their size was reduced the least. It seems that the effect of human activity on consciousness vortexes is independent of the number of triads. However, the change in size follows the same tendency as those of Earth meridian and chakra vortexes.

The data set from Taiwan also clearly illustrates the effect of human activity on the size of vortexes. The size of vortexes in nature is much larger than in cities. The situation in the city parks is better than in the cities themselves, but vortexes in such areas are still lower energy than those in nature. Taiwan is a young nation. It developed its technologies and modern constructions mainly in the past 200 years. Human activities deplete the vortexes and ultimately will also affect the vortexes outside of cities. Consequently, the energy in the vortexes in nature will begin to decrease as well. In Western Europe, the process of influencing the land has happened over eons. Therefore it is not surprising that the sizes of the vortexes has been reduced considerably more than in other places in the world.

From that perspective, it is interesting to look at Mallorca. Mallorca is one of the Balearic Islands off the east coast of Spain. As we have seen in chapter 8, this island is interesting in many ways. However, I was quite surprised by the size of the chakra vortexes. Their size was one of the highest measured—almost as high as vortexes found in nature in Taiwan. The majority of the island is cultivated, and most likely this happened over a long period of time. Apparently the degree of disturbance is such that the chakra vortexes were not affected as much as would have been expected. The size of the meridian vortexes, on the other hand, is comparatively small when compared to other countries, for which I have no explanation.

In summary, this data shows that human activities have a decreasing effect on the amount of energies in the three systems that are important for us. It may be possible that there are other explanations for the decrease in vortex size, but all data seems to indicate that human activities are a key factor.

While we do decrease the size of the vortexes, we also have the ability to restore their energies. To illustrate the power we have to restore the size of the vortexes, here are two examples: One example is that of a series of large-scale activations, and one is on a much smaller scale. The large-scale activations took place in the Sedona area. Table 7 shows data from Sedona from before 2002. From that year until 2006, much work was done on the vortexes. Smaller and larger groups connected with the earth to do ceremonies for healing and balancing Earth energies. In table 8, we can see that these activities have had quite an effect on the size of the vortexes.

In April of 2006, another large-scale Earth activation was organized by Adam Yellowbird, director of the Institute for Cultural Awareness (ICA).[1] This event was attended by several hundred people. Their intent was to activate the energy in the Sedona area by creating energies without telling the participants about this intention. We measured the size of the vortexes before the ceremony (which took place at the beginning of April 2006) and almost a month after the ceremony (toward the end of May 2006). Even after almost a month, the increase in size was still very noticeable.

In table 8, the data from the beginning of April 2006 shows that since 2002, different activities have induced an increase in size of the vortexes. The ceremonies during Earth Day expanded the vortexes even further, and the meridian vortexes reached their optimum states toward the end of May 2006. There was much enthusiasm among the organizers and participants when they realized that their work indeed had a powerful effect on the energies of the earth. After April 2006, no

When measured	Meridian %	Chakra level 4 %	Consciousness eleven triads %	Consciousness twelve triads %
Before 2002	81.8 (24)	44.1 (18)	57.5 (7)	52.1 (11)
Beginning of April 2006	97.7 (14)	75.9 (21)	70.7 (11)	71.4 (11)
End of May 2006	100.5 (14)	87.4 (21)	89.8 (11)	81.8 (11)
February 2009	93.4 (14)	84.3 (21)	78.7 (11)	84.5 (11)

Table 7: Measurement of the size of four types of vortexes expressed as percent of the optimum size in Sedona, Arizona, in four different periods (number of measurements).

large ceremonies have been held in the Sedona area. However, activities of smaller groups and individuals have kept the size of the vortexes in the Sedona area quite stable. As shown in table 7, only a small shift in size was observed at the beginning of 2009. The largest decrease was with the eleven triad vortexes while the twelve triad vortexes even increased. It seems that people unconsciously connect deeper with twelve triad vortexes than with eleven triad vortexes. Is this another sign of the shift in consciousness? It seems that this is the case. In chapter 6, we saw other data that showed the same tendency: The energies in the lines of triad grids with six to eight triads decreased while those with nine to twelve triads increased (see table 4). Table 4 also showed that the highest increase is in the lines of the twelve triad lines. The data also shows that the vortexes of the twelve triad grid have the highest increase in size (see table 7). This information supports the idea of a shift in awareness toward the higher frequencies of third-dimensional consciousness.

Large-Scale and Small-Scale Effects

The given examples refer to large-scale activities featuring several hundred people with a clear focus. However, we have discovered that we do not need large groups to have an effect on the size of vortexes—one example I mentioned in my book on crystal skulls.[2] Every week we have a crystal skull meditation in our house. One day I decided to follow the changes in size of two vortexes on our property, about 20 and 50 yards (18 m and 46 m) away from the place of meditation. I did not measure the size of the vortexes immediately after the meditations because the size would have been off the scale. I measured them the following day. The results showed that after every meditation, the size of the vortexes increased (see fig. 13.1). Because the energy disperses through the lines during the week, the size of the vortex begins to decrease again. However, vortexes do not decrease to the size they were before the meditation, and consequently our vortexes have slowly increased in size over time.

When we started taking measurements in 2006, the chakra two vortex was about 45 percent of its optimum and the twelve triad consciousness vortex was 72 percent of its optimum. When I measured the size of the vortexes in January 2009, the chakra two vortex was 91 percent of its optimum and the consciousness twelve triad vortex was 99.6 percent. Even though the energy dissipates through the lines, small-scale weekly meditations of on average nine to ten people over time reactivated these vortexes back to their optimal condition. Even when you meditate alone, you will improve the energetic environment in which you live. In addition you will also improve your neighbors' environments.

In summary we can say that every time we meditate, alone or in groups, we contribute to healing and balancing the Earth energy systems, thus providing a better environment for ourselves and others. There are several studies that show how life in cities improves when enough people meditate. Most of these studies

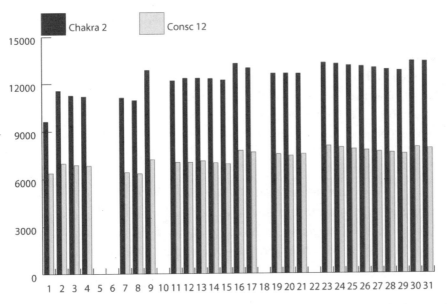

Fig. 13.1: The effect of weekly meditations on the size of two vortexes near the house of the author.

were induced by the Transcendental Meditation organization, but were carried out by independent researchers. An example of this type of research was done in Washington, DC during the National Demonstration Project in 1993.[3] Over a period of three months, researchers looked at the weekly violent crime rate in Washington, DC in relation to the number of people who practiced transcendental meditation. There is a highly significant correlation between the decrease in violent crime and the increasing number of people meditating. The violent crime rate was reduced by 23.3 percent during the week when the highest number of people meditated (week nine). I believe that the decrease in the crime rate was a consequence of the improvement of the quality of the environment due to the activation, balancing, and changes in the different Earth grid systems that occurred as a consequence of these meditations.

Human Effects on Other Grids

We already mentioned that, even though we cannot back this up with quantitative data, we do affect every grid system on Earth. We can create communication lines and we can increase the number of triads in these lines. We play an important role in the creation of the crystalline grids and we have the ability to affect the information contained in the morphogenetic grids. We can say that we have a powerful effect on the environment we live in and that we ourselves determine the quality of that environment through our effects on the different grid systems. Therefore it becomes very important to be aware of our actions, our thoughts, and our emotions because they all have an effect on the energetic environment we live in. We share this environment with all other creatures who live on Earth. We know the effect we have on other species through the destruction of habitats: We have eradicated many species of plants and animals. We do not know what effects we have on other species through the energetic changes we have induced. However, there is no doubt that a loving and balanced environment will benefit all species. We have the ability to create such a positive environment. It is time that we individually and collectively begin to do so.

ENDNOTES

1. The Institute of Cultural Awareness is a nonprofit organization "providing a safe and healthy environment for cultural exchange and healing." ICA is dedicated to "preserving sacred sites and honoring indigenous traditions while bridging the gap between the elders and the children" (from the ICA mission statement at *ICA*, http://www.ica8.org/pages/About_ICA.shtml). The Institute also organizes Earth Dance events. For this and other activities, visit *Earth Works for Humanity* at http://www.earthworksforhumanity.org/.

2. Jaap van Etten, PhD, *Crystal Skulls: Interacting with a Phenomenon* (Flagstaff, AZ: Light Technology Publishing, 2007), 87-88.

3. John S. Hagelin, Maxwell V. Rainforth, David W. Orme-Johnson, Kenneth L. Cavanaugh, Charles N. Alexander, Susan F. Shatkin, John L. Davies, Anne O. Hughes, and Emanuel Ross, "Effects of Group Practice of the Transcendental Meditation Program on Preventing Violent Crime in Washington DC: Results of the National Demonstration Project, June-July, 1993," *Social Indicators Research* 47, no. 2: 153-201. Information from this article is also available on the Internet at http://www.istpp.org/crime_prevention/.

14

HOW EARTH ENERGIES
SUPPORT HUMAN EVOLUTION

UNIVERSAL LAW TELLS US THAT EVERYTHING IN THE UNIVERSE IS CONTINUOUSLY changing. Nothing is constant, with the exception of the law of change and the three other universal laws.

- The **first law** is that everything that exists always will. This means that once something is created, it may change but independent of its form it will always be there. Our form may change, but our consciousness will always exist.
- The **second law** is that all is one and the one is All That Is. Although we each have our own consciousness we are at the same time also one with all. Seen from our third-dimensional perspective, this is experienced as a paradox; we can only experience the truth of this statement from a oneness perspective.
- The **third law** is what I prefer to call the law of resonance. All energy interactions are based on this law. Everything is energy, which means that resonance takes place continuously on all possible levels. This is a basic law of physics. This law is also known as "what you send out is what you get back,"[1] or the law of attraction.[2] It is also the secret of *The Secret*.[3]

Everything that exists is continuously unfolding itself. This enfolding is the expression of the Creator. This expression of the Creator is infinite and consequently change is also infinite. Seen from the perspective of our awarenesses, change in living beings seems to have a direction, and we call this evolution.

When we look at human evolution, its direction does not always seem to be clear. We see civilizations rise and fall. If evolution is supposed to show progress, what progress has human evolution made? Was technology progress? In some ways it may be, but it came at the price of losing our connection with the world around us.

Human evolution seems to have certain phases. Initially there were developments in feeling, sensing, and connecting with the world. We still see this reflected in the traditions of many cultures. Next came evolution of logic and the mental aspects. Our modern society reflects these developments. We now seem to be moving toward an integration of these two aspects to create a new human being. This is the new phase in human evolution: the evolution of awareness of our total potential instead of only certain aspects of the potential. We can connect with this potential if we are able to transform the tendency to live in duality: the experiencing of separateness and of thinking in terms of opposing energies, by which we mean thinking in terms of right/wrong and either/or.

In this era, we begin to move toward a different way of thinking. We see everything as part of a whole. We recognize that each truth is a valid truth for the one holding that truth. We begin to accept differences as aspects of the one and think in terms of, "This is valid and that is also valid," even though this does not mean that we choose to accept those aspects as our own. This is thinking in terms of and/and.

Although there are signs of change, most people live in third-dimensional reality, in which they tend to believe that their sensory perception is their reality, the true world. This belief leads us as a species to sink deeper into the lower vibrations of this reality, which are mostly fear-based energies. We tend to believe what our senses tell us and what others tell us to believe. Consequently we have created an illusionary physical reality that we believe to be real. As part of this illusionary reality, we experience separation and disconnect from the world around us, especially from Earth and from the universe. Our separation is so entrenched that we unwittingly destroy the very environment we depend on. From a spiritual point of view, we have not evolved but rather have devolved from higher awareness into our current state.

In the past forty years, we can observe an increasing shift toward higher vibrations. We believe again in an existence beyond the five senses, and it seems that we have shifted from spiritual devolution to spiritual evolution. We have become increasingly aware that we are spiritual beings having a human experience, spiritual beings who are deeply stuck in the illusion of the physical world and all the beliefs connected with that world. This awareness allows us to change and let go of these limited beliefs.

Although modern humans have lost their connection with Earth, the knowledge that Earth is important for our well-being has not been lost completely. Many cultures have maintained their respect and love for Mother Earth/Pachamama and are again sharing that with the world, inspiring many people to reconnect with our Mother. People of all colors and ages are holding ceremonies, prayers, and meditations to connect with her and to deepen the connection. We begin to again honor the uniqueness of each and everyone. The information provided in this book may support us to find our own unique way of connecting with Mother Earth and to feel again gratitude for all she offers us in support of our personal and collective journeys. These feelings may lead to an attitude of taking full responsibility for what we do, think, and feel and also for what we have done individually and collectively. This may lead to true change. Change does not involve healing Earth. The concept that we need to heal Earth is an illusion. The Earth does not need healing. Human beings need healing so that we will be able to fully accept responsibility for what we have created on Earth and also accept the responsibility for transforming and changing what has been brought out of balance by our past actions. In this way, we and Earth will come into harmony again and we can experience the full connection that exists between Earth and ourselves.

The Creation of Different Realities

The study of communication lines is one of the most powerful tools used to study human consciousness and how it has expressed itself over time. We looked extensively at the subject of communication lines in chapter 8, but here I share in more detail my interpretation of the story that the grids of communication lines are telling us. I am aware that it is an unusual story, and therefore I invite you, as I have done before, to feel whether or not you can resonate with what is shared.

As I mentioned, change is a constant in the universe. Change always enriches us independent of what we think about said change. We can define it as positive or negative, but change itself is simply an experience and an opportunity for growth. When we see change as negative—and we frequently do so—we may devolve instead of evolve. In each moment, we have the choice to determine how we see and experience our lives.

Devolution on a spiritual level happens both individually and collectively. We all have experienced or may still experience devolution on a personal level. To demonstrate what I mean by personal devolution, I have chosen to provide a short description of my own life.

My Own Spiritual Devolution and Evolution

I grew up in the Netherlands in the period after World War II. My parents were devoted Catholics, but I never resonated with what I heard and experienced in church and school. I had the good fortune to have spent my childhood years walking and playing in a forest before I was old enough to go to school, and that created the basis for a deep connection with nature. My love and appreciation for nature did not change when we moved to the city when I was almost six years old, not even when I had to go to school. I was a good student and obeyed the rules even while holding an inner resistance against them. But I did not dare to rebel. I became a typical left-brained person, logical and analytical, and I did well in school and later at the university. I had become a master at hiding my emotions, my insecurity, and my growing lack of self-worth. When I left home at age eighteen, I no longer went to church, and I stayed far from any form of religion. I did not know the difference between religion and spirituality, and by the time I was thirty, my spiritual development was zero. From my spiritual connection to nature as a child, I had devolved into an individual without any awareness of spirituality.

After my thirtieth birthday, my life changed. I became interested in yoga and transcendental meditation and read as many books on spirituality as I could get. My thirtieth year marked the shift from spiritual devolution to a spiritual evolution, and this process of spiritual evolution continues to this day. My story is not exceptional. On the contrary, many people have similar stories to tell. What happens within an individual life is also happening for humankind as a whole. In this case, the time scale is of course quite different.

The Devolution and Evolution of Earth and Humankind

I will now share with you my interpretation of the story of the devolution of humankind based on the study of the different communication line grids. I mentioned before that many people have created different communication line grids. I believe that these grids can be divided into five main groups. These groups are:

- Modern times (the past 13,000 years)
- Atlantis
- Lemuria
- sacred geometry people
- white-robed people

During the study of the energies of these communication line grids, the energies became more recognizable and alive. In modern times many different peoples have created communication lines, and each tribe and people created lines with a different energy. Lines are connected between megalithic sites; between churches, cathedrals, and temples; and between many other structures. Nonetheless these energies have a similarity that makes them different from the other four groups. They belong to our reality.

By reality I mean a reality that we can perceive with our senses. Some people experience a more extended version of physical realty based on their ability to perceive through the sixth sense. However, for most of us, reality is mainly based on the third-dimensional physical world. We create this reality collectively. It is an agreed-on, shared reality, a reality of our minds, a reality of illusions based on the belief that what we perceive through our five senses is *the* reality. Of course there are individual, group, and tribal differences in the way reality is perceived, but these differences are not fundamental. We share the same basic reality, and the communication lines we create hold the same fundamental vibrations that characterize this reality. As we have seen, the energies that determine this reality are held in the triad grids.

When we talk about Atlantis and Lemuria, we try to define these possible worlds in terms of our current reality. These attempts result in many different opinions about Atlantis and Lemuria, especially regarding where they were located. As we read in chapter 8, there is an agreement that certain areas can be called Lemurian or Atlantean. We come to these conclusions even though there is no concrete evidence. I also mentioned the possibility that Atlantis and Lemuria belonged to a different reality, since there is no physical evidence for their existence in this one.

Before we continue, let us look at the idea of reality in more detail. Reality is created by consciousness, that aspect of consciousness that we call awareness. Awareness is in turn determined by our belief structures. Earlier we looked at morphogenetic fields. These fields hold possibilities for a high if not infinite number of expressions of human reality. A number of these possible expressions have been realized and their energy/information can be found in the morphogenetic grids. Once the energy/information is part of these grids, the probability that a certain experience or expression will happen increases. The information in the human morphogenetic grids (the triad grids) does not only determine form and behavior but also how consciousness tends to express itself in this reality. Rupert Sheldrake states that we are determined by chemical and physical causation, which we share with animals and plants, but that we also have conscious causation.[4] This last aspect is very interesting. Basically conscious causation means that we can actively induce changes in this reality. This may happen in a conscious or unconscious way, but we can alter the way in which reality is expressed. This change needs to stay within the possibilities of the morphogenetic field, but it can change the probability of certain expressions. On an individual level, this could mean that a person perceives reality in such a different way that we have the tendency to call such a person abnormal. In serious cases of abnormality, we lock such people up in institutions.

What Happens When We Shift Human Reality?

But what happens when instead of an individual, a whole group of people shift their perceptions of reality? I believe that it is possible for a group of people to change a reality collectively to such a degree that they disconnect from their original reality. In such a situation, a group can create a different Earth reality. Such an Earth reality is out of phase with the reality they were originally connected to, and people who are out of phase can no longer perceive the reality they originated from. However, we are still able to sense these realities, which then lead us to embark on a search, like (for example) the search for Lemuria and Atlantis. I believe that Atlantis and Lemuria are indeed other realities that we are no longer are able to perceive. It is not clear what induced these shifts. These realities are still based on the same morphogenetic fields. However, they differ through sub-grids of the morphogenetic grids formed by the communication lines.

The same is true for the other two communication line grids I have found and that I've named the sacred geometry people and the white-robed people. The energies in these grids are even more different than those in the Atlantean and Lemurian grids, and in my opinion form two more realities, making the total number five. The question may arise: What does this have to do with the process of devolution? The answer is within my hypothesis, which is based on the different energies found in the communication lines. I share this hypothesis in the form of a story.

The first beings to come to Earth in order to experience physical reality came from the stars. Stories of many different cultures from all over the world are in alignment with this belief. They describe how their ancestors came from the stars. There are many portals that connect us to the different star systems, making a connection with home possible. The energies in the grid system of the white-robed people suggest that they may have been the ones who came from the stars. They obviously maintained a high level of consciousness. They are still connected with their spiritual selves, maintaining this connection during their physical experience. They do not posses technology because they are able to create all they need due to their understanding of the cosmos. They are mainly a state of being, and therefore we can say that they approach life from a feminine point of view.

The communication line grids of the sacred geometry people also reflect that they were able to maintain a high level of consciousness. However, they looked at the world from a more scientific and mental perspective, which means from a masculine perspective. Based on their energies, a psychic has given these people the name of "techno people." They were the first group to separate from the white-robed people, who did not have technological developments. This separation may have been a choice to allow people to experience this physical reality in two different ways: from a feminine perspective and from a masculine perspective. One is not better than the other; they were simply two different ways to experience the same reality. Due to this separation, two different realities were created, each with their own unique vibrations.

Living in a physical reality made it increasingly difficult to stay in connection with Source, the infinite consciousness. Due to its lower vibrations, the material physical world has a tendency to make people forget who they are, and as a consequence, they get caught in the lower physical vibrations. I believe that there were two groups who got caught in the physical realities connected with lower vibrations. They were growing out of phase with the reality from which they'd descended. A group separated from the white-robed people, and they became the Lemurians; the Atlanteans split off from the sacred geometry people. Two more realities were created. I believe that Atlantis and Lemuria are two worlds, two realities that are out of phase with one another and with the other two realities. Now four realities exist, each with their own communication line grid system. We do not find physical remnants of these civilizations because their realities are not part of ours. The structures we call Lemuria and Atlantis have been created by those who descended from these two realities, which brings us to the fifth and current reality.

The reality we now live in has a lower vibration than any of the previously mentioned realities. A group of Atlanteans and of Lemurians lost the connection with their civilization and grew out of phase. Interestingly, this lower vibrational reality we live in brought aspects of Lemuria and Atlantis together. Such a shift in reality may be caused by disasters, which may explain the stories of the destruction of Atlantis and Lemuria. In summary we see that the human race descends in frequency over time, losing its connection with its original state. In the same way, the same thing can happen in a person's life as what happened on a large scale with the human race. In these times, the human race moves from the devolution phase to the evolution phase.

Does this story sound far-fetched? Maybe it does, but it is in alignment with the energies of the different communication line grids. It also explains the visions that I and others have had of the white-robed people. It may also explain why we feel so connected with Atlantis and Lemuria, because our vibrations are again increasing, making it easier to connect with these realities. The same will be true for the realities of the sacred geometry people and the white-robed people. When we raise our vibration, we may be able to connect with these other realities and integrate them in such a way that we can shift into a completely new reality based on mastery of third-dimensional physical reality.

Circles and the New Earth

Recent crop circles seem to confirm the idea of a new Earth that may separate from the old one.[5] According to researchers, in 2010 there were at least six crop circles that showed this theme. I wanted to remove the hypothesis of the five realities from this book, but I viewed the crop circles of 2010 as the universe giving me an encouraging sign to leave my hypotheses of different realities in. Let us be open to the possibility that realities can be separated, and let us play with this idea.

Human Evolution in the Now

There are many signs that interest in spirituality is increasing. Books, workshops, conferences, movies, and documentaries are abundantly available for the spiritual seeker, and their numbers are only increasing. A clear sign that reflects the growing interest in spirituality is what is called the New Age movement.[6]

The term "New Age" is given to a movement that includes spirituality of all sorts and science, but it is not directed by a particular person or group. It is almost as diverse as the number of people who are a part of it. The New Age is characterized by the realization that we are our own best teachers and guides. It is a time in which we experience the freedom of following our own paths, guided by our own inner wisdom. This does not mean that this is what everyone is doing. There are still many people who follow gurus, avatars, teachers, and other outside guidance.

However, more people are beginning to realize that although they can learn from others, they have to follow the guidance of their own hearts.

An important part of the New Age movement is our reconnection with Gaia, the superorganism, Mother Earth. This book is meant to increase awareness of the different energies Earth makes available to us and to realize the importance of such reconnection. Through reconnection, we can begin to again experience how each of these Earth energies supports us both individually and collectively on our spiritual evolutionary paths. We have already mentioned how certain grids can help to align our energy systems and how others help to expand our awarenesses. The key to human evolution, however, is the morphogenetic grids.

Morphogenetic Grids and Human Evolution

We have the potential, as defined in the morphogenetic field, to be joyful, happy, abundant, and full of love. However, few humans experience these wonderful feelings, and definitely not on a permanent basis. As we have seen, form and behavior are determined by the morphogenetic grids. This means that we have brought into the grids many behaviors and feelings that prevent us from being happy, joyful, abundant, and full of love. We are collectively stuck in the emotions that we have brought into the grids, preventing us from experiencing our potential. Realizing this can make us sad. It can also help us to see that we have an opportunity for change. We can step into our power, connect with the field of our potential, and change the program in the morphogenetic grids. Doing so helps us, but it also gives others the possibility for change. It is this type of change that is empowering and creates a new reality. It may sound easier than most people are willing to believe. I believe that it is as easy as I describe. However, we have to be determined and never give up. In every moment, we have a choice. The question is simple: What do you choose?

I have mentioned that the human morphogenetic grid is the triad grid. Chapter 6 and chapter 13 indicated that there has been a shift toward the highest level of the triad grid, level twelve. There is no doubt that this shift is a reflection of a general shift in consciousness. Let us remember that the data I collected came from Sedona. There are other areas that have shifted to the highest level of our collective consciousness, and there are still many areas in the world where this is not yet the case. The more the highest level is activated, the larger the effect will be on humanity as a whole.

The New Children

There is another phenomenon that supports the process of a shift in the morphogenetic grids, and that is the birth of an increasing number of new types of children. These children seem to have qualities that are different from those of the overall population. The need to describe them has led to several new terms: Indigo children, Crystal children, Star children, Angels on Earth, and Transitional Children. I will not describe the characteristics of these different types of children because others have done so already.[7] The appearance of these new children is, in my opinion, the evolution of awareness in action.

These children express and display qualities and abilities that appear to be the next step in human evolution. They have these abilities not so much because they are different in potential but because they are able to maintain their special abilities instead of losing them to the mass consciousness. They are showing us abilities that are inherently human but have disappeared from our society to a large degree. In other words, they seem to be more connected with the morphogenetic field than with the grids. Consequently, they bring more information from the field into the grids, contributing to the shift in awareness.

I believe that the evolution through the new children is actually an acceleration of a process that has been evolving for a long time. One way to demonstrate this is by answering a few questions. These questions are based on generally described characteristics of Indigo and other new children. Although there are many tests to be found on the Internet, I have summarized my own version, using also some of the aspects I see with my grandchildren and other children. The questions resulted in the following test:

- Are you searching for a deeper meaning of life?
- Do you feel like you do not belong to this world?
- Do you feel like a stranger in your family?
- Do you feel resistance to conforming to the ways of society?
- Are you searching for like-minded people and feel disconnected from those who are not?
- Are you strong in defending what you feel as truth?
- Are you challenged by people who force authority on you?
- Do you have strong intuition?
- Are you extremely emotionally sensitive?
- Do you feel you have a mission to fulfill?
- Do you have problems following rules you do not understand or do not make logical sense to you?

- Do you dislike work that seems like meaningless routine?
- Do you have trouble focusing on assigned tasks or possibly have been diagnosed as ADD?

When I took this test, I had to say yes to all the questions, and I have no doubt that many who read this part of the book will say yes to many of these questions as well. I am far from being a child or even a teenager. Does this mean that there always have been Indigo children? It seems so. Kabin Jaffe and Ritama Davidson wrote a book called *Indigo Adults: Forerunners of the New Civilization.*[10] They recognize that there are adults who have Indigo characteristics. I define this phenomenon differently. There are people who have chosen the path of expanding awareness. They have become the forerunners, teachers, and healers. Sometimes they are called the lightworkers. The name is unimportant, but this group of people has fed the morphogenetic grids with information that allows the new children to maintain their abilities more easily than they could in the past. This grid enables the new children to express more of their inherent qualities, which are actually human qualities that have been forgotten. These qualities are awakening in us now on a larger scale and herald the time of a new civilization.

When you take the test, if you also answer most of the questions with a yes, that does not necessarily mean that you are an Indigo. I believe that it is more a reflection of an expanded awareness that makes you different from the masses. I also believe that more people will begin to expand their awareness and soon they too will answer most of these questions with a yes. In a sense, humankind is on its way to becoming Indigo.

Although we may see certain developments, this does not mean that the process will evolve smoothly. Many parents do not recognize that their children are special, and even when they do, society tries to fit them into the old systems like school and religion. The consequent problems create diagnoses of learning disabilities and monikers like "problem child." Parents—but especially our educational, medical, and psychological institutions—are not ready to work with these children. Many are diagnosed with Attention Deficit Disorder (ADD) or Attention Deficit Hyperactivity Disorder (ADHD) and are given medications like Ritalin. Although it may be supportive for a certain moment for certain children, I do not believe this is optimal. It is not the children but the institutions that need to change. We see in front of our eyes how established systems delay a natural development that is part of our evolution. Fortunately in these systems, we also see signs of change.

The range of special abilities of the new children varies tremendously. In Meg Blackburn Losey's *Conversations with the Children of Now*, we can read about some very special children.[11] One of these children who has become well-known is Grandma Chandra. She is an omnidimensional being in a severely physically challenged body, and she is often called a living miracle.[12] In the description of her life, it is mentioned that in 2004 she flew to Taos, New Mexico, to assist Chief Golden Eagle (aka Black Spotted Horse) on the energies of the 11:11 phenomenon to promote changes in the Earth's morphogenetic field.[13] Although I do not know whether they focused on the field or on the grids, this statement reveals an awareness that changes need to happen through the morphogenetic system.

Grandma Chandra is not the only one who is doing her work under severely handicapped conditions. Another group of physically and emotionally handicapped people are autistic people. I believe strongly that autistic people also show us a different way of perceiving reality. They help us to get out of our boxes, out of our self-limiting belief structures. All people who are different give us an opportunity to change our limiting ideas, open our hearts, and learn new ways to see and experience reality.

Autistic people, especially those who do not speak, seem to be connected with higher dimensions. They close themselves off from our lower-dimensional world in order to maintain their fifth-dimensional connection. They are waiting for the world to be ready to receive their gifts and their contribution to the evolution of humankind. They are the ones who will bring into the morphogenetic grids the possibility for nonautistic people to move from the third through the fourth and on to the fifth dimension.

I was fortunate to have had the opportunity to meet one of these severely autistic people, a woman who cannot speak. Together with her mother, she found a way of communicating called facilitated communication. She was able to communicate her ideas and feelings, resulting in a wonderful book.[14] In this book, she shared her realization that she and others have chosen their physical limitations to hold the "autism spark," their fifth-dimensional connection. She feels that it is time to bring her spark into this reality. This spark may enable the development of the fifth-dimensional grid that I am still unable to detect. To move fully into fourth-dimensional consciousness, the potential of the next step—to fifth-dimensional consciousness, as defined in a grid—needs to be present. However, it is possible that the fifth-dimensional consciousness is not an aspect of the physical Earth because the fifth dimension is not physical.

In summary we can say that there are many new children with a wide range of abilities who show us different aspects of our evolution. They hold the promise of a different and beautiful future.

The Shift, 2012, and Human Spiritual Evolution

There are many predictions that talk about a time of change. In our current time, predictions have culminated in the idea of the year 2012. I do not believe that a particular date will function as a switch into something new. That would be the same as swallowing a pill against pain and believing yourself to be better. Change and shifts occur through consciousness, which facilitates change. In order to create this state of consciousness, we need to become aware of ourselves and be willing to change all that does not come from a state of love. We do not need to fixate on 2012 to become aware that we live in a transitional time. This is a time of opportunities, but it is also a time of taking responsibility for what we have created, both individually and collectively.

What does this mean, taking responsibility? It means that we need to transform, change, and clean up all that we have set into motion in the present and in the past, especially all that is not in harmony and resonance with love and all that creates separation instead of oneness. It also means that we have to take care of all energies that we have imprinted on this world that are based on fear, greed, and lack—lack of love and lack of respect. Regarding the subject of this book, it means we need to bring the lower subtle energy grids of the earth back into balance. It means we need to expand the higher subtle energy grids that we have reduced in size. We have a responsibility to become who we truly are: a bridge between the grids and the fields, between the physical and the spiritual, between heaven and earth. By doing this, we will make the shift possible. This will take as long as it takes and is not dependent on a date. It is dependent on us—on human beings.

Something new can only be created when the old is sufficiently mastered. That is why those on a spiritual path go through different transformational processes. This is also true for humankind as a whole. Assuming that the story of the five realities is true, our reality has descendants of those who chose a feminine path and those who chose a masculine path. I believe that the process we are in is about the integration of these two approaches but also includes the neutral aspect we call the child. We can only experience oneness when we integrate all three of these aspects. Peoples from the four other realities knew that, and therefore created structures representing the three universal principal energies: feminine, masculine, and child.

In our society, technology and science represent the masculine approach. Indigenous peoples hold the feminine path. The only chance to overcome the duality of our third-dimensional world is to embrace and learn from both. This perspective may enable us to bring back the innocence of the child and complete the triad. The importance of the communication line grids is that they hold information from our ancestors and therefore can help us reconnect with information that can support us in the process of integrating past and present as well as feminine, masculine, and child so that we can finally experience oneness. May we all contribute to this unique phase in the development of the human species. May we connect with our hearts so that we can find our true selves and contribute to this evolutionary process by sharing our unique gifts. We are all needed.

ENDNOTES

1. The concept that "what you put out is what you get back" is very common in these contexts. For example, it is an aspect of the principles shared by Bashar through channel Darryl Anka in "Bashar's Basic Message," *Bashar Communications*, accessed February 4, 2011, http://www. bashar.org/aboutprinciples.html.

2. Esther and Jerry Hicks, *The Law of Attraction* (Carlsbad, CA: Hay House, 2006).

3. Rhonda Byrne, *The Secret* (Hillsboro, OR: Beyond Words Publishing, 2006).

4. Rupert Sheldrake, *A New Science of Life: The Hypothesis of Morphic Resonance* (Rochester, VT: Park Street Press, 1995), 202-206.

5. Scott Mowry, "New Crop Circles Found in England May Offer Proof that a New Earth Is about to Unfold," *Miracles and Inspiration* (July 31, 2010), accessed February 4, 2011, http://www. miraclesandinspiration.com/news_cropcircles.html.

6. See "New Age," *Wikipedia*, last modified February 4, 2011, http://en.wikipedia.org/wiki/New_Age

7. Meg Blackburn Losey, MscD, PhD, *The Children of Now* (Pompton Plains, NJ: New Pages Books, 2007).

8. Serenity Hope, "How Can You Tell if You Are an Indigo?" *Indigo Children*, http://www.namas-tecafe.com/evolution/indigo/#canyoutell.

9. Ibid.

10. Kabir Jaffe and Ritama Davidson, *Indigo Adults: Forerunners of the New Civilization* (New York: iUniverse, 2005).

11. Meg Blackburn Losey, MscD, PhD, *Conversations with the Children of Now* (Pompton Plains, NJ: New Pages Books, 2008).

12. Ibid., 27.

13. Ibid., 29.

14. Gayle Barkley Lee and Lyrica Mia Marquez, "AWEtizm: A Hidden Key to Our Spiritual Magnificence" (unpublished manuscript, November 2009).

BIBLIOGRAPHY

Anka, Darryl. "Bashar's Basic Message." *Bashar Communications*. http://www.bashar.org/.

Becker, Greg, and Harrey Massey. *The Living Matrix: The Science of Healing*. Directed by Greg Becker. Hillsboro, OR: Beyond Words Publishing, 2009. DVD.

Bird, Christopher. *The Divining Hand: The 500-Year-Old Mystery of Dowsing*. Atglen, PA: Whitford Press, 1993.

Blackstock, Regina. "Dolphins and Man.....Equals?" *Little Townmart* (2004). http://www.little-townmart.com/dolphins/.

Blake, Ian. "Aleister Crowley and the Lam Statement." *The Excluded Middle* (1996). http://www.excludedmiddle.com/.

Bohm, David. *Wholeness and the Implicate Order*. London: Routledge, 1980.

Bohm, David, and Basil J. Hiley. *The Undivided Universe*. London: Routledge, 1993.

Boudillion, Daniel V. "Aleister Crowley's Lam and the Little Grey Men." *boudillion.com* (August 15, 2003). http://www.boudillion.com/.

Brennan, Barbara Ann. *Hands of Light: A Guide to Healing Through the Human Energy Field*. New York: Bantam Books, 1988.

Bryant, Page. "Sacred Sedona." In *Sedona Vortex Guide Book*. Light Technology Research. Flagstaff, AZ: Light Technology Publishing, 1991.

Bueno, Mariano. *Stoorvelden in onze woning*, Trans. Nicole Gilissen (Euroterm, Maastricht, NL). [Disturbing fields in our house]. Deventer, NL: Ankh-Hermes, 1990.

Burmeister, Alice, and Tom Mente. *The Touch of Healing: Energizing Body, Mind, and Spirit with the Art of Jin Shin Jyutsu*. New York: Bantam, 1997.

Bursell, Kaare. "Healing with the Day." *The Alchemycal Pages*. http://www.alchemycalpages.com/heal10.html.

Byrne, Rhonda. *The Secret*. Hillsboro, OR: Beyond Words Publishing, 2006.

Callahan, Philip S. *Exploring the Spectrum: Wavelengths of Agriculture and Life*. Kansas City, MO: Acres U.S.A., 1994.

"The Canary Islands." *Spanish Website*. http://www.ctspanish.com/.

Carroll, Lee. "The Celebration! What's next?" *Kryon* (December 8, 2002). http://www.kryon.com/.

Cerve, Wishar S. *Lemuria: The Lost Continent of the Pacific*. San Jose, CA: Supreme Grand Lodge of AMORC, 1931 and 1982.

Charpentier, Louis. *The Mysteries of Chartres Cathedral*. Translated by Sir Ronald Fraser. Research into Lost Knowledge Organisation. Suffolk, UK: Rilko Books, 1966.

Childress, David Hatcher, ed. *Anti-Gravity and the World Grid*. Kempton, IL: Adventures Unlimited Press, 1992.

Christensen, Ronnie. *Passengers*. Directed by Rodrigo García. Culver City, CA: TriStar Pictures, 2008.

Coon, Robert. *The Rainbow Serpent and The Holy Grail: Uluru and the Planetary Chakras*. Warburton, VIC: Robert Coon, 2008.

———. *Earth Chakras: The Definitive Guide*. Warburton, VIC: Robert Coon, 2009.

The Crossroads Institute. "Brainwaves and EEG: The Language of the Brain" *The Crossroads Institute*. http://www.crossroadsinstitute.org/.

Deliso, Tom. "The Spiritual Chakra 8 to 12." *Hermes Trismegistus Wisdom's Door Website Collection Volume 1.* Dunnellon, FL: Hermes Trismegistus / Tom DeLiso, 2008. http://www.wisdoms-door.com/.

Dongo, Tom, and Linda Bradshaw. *Merging Dimensions: The Opening Portals of Sedona.* Sedona, AZ: Hummingbird Publishing, 1995.

D'Silva, Lauren. "Geopathic Stress." *BellaOnline* (2008). http://www.bellaonline.com/articles/art39881.asp.

Emoto, Masaru. *The Hidden Messages in Water.* Translated by David A. Thayne. Hillsboro, OR: Beyond Words Publishing, 2004.

Fidler, J. Havelock. *Earth Energies: A Dowser's Investigation of Ley Lines.* Northhampshire, UK: Aquarian Press, 1988.

Fischer, Hanns. *Aardstralen en de Wichelroede* [Earth radiation and the dowsing rod]. Den Haag, NL: De Mystieke Wereld, 1938.

Furlong, David. *Working with Earth Energies: How to Tap into the Healing Powers of the Natural World.* London: Piatkus, 2003.

Gannon, Tom. "White Buffalo (Calf) Woman: (Ptesan Winyan) (Wohpe)." *TGC* (February 23, 2009). http://incolor.inebraska.com/tgannon/.

Gardner, Philip, and Gary Osborn. "The Grid Lines of Force: Their Ancient Discovery and Primitive Use." *World-Mysteries.com* (2008). http://www.world-mysteries.com/.

Giese, Paula, ed. "White Buffalo Calf Woman Brings the First Pipe: As Told by Joseph Chasing Horse." *Native American Indian: Art, Culture, Education, History, Science* (1995). http://www.kstrom.net/isk/.

Groce, Duane. "The Twelve Chakras." *The Inner Switchboard: A Path to Healing* (2007). http://www.innerswitchboard.com/.

Hagelin, J.S., M.V. Rainforth, D.W. Orme-Johnson, K. L. Cavanaugh, C.N. Alexander, S.F. Shatkin, J.L. Davies, A.O. Hughes, and E. Ross. "Effects of Group Practice of the Transcendental Meditation Program on Preventing Violent Crime in Washington DC: Results of the National Demonstration Project, June-July 1993." *Social Indicators Research* 47, no. 2: 153-201.

Hicks, Esther, and Jerry Hicks. *The Law of Attraction: The Basics of the Teachings of Abraham.* Carlsbad, CA: Hay House, 2006.

Hodson, Geoffrey. *The Kingdom of the Gods.* Adyar: Theosophical Publishing House, 1980.

Icke, David. *Infinite Love Is the Only Truth: Everything Else Is Illusion.* Ryde, Isle of Wight, UK: David Icke Books, 2005.

The Institute for Cultural Awareness. "About Us: Mission." *ICA.* http://www.ica8.org/.

Isabelle, Susan. *On Assignment with Adama.* Bloomington, IN: Author House, 2005.

———. *Return The Goddess, The Lemurians Shall Come.* Bloomington, IN: Author House, 2007.

Jacka, Judy. *The Vivaxis Connection: Healing through Earth Energies.* Charlottesville, VA: Hampton Roads Publishing Company, 2000.

Jaffe, Kabir, and Ritama Davidson. *Indigo Adults: Forerunners of the New Civilization.* New York: iUniverse, 2005.

Kaptchuk, Ted J. *Chinese Medicine: The Web that Has No Weaver.* London: Rider, 1983.

King, Soluntra. "Earth's Grids and Portals." Excerpt from *Crystals: Gateways of Light and Unity* in *Evenstar Creations* (2001). http://www.evenstarcreations.com/.

Knierim, Thomas. "Spacetime." *The Big View.* http://www.thebigview.com.

Kross, Brian. "If Atoms are 99.999999999999% Empty Space Then Why Don't Things Pass Right through Them?" *Jefferson Lab.* http://www.jlab.org/.

Lee, Gayle Barkley, and Lyrica Mia Marquez. "AWEtizm: A Hidden Key to Our Spiritual Magnificence." Unpublished manuscript, November 2009.

Lemurian Fellowship. *Into the Sun.* Ramona, CA: Lemurian Fellowship, 2006.

Lewis, C.S. *The Chronicles of Narnia.* New York: HarperCollins Publishers, 2001.

Lipton, Bruce. *The Biology of Belief: Unleashing the Power of Consciousness, Matter and Miracles.* Fulton, CA: Elite Books, 2005.

Lonetree, Benjamin. "Seven Subtle Variations: A Scientific Study of Schumann Resonance, Geomagnetics and Vortex Energy in Sedona." *Sedonamolies.* http://sedonanomalies.com/.

Losey, Meg Blackburn. *The Children of Now*. Pompton Plains, NJ: New Page Books, 2007.

———. *Conversations with the Children of Now*. Pompton Plains, NJ: New Page Books, 2008.

Lovelock, James. *Gaia: A New Look at Life on Earth*. Oxford: Oxford University Press, 1979.

_____. *The Ages of Gaia: A Biography of Our Living Earth*. New York: W.W. Norton, 1988.

Lutz, Antoine, Lawrence L. Greischar, Nancy B. Rawlings, Matthieu Ricard, and Richard J. Davidson. "Long-Term Meditators Self-Induce High-Amplitude Gamma Synchrony during Mental Practice." *PNAS* 101, no. 46 (November 16, 2004): 16369-16373.

Lyster, Karen. "Stargate: The Real One?" *UFOs: The Beginning of a New World*. http://www.karen-lyster.com/.

Mann, Nicholas R. *Sedona Sacred Earth: A Guide to the Red Rock Country*. Rev. ed. Flagstaff, AZ: Light Technology Publishing, 2004.

McTaggert, Lynne. *The Field: The Quest for the Secret Force of the Universe*. New York: HarperCollins Publishers, 2001.

Melchizedek, Drunvalo. *The Ancient Secret of the Flower of Life*. Vol. 1. Flagstaff, AZ: Light Technology Publishing, 1998.

———.*The Ancient Secret of the Flower of Life*. Vol. 2. Flagstaff, AZ: Light Technology Publishing, 2000.

Morton, Sean David. "Chakras of Planet Earth." *Toronto Dowsers* (September 2004). http://www.dowsers.info/.

Motoyama, Hiroshi. *Theories of the Chakras: Bridge to Higher Consciousness*. Wheaton, IL: The Theosophical Publishing House, 1981.

Mowry, Scott. "New Crop Circles Found in England May Offer Proof that a New Earth Is about to Unfold." *Miracles and Inspiration* (July 31, 2010). http://www.miraclesandinspiration.com/.

Myss, Caroline. *Anatomy of the Spirit: The Seven Stages of Power and Healing*. New York: Three Rivers Press, 1996.

Nave, C.R. "Magnetic Field of the Earth." *HyperPhysics*. Georgia State University. http://hyperphysics.phy-astr.gsu.edu/.

Nichols, Preston B., and Peter Moon. *Pyramids of Montauk: Explorations in Consciousness*. Westbury, NY: Sky Books, 1998.

Oschman, James. "What is 'Healing Energy'? Part 3: Silent Pulses." *Journal of Bodywork and Movement Therapies* 1, no. 3 (1997): 179-194.

Pearsall, Paul. *The Heart's Code: Tapping the Wisdom and Power of Our Heart Energy*. New York: Broadway Books, 1998.

Phillips, Tony. "Earth's Inconstant Magnetic Field." *NASA Science*. http://science.nasa.gov/.

Pinkham, Mark Amaru. *The Return of the Serpents of Wisdom* Kempton, IL: Adventures Unlimited Press, 1997.

Puryear, Herbert B., and Mark A. Thurston. *Meditation and the Mind of Man*. Rev. ed. Virginia Beach: A.R.E. Press, 1978.

Quan Yin, Amorah. "The Crystalline Cities of Light." *Pleiadian Lightwork* (2007). http://www.amorahquanyin.com/.

Richardson, Patrisha. "Subtle Bodies and Chakras." *Transforming Darkness into Light : A Guidebook for Spiritual Seekers*. Emeryville, CA: Absolute Truth Publications, 2000.

Rose, David. "Cancer Cases 'to Increase a Third by 2020.'" *The Times*. December 4, 2007. http://www.timesonline.co.uk/.

Rubin, Bruce Joel. *Ghost*. Directed by Jerry Zucker. Hollywood: Paramount Pictures, 1990.

Sahag'n, Carlos Lazcano. *Exploring a Forgotten World: Lost Sites of the Paquimè Culture*. Mexico City: Grupo Cementos de Chihuahua, 1999.

Sams, Jamie, and David Carson. *Medicine Cards: The Discovery of Power through the Ways of Animals*. Santa Fe, NM: Bear and Company, 1988.

Sankey, Mikio. *Esoteric Acupuncture, Volume I: Gateway to Expanded Healing*. Kapolei, HI: Mountain Castle Publishing, 1999.

Schumann, W.O. "‹ber die strahlungslosen Eigenschwingungen einer leitenden Kugel, die von einer Luftschicht und einer Ionensph‰renhulle umgeben ist." *Zeitschrift f,r Naturforschung* 7a (1952): 149-154.

Scott-Elliot, W. *The Lost Lemuria*. London: The Theosophical Publishing House, 1904. Reprinted as *Legends of Atlantis and Lost Lemuria*. Wheaton, IL: The Theosophical Publishing House, 1972.

Sheldrake, Rupert. *A New Science of Life: The Hypothesis of Morphic Resonance*. Rochester, VT: Park Street Press, 1995.

————.*The Presence of the Past: Morphic Resonance and the Habits of Nature*. New York: Crown Publishing, 1988.

Smith, Michael. *A Year in the Field: Apprenticeship in the Energy Arts*. Gilroy, CA: Bookstand Publishing, 2009.

Smith, Tony. "Schumann Resonances, Geomagnetic Reversals and Human Brain States." *Lowndes County Historical Society and Museum*. http://www.valdostamuseum.org/.

St. Claire, Eva, and Peter Carlton. *Geopathic Stress: Unlock the Key to your Health*. Toronto: Savoy House, 2001.

StarStuffs. "Earth Chakras." *StarStuffs* (2007). http://www.starstuffs.com/.

Stillman, Ed. "Dowser's Brain-Wave Study: Your Key to Dowsing Independence and toward a Unified Theory for Dowsing Success." *Sedona Journal of Emergence* 10, no. 10 (October 2000): 71-78.

Strawberry World and CDM. "Short History of Gran Canaria." *Strawberry World: Gran Canaria*. http://www.spain-grancanaria.com/.

Streiber, Whitley. "Did Magicians Cause UFO Sightings." *Unknown Country: The Edge of the World* (July 20, 2005). http://www.unknowncountry.com/.

Talbot, Michael. *The Holographic Universe*. New York: HarperPerrenial, 1992.

Tiller, William A. "Subtle Energies." *Science and Medicine* 6, no. 3 (May/June 1999). http://www.tillerfoundation.com/

Underwood, Guy. *The Pattern of the Past*. London: Sphere Books, 1972.

Van Etten, Jaap. *Crystal Skulls: Interacting with a Phenomenon*. Flagstaff, AZ: Light Technology Publishing, 2007.

Vleer, Wigholt. *Leylijnen en Leycentra in de Lage Landen*. Deventer, NL: Ankh-Hermes, 1992.

Walton, Bruce, ed. *Mount Shasta: Home of the Ancients*. Pomeroy, WA: Health Research, 1985.

Webb, Avril. "Geopathic Stress in Our Homes." Reprinted as PDF at http://www.sheerprevention.co.uk/.

Whitfield, Sherry. "The Ancient Crystal Skull Synergy." *Blue Star Traders*. http://www.crystalskull.net/.

Wikimedia Foundation. "Cetacean Intelligence." *Wikipedia*. Last modified January 19, 2011. http://en.wikipedia.org/wiki/Cetacean_intelligence.

————. "Earth's Magnetic Field." *Wikipedia*. Last modified January 31, 2011. http://en.wikipedia.org/wiki/Earth%27s_magnetic_field.

————. "Location Hypotheses of Atlantis." *Wikipedia*. Last modified January 30, 2011. http://en.wikipedia.org/wiki/Location_hypotheses_of_Atlantis.

————."New Age." *Wikipedia*. Last modified February 4, 2011. http://en.wikipedia.org/wiki/New_Age.

————."Rupert Sheldrake." *Wikipedia*. Last modified January 28, 2011, http://en.wikipedia.org/wiki/Rupert_Sheldrake.

————. "Schumann Resonances." *Wikipedia*. Last modified January 14, 2011. http://en.wikipedia.org/wiki/Schumann_resonance.

————. "Talaiot." *Wikipedia*. *Wikipedia*. Last modified August 12, 2010. http://en.wikipedia.org/wiki/Talaiot.

————."Unexplained Disappearances." *Wikipedia*. Last modified January 2, 2011. http://en.wikipedia.org/wiki/Unexplained_disappearances.

Wolf, Fred Alan. *Parallel Universes: The Search for Other Worlds*. New York: Touchstone, 1988.

Wright, Brad, and Jonathan Glassner. *Stargate SG-1*. Century City, CA: Metro-Goldwyn-Meyer, 1997-2007.

𝔏*Light Technology* PUBLISHING **Presents**   229

TO ORDER PRINT BOOKS
Visit LightTechnology.com, Call 928-526-1345 or 1-800-450-0985,
or Check Amazon.com or Your Favorite Bookstore

BOOKS THROUGH JAAP VAN ETTEN

Crystal Skulls
Interacting with a Phenomenon

Discover your energetic connection with crystal skulls. Learn how to utilize these energies for your personal growth and how these special energies affect your awareness and expand your consciousness.

Dr. van Etten's book reveals the skulls' ancient mysteries, their different characteristics and special energies, and the effects they have on humans and on Earth.

A few of the many theories surrounding these skulls are that they are shaped by higher or alien powers, they come from another world, or they are from an ancient Mayan civilization. Enhanced by 16 pages of color photos, this book invites you to delve deep into the mystical world of the crystal skulls.

$19.95 • 240 PP. • Softcover
ISBN-13: 978-1-891824-64-7

TOPICS INCLUDE

- Characteristics of Crystal Skulls
- Some Famous Crystal Skulls and Their Caretakers
- Contemporary Crystal Skulls and How to Find Yours
- Why a Skull Shape?
- How to Categorize Crystal Skulls
- Piezoelectricity
- Original, Singing, Fully Activated, and Contemporary Crystal Skulls
- The Legend of the 13 Crystal Skulls
- The Effects of Crystal Skulls on Human Beings

🜍 *Light Technology* PUBLISHING *Presents*   231

TO ORDER PRINT BOOKS
Visit LightTechnology.com, Call 928-526-1345 or 1-800-450-0985,
or Check Amazon.com or Your Favorite Bookstore

BOOKS THROUGH JAAP VAN ETTEN

Birth of a New Consciousness
Dialogues with the Sidhe

We usually base our perception of reality on what our five main senses receive, particularly our visual interpretation of the world, but the world we live in actually consists of many different worlds, most of which are invisible to us. All these worlds are part of Gaia and make up the reality we live in.

This book contains dialogues with the Sidhe, a race of human-like beings who are our direct relatives. Invisible to us, they occupy one of the subtle worlds of Gaia.

As the Sidhe and the author share their views on their respective worlds, explore the similarities and differences and gain a different perspective. Learn to recognize our respective gifts and self-induced limitations.

By collaborating with beings from the subtle realms, such as nature spirits and unicorns, we can create a new consciousness — and a new world. Embark on the journey available to every soul who comes to Earth, and raise your vibration and expand your view of reality.

Dialogues with the Sidhe
Jaap van Etten, PhD

$16.95 • Softcover • 6 x 9 • 192 PP.
ISBN 978-1-62233-033-1

CHAPTERS INCLUDE

- Meeting the Sidhe
- Getting to Know Each Other
- Our Origins and the Influence of the Stars
- The Separation
- Thoughts and Emotions
- Energy Systems and Healing
- Procreation and Hereditary Factors
- Teaching and Learning: the Education Systems
- Relationships with Plants and Animals
- Crystalline Energies